Acclaim for Bill Gutman's

PARCELLS

"Gutman makes it abundantly clear [that Parcells] is a cut above the rest of the pack. . . . Just the thing to pick up and read on a Monday night."
—*Washington Post Book World*

"Taking readers through Parcells's peripatetic coaching journey, Gutman sheds light on his subject's offbeat brand of genius. The author's wide-ranging knowledge and generous insights make this solid reading for Parcells fans and detractors alike."
—*Kirkus Reviews*

"Gutman weaves a readable and effective overview that will make fans alternately smile and wince as they relive the Tuna's success.
—*Boston Herald*

"Gutman gives fans of Parcells' teams a pleasant ride down memory lane."
—*Hackensack Record*

"Sportswriter Gutman's biography is a good read about a hardnosed, uncompromising man. An engaging story describing the motivation that drove Parcells to become one of the most successful coaches in pro football."
—*Library Journal*

"Expect considerable demand among NFL fans for this thoroughly readable examination of a larger-than-life sports personality."
—*Booklist*

Also by Bill Gutman

The Giants Win the Pennant! The Giants Win the Pennant: The Amazing
1951 National League Season and the Home Run That Won It All

When the Cheering Stops

Magic Johnson: More Than A Legend

Tiger Woods: A Biography

Sammy Sosa: A Biography

Michael Jordan: A Biography

The Pictorial History of NCAA Basketball

The Golden Age of Baseball: 1941–1964

Ken Griffey, Jr.: A Biography

Shaquille O'Neal: A Biography

Brett Favre: A Biography

The Musical Life of Duke Ellington

Pistol Pete Maravich: The Making of a Basketball Superstar

PARCELLS

A BIOGRAPHY

Bill Gutman

CARROLL & GRAF PUBLISHERS
NEW YORK

Selections from *Parcells: Autobiography of the Biggest Giant of Them All* by Bill Parcells with Mike Lupica, reprinted by permission of Bonus Books, Inc., 160 East Illinois St., Chicago, 1987.

First Carroll & Graf cloth edition 2000
First Carroll & Graf trade paperback edition 2001

Carroll & Graf Publishers
A Division of Avalon Publishing Group
161 William Street
New York, NY 10038

Library of Congress Cataloging-in-Publication Data is available.
ISBN: 0-7867-0934-0

Manufactured in the United States of America

In Memory of My Parents
George and Violet Gutman
and
for My Wife, Cathy,
With Unending Appreciation

Acknowledgments

T O WRITE A BIOGRAPHY OF A CHARISMATIC, SOMETIMES CONTROVER-
sial public figure who is also a very private individual and (at the
time of the writing) still active in his profession can be a daunting
task. Not everyone you want to speak with wants to speak with you. Fortunately, there were enough people willing to share their memories, recollections, and feelings about Bill Parcells so that I could construct what
I hope is a well-rounded and accurate portrait of a great football coach
and sometimes enigmatic man.

For openers, I would like to thank a group of Jersey guys for talking
about the Jersey guy they knew as a teammate and friend. They include
boyhood friends Tom Godfrey and Walter "Butch" Bartlett, and Larry
Ennis, who played semi-pro baseball with a young Bill Parcells. The author is especially grateful to Mickey Corcoran, who not only coached the
teenage Parcells at River Dell High School but also became a lifelong
influence, advisor, confidant, and friend. The information he provided was
invaluable.

I would also like to acknowledge the sports information departments at
Colgate University, Wichita State University, the United States Military
Academy, Vanderbilt University, Florida State University, Texas Tech
University, and the United States Air Force Academy for providing infor-
mation and helping to locate former teammates and coaches.

Those I spoke with from Parcells's college years also provided insights
and anecdotes about a fine collegiate tackle who soon began evolving into
a coach with a thorough knowledge of the game and unique style of dealing
with his players. They include Len Clark, who played alongside Bill at
Wichita State; Steve Sloan, who hired Bill as one of his assistant coaches
at both Vanderbilt and Texas Tech; and Jim Bowman, who was at the Air

Force Academy when Parcells took his first head coaching job there in 1979. Both Greg Frazier and Richard Arledge were players on the Texas Tech team when Parcells served as defensive coordinator. Their candor provided additional insight into the development of a young coach and some of the adjustments he had to make.

Finally, there was the pro game. My thanks to the media relations department of the New England Patriots and to Pat Hanlon, media relations director of the New York Giants, for providing information on the availability of players familiar with the coach, his personality, and his style. Former giants Harry Carson, Phil McConkey, Brad Benson, George Martin, O. J. Anderson, and Dave Jennings were all open and honest, willing to share their recollections of the Giants years under Parcells and what he brought to the team during his coaching tenure.

I also appreciate the time given me by former NFL coaches Chuck Noll, Marv Levy, and Chuck Knox, all of whom talked about their long and successful careers in the National Football League and gave me valuable insights into a very demanding and pressure-packed profession.

Last but not least, I would like to extend a special thanks to *Boston Globe* columnist Will McConough, who shared his thoughts about his long friendship with Bill Parcells as well as his in-depth knowledge of Bill's tenure and subsequent departure from the New England Patriots. He was also the only member of the working press to extend me the courtesy of a callback and, subsequently, an interview. Thanks again, Will.

Table of Contents

Prologue

The early morning sun glistened through the deep blue California sky and onto the green grass of the stadium below. While much of the country was in the midst of a cold and angry winter, the Rose Bowl stood as it had since 1923—a huge, open-air football arena basking in the warmth of a January day in Pasadena. In a matter of hours, however, the stadium would be awash with activity and filled with more than 100,000 football fans as the National Football League prepared to stage the biggest gridiron extravaganza of them all—the Super Bowl.

For New York Giants coach Bill Parcells, bringing his team across the country to the Rose Bowl probably seemed a bit strange. Given his choice, he surely would rather have played at Giants Stadium. In fact, in more than twenty years of coaching, Parcells had never walked through the hallowed doors and onto the perfectly manicured gridiron of one of the most famous football stadiums in the land. Not once. But when the Super Bowl became a national event following the 1967 season, the powers that ruled the NFL decided the game would be played at a neutral, warm-weather site. That way, they felt the game would be closer to a true test of talent and wouldn't be derailed by the possibility of subzero temperatures, a rock-hard frozen field, numbing wind-chill, or even a howling blizzard. Play the January game in Green Bay, Minnesota, Chicago, or even New York and these factors were all possibilities. And, of course, they were also aware that the marketing potential of a warm-weather site would surely wind up generating a much fatter cash cow for the burgeoning business of professional football.

That's why Bill Parcells had to take his team away from Giants Stadium and travel far from his own roots to a stadium best known for hosting the oldest of the postseason college bowl games. All that notwithstanding, the forty-five-year-old coach was ready to call the shots for a team on the brink of the National Football League championship. After a long and arduous coaching road, he was about to take the final step toward the pinnacle of his profession in just his fourth year at the helm of an NFL ballclub.

Not that he hadn't already proved his mettle, having taken the Giants from an abysmal 3–12–1 record his first year and turned them into a 14–2 juggernaut by 1986. To tell the truth, it didn't matter if this game was played in Giants Stadium, in the Rose Bowl, or on a grassy meadow somewhere in Iowa. To any coach worth his salt, it's not where you play, but how you play. Bill Parcells had been getting football teams ready to play all his life, or so it must have seemed. Whether it was his first official job as linebackers coach at tiny Hastings College, or returning to his old high school to help put in a new defense, or working an unlikely first head coaching gig in the staid atmosphere of the Air Force Academy, he always did everything with a purpose, a purpose that had an inexorable, singular end. To win!

The Giants team that came to Pasadena on January 25, 1987, would become known as a prototypical Parcells team. It featured a punishing running game with a well-oiled complementary passing attack, and a rock-ribbed, stingy defense led by a quick yet bruising linebacking corps. It had one out-of-this-world player in Lawrence Taylor, and star-quality performers such as Phil Simms, Joe Morris, Mark Bavaro, Harry Carson, and Carl Banks. The remainder of the players, no matter what their innate football talent, were handpicked by the coach and on the team for a reason. Every single player, from the superstar Taylor to the last guy on the bench, had one thing in common. They all believed deeply in Bill Parcells, convinced that if they played to the utmost of their ability and followed the game plan laid out by their coach, they would win.

Sure, Denver had a fine team. The Broncos were led by a young, strong-armed quarterback named John Elway. On any given Sunday, Elway's explosive right arm could hang a defense out to dry. But on this day,

Parcells and his Giants brought their "A" game to Pasadena. After a close first half in which the Broncos led by just one point, at 10–9 the New Yorkers broke it open in the third quarter, scoring seventeen unanswered points, then went on to a convincing, 39–20 victory and the championship.

For Bill Parcells, the game seemed to mark the end of a journey. A coaching odyssey spanning more than two decades had brought him to this place—where his coronation for all to see culminated in getting a barrel of Gatorade dumped over his head in the Rose Bowl. That symbolic shower meant he was a champion, that he had led his team to the top of the football world. Now, at last, he was in a position to write his own ticket. Coaching the team whose home field was just minutes from the place he grew up, the team he had rooted for as a kid, had always been his ultimate dream. It seemed, now, that he could remain a Giant forever.

September 12, 1999—East Rutherford, New Jersey

An almost deafening roar erupted from the crowd at Giants Stadium as the New York Jets ran onto the field to meet the New England Patriots in the opening game of the 1999 season. Fans of the team known as "Gang Green" sensed this was finally their time to shine. Collectively, they could feel it. After years of frustration, the Jets' followers finally had a team good enough to make it to the Super Bowl, something that hadn't happened since a brash young quarterback named Joe Namath had engineered the NFL's biggest upset by leading the former American Football League team to a Super Bowl victory over the established Baltimore Colts in January 1969.

These Jets had posted a 12–4 record in 1998 and had made it all the way to the American Football Conference championship game before losing to the Denver Broncos. There was no reason to think the team wasn't ready for that final step in '99, the one that would return them to the top of the football world. Besides fielding a team of talented players, the Jets had a head coach who had made a habit of taking his teams to the Super Bowl. His name was Bill Parcells.

It had been nearly thirteen years since the same Bill Parcells stood on the turf of the Rose Bowl, dripping with Gatorade, wearing an ear-to-ear grin that could only come from coaching a team to a championship. No longer the new kid on the block, Parcells was now fifty-eight years old, working at what he had said would be his final coaching stop. The man who had seemed destined to be a Giant forever was now the boss of the crosstown Jets, his third professional team. From the time it took to win a Super Bowl with the Giants back in 1987 and then bring the current Jets to the brink of the same success, his reputation had grown to the point where his coaching exploits were looked upon as legendary.

Want to turn a loser to a winner? Hire Parcells. Want to bring respect to a franchise? Hire Parcells. Want your team in the Super Bowl in the shortest time possible? Hire Parcells. Want to transform a ragtag collection of underachievers into a tough and hungry group of winners? Hire Bill Parcells. In the eyes of many, he had become the best.

The Giants were 3–12–1 Parcells' first year. Three years later they were in the Super Bowl. The New England Patriots were 5–11 his first year. Three years later they were in the Super Bowl. The Jets were an abysmal 1–15 the year before he signed on. Amazingly, he made that team a 9–7 winner his first year, and the season after that had them a game away from the big one. As a coach, he was looked upon as a kind of miracle man. For those reasons, many felt that in his third year at the helm of the Jets the team was almost surely Super Bowl-bound. That was before the season's first game even started. Once it began, the fans continued cheering for what they felt would be the first step of the final journey.

With a little more than seven minutes left in the second quarter of the opening game, the Jets were driving. Veteran quarterback Vinny Testaverde, who had produced his greatest season under Parcells a year earlier, had already completed ten of fifteen passes for ninety-six yards and was leading the offense with confidence. Though the Jets trailed 10–7, this drive, which had the club at the Patriots' 25–yard line, was likely to result in either the go-ahead touchdown or tying field goal. The Jets then called a running play and Testaverde handed the ball to tailback Curtis Martin.

Martin charged into the line. As he did, a Patriots tackler poked the ball loose. Fumble! Standing almost ten feet behind the play, with nobody around him, Testaverde did what every football player is taught—when you see a fumble, go after it! He made a quick move to pursue the loose ball, but before he could take a full step, he suddenly crumpled to the ground. No one noticed until the play was blown dead. When everyone realized what had happened a strange, almost eerie hush fell over the filled, 75,000-seat stadium.

Testaverde was on his knees, bent over, helmet touching the turf. He was pounding the artificial surface repeatedly with his fist. It had to be bad. It *was. Once he was examined by doctors, the team received the news. Their star quarterback had ruptured his left Achilles tendon. He would need immediate surgery. With the clock showing 7:12 remaining in the second quarter of the first game, the Jets had lost their quarterback for the entire year.*

On the sidelines, Bill Parcells grimaced when he saw his quarterback carted off. Not to worry, most observers felt. Parcells would find a way to fix it, find a way to make his team win. Even the coach, with all those years of experience behind him, felt there was a way to fix things. In football, there was always a way.

What no one realized then, what no one could realize, was that Bill Parcells was about to embark on the longest and ultimately strangest season of his coaching life, a roller coaster ride that would continue its journey even after the games had ended.

Introduction

B ILL PARCELLS IS A MAN OF MANY FACES. HE CAN CHARM YOU WITH an unexpectedly broad smile or destroy you with a withering glance that can make even a mammoth defensive tackle want to run and hide. At press conferences, he can cause the most experienced reporter to feel like a kid failing journalism school by reacting to an inquiry with a look of extreme disgust, quickly adding, "Now *that's* a dumb-ass question." As a coach, he can walk up to a player one day and hug him and kiss him on the head, yet the very next day give the same player a blistering dressing-down in front of the entire team.

He has been called both a master psychologist and a shameless manipulator, a coach with a vision of a winning team who is determined to assemble, then mold, the players he has chosen to be part of it. He has also been depicted as a coach who plays constant mind games with his players, his goal being to break them down mentally then reconstruct them in his image. He has been called a master motivator—an obvious compliment—and a coach who motivates by fear—a not-so-endearing quality. Through it all, however, Bill Parcells has remained steadfast in his never-changing goal: to produce winning football teams good enough to contend for a title.

"I know what a championship team is supposed to look like and I'm [always] trying to get to that end," he has said, on numerous occasions.

1

But at other times, he has also proclaimed, "I know what it takes to survive in this business."

Survive and prosper. With Bill Parcells, those two singular elements have always made not-so-strange bedfellows. In fact, Parcells has done a great deal of both since entering the coaching profession as a twenty-three-year-old fresh out of college in 1964. It was more a matter of survival at first as he made the many requisite stops along the collegiate way—an assistant here, an assistant there, then a coordinator, and finally a head coach. During that early period the Parcells style began to evolve, but the timing wasn't always right and his players couldn't always separate the method from the madness. He had to have his way even then, and often wouldn't or couldn't make allowances, much less compromise. He coached in the East, the Midwest, the South, and the Southwest, distinctly different regions of the country where there are wide variations in culture and custom. While his hard-boiled, often abrasive style—part of the Parcells mystique today—remained constant, it was not always welcomed.

Former players sometimes found him rude and unyielding. His methods of motivation didn't always jibe with theirs, leading one player to knock him down in the locker room before a game with a well-placed punch. Yet in looking back, many of these same players admit, sometimes grudgingly, that while they didn't like him, Bill Parcells knew more about football than any coach they ever had.

Before moving from the collegiate to the professional ranks, Parcells took a year off, dealing with a crisis of conscience after he realized the carpetbagging life of a college assistant, always looking for that better job, was taking a toll on his family. He tried selling real estate, but found he was spending all his spare time in the fall and winter watching football games. It was his wife, Judy, who finally realized that her husband could only be happy doing one thing. As soon as she gave him the word, Bill Parcells was back in coaching. Only this time he went to the place he really wanted to be, the NFL.

He began as an assistant to Ron Erhardt with the New England Patriots in 1980. A year later, he left to join Ray Perkins's staff with the New York Giants as defensive coordinator and linebackers coach. Bill Parcells had finally come home. When Perkins resigned to take the head-coaching job at the University of Alabama after the end of the 1982 season, Parcells became the Giants' main man. Finally, the pro football world, and subsequently the entire sports world, would begin to notice the big, somewhat paunchy head coach with the penchant for turning losers into winners.

But it wasn't until the Giants won their first-ever Super Bowl, following that 14–2 1986 season, that Bill Parcells really emerged. Named Coach of the Year, he was sought out for interviews, with both the style and substance of his obviously winning system coming under much closer scrutiny. Parcells and the Giants were on the football map. They had two more fine seasons in 1988 and '89, then crested again with a 13–3 mark in 1990, the culmination of that year being a second Super Bowl triumph. By then, the coach's no-nonsense approach to the game was well known, as was his unique and sometimes contradictory relationship with his players.

"He was like a general," said star running back Joe Morris. "He has to be in control."

"[Coach Parcells] is sometimes the nastiest person you ever met," is the way former Giants' offense lineman Bob Kratch described him. Yet Kratch played for Parcells with both the Giants and New England Patriots.

And Jeff Hostetler, the backup quarterback who led the team to its second Super Bowl victory, didn't exactly make it sound as if memories were made of this when he said, "I have nothing but great things to say about the man as a coach, but I didn't enjoy one minute of my time with him. I know that sounds strange, but that's how it is when you're around Bill Parcells."

Tough and uncompromising, with an asp-like tongue that can sting, injure, and sometimes even destroy the biggest of men, Parcells won't deny the existence of his venomous side.

"If you're sensitive," he has said, "you will have a hard time with me." Then he adds, "The only players I hurt with my words are the ones who have an inflated opinion of their ability. I can't worry about that."

But there is another side to the Parcells personality as well. Despite his reputation for being manipulative and for playing mind games, he is still considered a player's coach, a guy who's comfortable around young athletes, whether interacting with them on the field, in the weight room, or in the locker room. Former Giants tackle Brad Benson put it this way:

"The unique thing about Coach Parcells is that he has a self-security. He can be a player's coach, yet when we get back in that locker room and he has to regain control of the team, he can do that."

Parcells apparently feels the dichotomy is necessary, that you can't have one without the other. "Coaching is about human interaction," he has said, "and trying to know your players. If you respect a player and he respects you, then you have a relationship, and in a relationship all commentary is allowed."

So Bill Parcells's reputation as a coach was pretty much set by 1990. His team had won a second Super Bowl and people were beginning to learn more about his often controversial and unique coaching style, especially his dealings with his players. In reality, however, the story was just beginning.

Several months after his team's triumph over the Buffalo Bills in Super Bowl XXV, Parcells shocked the football world by suddenly resigning from the one job he had always coveted. Though he wouldn't go into specific reasons at the time, it was soon apparent that the coach was stepping down for health reasons. At the age of forty-nine, Bill Parcells had to deal with a new and unexpected foe—his own heart.

"I didn't want to leave football," he would say, years later. "But I knew I had to do something. I knew I couldn't keep going like I was or I wasn't going to make it."

Over the next two years he did what many ex-players and former coaches do upon retirement. He became a television analyst, a genial presence who probably smiled a lot more than he did when he was coaching. During that time, he also underwent what is euphemistically called "four heart procedures." The final one was single bypass surgery and upon his recovery, Bill Parcells received a pleasant surprise. His doctors cleared him to coach again.

This marked the beginning of the second phase of his career, and he wasted precious little time jump-starting it. On January 21, 1993, he became the twelfth head coach of the New England Patriots. The Parcells presence would be on the sidelines once again, only this time away from his beloved Giants, taking control of a team that had just completed a terrible 2–14 season and a 14–50 four-year run. The Patriots, looking to turn things around, had hired a coach who had taken the Giants from 3–12–1 his first year to 14–2 and a Super Bowl triumph in year four. In essence, Bill Parcells was being asked to work the same kind of magic a second time.

He started his tenure in New England by drafting a strong-armed quarterback out of Washington State, Drew Bledsoe, and building from there. Once again he was demanding, uncompromising, insulting, and always looking for his type of player. As usual, the proof was in the pudding. For a second time, the results said he was doing something right. After a 5–11 get-acquainted year, the Patriots went to 10–6, had an off year at 6–10, and then, in 1996, won their division at 11–5 and made it all the way to the Super Bowl. It had taken him just four years to reach the top for a second time. Though the Pats were beaten by the Green Bay Packers for the title, Parcells was a hero in New England and, so it seemed, could once again write his own ticket.

There was however, a convoluted side to the story. While the fans were cheering their team and hoping for a Super Bowl champion, Bill Parcells was already embroiled in a behind-the-scenes war with Patriots owner Robert Kraft. The central issue: control. To those who knew Parcells, that wasn't a surprising revelation. For more than a year, Kraft had been removing much of his coach's say over player personnel, the issue coming to a head even before the 1996 season began. There had been similar rumblings during Parcells's stay with the Giants, when the coach sometimes found himself at odds with General Manager George Young. Now, more firmly established as both winning coach and compelling personality, Parcells wasn't about to live with what he felt was an untenable situation.

"If they want you to cook the dinner, they at least ought to let you buy the groceries," Parcells would say, with a grin.

But the animosity between the two antagonists, both strong-willed men, wouldn't go away and the situation wouldn't change. It was a fait accompli. Parcells knew he couldn't stay, but Kraft didn't make it easy for him to leave. Finally, NFL Commissioner Paul Tagliabue became involved in a situation that had turned ugly. Not surprisingly, Bill Parcells didn't waver, didn't apologize, and didn't feel he had done anything wrong by signing a $14.4-million, six-year contract to coach the New York Jets. After some heated negotiations, the deal was done. Now he would be taking over yet another team in shambles. As Bill Parcells was leading the New England Patriots to the Super Bowl, the Jets were in the process of compiling an atrocious 1–15 record, the worst in the League. Could Parcells finally have been dealt a stacked deck as well as a tarnished reputation?

During the entire acrimonious episode in New England, he began to take some serious heat. There were accusations of disloyalty, with Parcells being called a coach who couldn't stay put, who was always looking for greener pastures. But as with any messy divorce, there were two sides to the story. Was "greener pastures" just another way of saying "new challenges"? Perhaps. Certainly he wanted control and had to have control, a free hand to deal with personnel in the way he wanted. More so than ever, he seemed to handpick his players, lose patience with others, and quickly weed out those who didn't fit the Parcells mold. As for moving on now three times in his pro career, he also had an answer for that.

"Maybe I am restless," he said, "but I don't necessarily see that as a bad thing. I was with the Giants a total of ten years [eight as head coach]. I just don't think nowadays you can do that anymore. The landscape of the business has changed a lot. After a while, it's like it is with the players. You've got to move on to something different."

So on he moved. Once again there were the usual mixed responses. Patriots quarterback Bledsoe, while acknowledging a debt to Parcells, said he really wouldn't miss him, wouldn't mind playing for someone else.

"He didn't say anything to any of the players [when he left]," Bledsoe said. "You'd like to think that when you go through some of the things we all went through with the guy, he'd at least say goodbye. But from the get-go, Bill has been about Bill. That's the way it is; that's the way he is."

New England linebacker Chris Slade took it several steps further when he said, "If they offered me ten million dollars to play and [Parcells] was still here, I wouldn't play."

Yet Patriots linebacker Willie McGinest, the Pats' top draft pick in 1994, described a different Parcells when he said: "Along with the yelling and discipline, I was close to Bill. A lot of people don't really understand [him] . . . Me and Bill were tight and that's not just as a coach. He was also a friend."

At his first Jets camp the feeling was unanimous. Everyone seemed glad he was there. Players who had agonized over losing the past several seasons suddenly had their perceptions changed. Wide receiver Key-shawn Johnson, the team's top draft choice in 1996, was already being viewed as a malcontent who did nothing but complain and buck authority. But Johnson was like his new coach. He had a burning desire to win. In Bill Parcells, he saw a man who could make it happen.

"I don't have a problem taking orders," Johnson said, answering his critics, "and I don't think any other real players do. We just want to take the right orders from the right person, and that's what you get from Bill Parcells."

Quickly, the process started again, dumping some players, acquiring others, changing the mindset of all those who returned. The Parcells magic worked faster than ever. The Jets went from 1–15 to 9–7, then from 9–7 to 12–4 and a spot in the AFC championship game. Parcells was just a step away from becoming the first coach ever to take three different teams to the Super Bowl. That's exactly what many thought would happen in 1999—until Vinny Testaverde, the quarterback that Parcells had resurrected a year earlier, was injured in the first game. With this and several other key injuries, the Jets did something that no established Parcells team had ever done. They nosedived, began losing, and in doing so tested the mettle of their proud coach more than ever before.

"We're not gonna run up the white flag," he said defiantly, after learning his quarterback was lost for the season.

For this fifty-eight-year-old man, who had said that the Jets would be his last coaching stop, the question quickly arose as to whether he would stick around for one more shot at the big one. There was speculation that if the Jets had won the Super Bowl in 1999, Bill Parcells would surely have stepped down. Testaverde's injury made that possibility a remote one right from the start. But the coach who seems to alienate as many people as he charms is far from a quitter.

"I enjoy being around young people," he said, at the start of the 1999 season. "It's probably what keeps me going. I still feel I belong in a locker room."

In 1999, Parcells found that the injury jinx had suddenly thrust him into the toughest coaching job of his life, trying to salvage a season for a team that had been expected to challenge for the Super Bowl. When the Jets lost six of their first seven games, it seemed over. The death of team owner Leon Hess before the season started, and the tragic loss of Parcells's friend and agent Robert Fraley during the season, made things even more difficult. In addition, the team was now for sale, the new owner still unknown. Despite all these negative factors, Parcells rallied his team, finally turning the quarterbacking reins over to an untried player about whom he had an old-fashioned, gut feeling. This was the leader he was looking for.

Ray Lucas came through, the Jets pulled together, and while not making the playoffs, amazingly salvaged their season with an 8–8, .500 finish. That's when Bill Parcells had another big decision to make—to finally step down or to continue for one more year. As was his wont, he made his decision quickly. He decided to retire from coaching, this time giving the story an ending. Just the act of retiring, however, turned out to be a complicated matter, wrought with several unexpected circumstances that made

for great drama. For a short time, Parcells's future hung in the balance
while this complex man had to once again take charge and make some
additional hard decisions. As always, it was very difficult for anyone to
predict what he would do, since he had changed his mind many times
before. It was as if he loved to keep them all guessing.

What is it, then, that makes Bill Parcells tick? His high school coach
and mentor, Mickey Corcoran, has said that "[Bill] was born to coach."
Sportscaster Jim Lampley, after interviewing Parcells for an HBO special,
said, "His whole life is about athletic competition." That always translates
to winning.

But is that all there is? Other coaches have been winners, too: Lombardi, Halas, Landry, Shula, Gibbs, Walsh, Johnson, Holmgren, and
Reeves, just to name a few. Each found his own style, a style that had
worked for him. None is an exact clone of the other. Parcells may be
unique in that he's won with a variety of styles, adapting his game plans
to the talent around him. He went from a ball-control offense and attacking
defense with the Giants to more of a passing attack and a containing
defense with the Patriots, and finally a combination of both (depending
on the health of his team) with the Jets.

It was once said that Clint Eastwood has remained a major motion-
picture star for so many years because no one really knows that much
about him as a person. In a sense, that description also applies to Bill
Parcells. Through all the years, despite all the analysis of his coaching
style and dealings with his players, and all the apparent contradictions in
his personality, he remains an intensely private man. Dave Meggett, who
played for him with the Giants, again with the Patriots, and briefly with
the Jets, was one who confirmed this perception.

"You think I know Bill Parcells?" Meggett asked, rhetorically. "I don't
think anyone knows Bill, even himself."

Another former player, who chose to remain anonymous, made this
telling statement. "[If Parcells] was named king of the world on Sunday,
he'd be unhappy by Tuesday."

Parcells's story is one of a man who loved sports almost from day one,
chose to become a coach, was eminently successful at it, and then found
himself a sports and media superstar, as well-known as any of his players.
It is also a story of development and evolution, of contradiction and controversy, and the kind of character it takes to win in one of the most
demanding professions in the country. Coaching an NFL team exacts a

price. It weeds out the weak and marginal, it frustrates those who can only find partial success, and it even wears down and ultimately changes the best of men. Perhaps that is why Bill Parcells, in one of those moments when nothing seemed to be going right, said:

"This game is going to kill me yet."

CHAPTER ONE

Sowing the Seeds, Jersey Style

I N THE 1983 FILM *EDDIE AND THE CRUISERS*, WHICH DEPICTS A GROUP of youngsters trying to make it as a rock band in the 1960s, the leader of the group, the fictional Eddie Wilson, keeps reaching out for more. He wants to create music that is new and different, ahead of its time; wants to find that perfect sound. His best friend and fellow band member Sal can't understand this quest for perfection and finally tells Eddie that they aren't special, adding, "We're just a bunch of guys from Jersey."

Bill Parcells has always liked to refer to himself as a Jersey guy. Sure, he grew up there and continues to make his home in the Garden State. But while he often uses his Jersey guy persona to say, *hey, I'm not really special, I just happen to be a football coach,* in reality he is closer to Eddie Wilson, a guy who is reaching for more, looking for new ways to win, striving for perfection. His roots, though, are definitely steeped in the New Jersey of the 1940s and '50s, and even when he spent the better part of two decades learning his craft at various compass points around the country, the good ol' Jersey guy was never very far away. His Jersey roots run deep.

Ironically, when Charles and Ida Parcells had their first son they didn't name him Bill. The future National Football League coach with the oh-so-familiar name was actually christened Duane Charles Parcells when he was born on August 22, 1941, in Englewood, New Jersey. The change to Bill came in his early teenage years when a number of people mistook him for another boy, a look-alike, who happened to be named Bill. Young Duane Parcells found he liked being called Bill. Somehow, it had a better ring to it than Duane. He took it as a nickname, and it stuck.

Both of Bill's parents also had Jersey backgrounds, only from an earlier era. His father, Charles Parcells, grew up in Hackensack, where he acquired the nickname "Chubby" and became an outstanding athlete. Oddly enough, he was anything but chubby, being tall, thin, and very athletic looking. His real name was O'Shea, but early in his life he was adopted by the sister of his real mother, who later married a man named Parcells. Fortunately, none of those difficult early times stopped Charles Parcells from becoming a doer and an achiever.

"Charles Parcells was a striking, impressive man," said Tom Godfrey, who met young Bill when the two played Babe Ruth League baseball together and has remained a friend ever since. "He was the type of guy you looked at and said, 'Wow, here's a successful man.' He had rod-straight posture, was tall and slender with a full head of white hair."

A multisport, multi-letter athlete at Hackensack High School, Charles Parcells went on to become a track and football star at Georgetown University. He was, however, much more than a campus jock. He was also a fine student who went straight from Georgetown U. to Georgetown Law. Upon getting his degree, he became an agent with the Federal Bureau of Investigation.

Ida Naclerio Parcells, also a Jersey girl, grew up in Woodridge, her home being just five minutes from the Meadowlands, the area that now houses Giants Stadium. She was of Italian heritage and enjoyed being a housewife, caring for her husband and eventually her children. Yet even before her children were born, Mrs. Parcells became concerned about her husband's profession. As the wife of an FBI agent, she suffered the trepidations most wives of law-enforcement officials suffer, of not knowing whether her husband would come home each night.

Out of deference and respect for his wife, Charles Parcells left the Bureau the day after his first son was born and went to work for U.S. Rubber. There were brief stops for the family in Pennsylvania and Illinois before they eventually settled in Hasbrouck Heights, New Jersey, which was south of Hackensack where Mr. Parcells grew up and north of Woodridge where Mrs. Parcells had lived. In a sense, they had come home, and now young Duane would begin to grow up a Jersey guy. Consequently, all his early memories are of New Jersey. Charles and Ida Parcells had three other kids after Bill, two more boys and then a girl.

Even before young Duane discovered sports, he learned an early lesson in perseverance and competitiveness from his father. One day five-year-old Duane was outside playing with some friends when he got into it with one of them. Within minutes he was home, telling his father that he had come up on the short end of a fight. The first thing Charles Parcells told him to do was to go back out there. If it meant another fight, so be it.

"You have to go back out there," Mr. Parcells supposedly said. "You always have to go back out there."

It wasn't long afterward that Duane discovered sports. It became his number-one love almost from the beginning. His father soon bought him his first bat and glove, a rite of passage for many a boy, especially in the postwar 1940s, when baseball truly was the national pastime. Living in New Jersey, it was inevitable that he would begin following the three local baseball teams—the Yankees, Dodgers, and Giants—often listening on an old table radio as the likes of Mel Allen, Red Barber, and Russ Hodges called the games in ways that imprinted the actions and personalities of the players forever in the minds and memories of young fans all around the metropolitan area. Yet even while following the so-called local teams, to the point where he knew every single player, Duane Parcells rooted even more for another team—the Boston Red Sox.

In those years, the Red Sox and Yankees were bitter American League rivals and the Sox could give the Bronx Bombers a run for their money, what with the likes of Ted Williams, Johnny Pesky, Bobby Doerr, Dom DiMaggio, Vern Stephens, Mel Parnell and Ellis Kinder. The Yanks countered with Joe DiMaggio, Hank Bauer, Yogi Berra, Phil Rizzuto, Vic Raschi, Eddie Lopat, and Allie Reynolds. The two teams were closely matched and many of the games were tantamount to war. It was an incredibly competitive rivalry and it pushed some of the right buttons in young Duane Parcells.

Before long, however, he wasn't content just watching. He soon began playing, joined by neighborhood friends and, shortly afterward, by younger brothers Don and Doug. Like most boys back then, they played all the sports, whichever happened to be in season at the time. They emulated their heroes in each, fantasizing about playing in the big leagues, and later in the NFL or National Basketball Association.

The first place Duane played was a vacant lot right across the street from his home. The lot was used by the Army for drills during World War II and was set between two aviation plants, Curtis Wright and Bendix. Looking back, *Bill* Parcells recalls that lot as the place young *Duane* Parcells began to love sports.

He pretty much discovered that love on his own. Despite Charles Parcells' athletic prowess and achievements, he never pushed any of his sons to play, never forced them into sports. He was about as far from the stereotypical "Little League father" as you could get. In fact, he rarely if ever talked about the good old days. He had some scrapbooks, but never opened them or showed them off to friends. There was a humility about him that precluded showcasing the things he had done in the past. Maybe that's why in later years his son would always field questions about the past, even the immediate past, with a terse, "That's ancient history." Yet, at the same time, Charles Parcells was a man of action who often told his sons, "Don't talk about it; do it!"

There were times when he was growing up that Duane would hear the inevitable comparisons around town, the ones that reminded him how good an athlete his father had been and that said, rhetorically, *wouldn't it be great if you could be as good as he was.* The important thing, however, was that he never heard it from his dad and, for that reason, it never bothered him.

It wasn't long before the Parcells boys and their friends played ball nearly all day long when they weren't in school. "Anything with a ball was good enough," Don Parcells remembered. He also remembered that older brother Duane was already taking charge, trying to set the rules and control the games.

"He used to tell me what to do, but I could outrun him," Don Parcells recalled. Then, kiddingly, he added, "It was a good thing I could outrun him, because otherwise I wouldn't be alive today."

By the time Duane was entering junior high school, the family decided to move. They went from Hasbrouck Heights to Oradell, a small town north through Hackensack and just past the slightly larger town of River Edge. There, they settled into a bi-level ranch-style home on Wildwood Drive. It was in Oradell where Duane Parcells began to be mistaken for the other boy, the look-alike named Bill. Before long, more of his friends and acquaintances were calling him Bill. Soon it became Bill permanently.

Oradell had fewer than seven thousand people when the Parcells family moved there. As in many other small northern New Jersey towns, a gradual transition had been taking place. What had been a traditional farming community for many years was now turning into a commuter suburb of New York City. More middle and upper-middle class families were moving in, new homes were being built, and additional businesses were springing up. The trains into the city were becoming busier, and there was an increasing traffic load crossing the George Washington Bridge every morning and evening.

Fortunately, there were still open spaces and thus many parks and fields, places where kids could go to have fun or play ball.

"Oradell had become a small, family-oriented town," Tom Godfrey recalled. "There were ball fields all over. In the summer we would just hang a glove on the handlebars of our bikes and go find a game. It was easy. If you wanted to play, you could always find a field with other kids ready to join you."

As the forties gave way to the fifties, young Bill began to add to the growing list of sports that fascinated and attracted him. Baseball was the first, but pro football wasn't that far behind. There was only one team in New York then, the Giants. At that time, they were still playing at the Old Polo Grounds, which was the home of the baseball Giants as well. By the time he saw his first game at the Polo Grounds in 1954, young Duane was being called Bill and also was eating, drinking, and sleeping sports. The Giants beat the Steelers that day, and Bill was hooked.

He began watching *Marty Glickman's Quarterback Huddle* on TV's Channel 5, as the longtime Giants announcer brought on many of the team's top players, such as quarterback Charley Conerly and safety Emlen Tunnell, as guests. It was a way to get to know the players and Bill Parcells watched faithfully every week. He had found a new favorite show. He also began going to more games with his Little League and later Babe Ruth League teams, usually seeing two or three a year. At the same time, he played all he could. He even played some sandlot football with Vince Lombardi, Jr., while the elder Lombardi was still an assistant coach with the Giants. That association made him feel even closer to the team and it was no surprise that he soon became a rabid Giants fan.

As much as he enjoyed watching the pro teams, it was when he was on the playing field that Bill Parcells felt increasingly good. Winning a game was extremely satisfying to him. Losing, by contrast, was plain lousy. He soon began to realize that to win as much as possible, he had to put himself in a position where he could control the outcome of the game. So he gravitated to control positions—quarterback in football, catcher or pitcher in baseball, center in basketball. Sometimes, however, he had to do even more. It was while he was playing Babe Ruth League baseball in the summer of 1955 when he first put these instincts into action and the sports personality of Bill Parcells began to emerge.

He was fourteen then, and one of his teammates was Tom Godfrey, who remembers meeting his new teammate for the first time.

"He was like a man at fourteen," Godfrey said. "I was more like a timid little twelve-year-old. It was apparent even at that young age that he was really a leader. He wanted to control everything on the field. At the end of practice he used to say, 'I'll take the catcher's stuff home; you guys just make sure you're here tomorrow.'"

Then came one of the early incidents from which the Parcells New Jersey legend grew. His team was winning by a single run and trying to protect its lead in the final inning. Bill was catching, as usual, but he began to worry when the opposition's best hitter came up with two outs. Tom Godfrey remembers:

"He called time out, took off his equipment, and then called the left fielder in and told him they were switching positions. Nobody said a word. It was just expected of him. Even then, he was taking charge."

The left fielder climbed into the catching gear, and Bill trotted to the outfield. Sure enough, on the very next pitch the batter hit a lazy fly in his direction that he caught easily. The only thing that kept the story from having a real Frank Merriwell ending was that he didn't make a leaping catch at the fence to save the game. But his instincts for looking ahead, for seemingly knowing what would happen, were uncanny for one so young.

"Being a leader just seemed to be inbred in him," said Tom Godfrey. "He undoubtedly would have been a leader in anything he did. But he found his niche in sports early and once he did, he was always playing ball. Even then, he was some kind of competitive. That's what set him apart from the average kid. He was always going to win at anything, whether it was the major sports or something like handball, racquetball, tennis . . . anything."

From that point on it was sports, sports, and more sports. The only other thing Bill made sure he had covered was his schoolwork. His father, being a student/athlete in his younger days, knew the importance of education and insisted his son not let his grades slip because of sports. Mr. Parcells taught Bill to strike a balance early, and it was a lesson well learned. Otherwise, Bill and his friends would do anything to play ball—finding a game at one of the many parks and fields, using the gymnasium whenever they could, or even shoveling snow off outdoor basketball courts in the winter so they could shoot hoops.

Walter "Butch" Bartlett met Bill when the two were in the eighth grade and played alongside him right into college. Butch, too, knew the kind of athlete his friend was right from the start.

"We were a hungry group," Bartlett recalls. "We played everything when we were young. In the summer we often went to the local recreation center and played baseball and basketball. It was a year-round thing then. No one specialized. We all played everything all the time. Bill was very demanding, even then, and it's obvious that he has stayed that way."

There were many days and nights when the two boys wound up at the Parcells home after a workout, something else that Butch Bartlett always remembered.

"His parents were very friendly with all the kids who came there," he said. "Bill's mom was a real Italian in that she was always cooking. And she kept the house immaculate. We spent all our time in the kitchen or downstairs in the rec room. I can still remember that there was always plenty to eat."

In the fall of 1956 Bill Parcells and his friends from Oradell were ready to begin high school as sophomores. Ordinarily, they would have been boarding a bus and traveling some five miles to Dwight Morrow High in Englewood. But because Oradell and River Edge were growing so rapidly, a new high school was built for students from both towns. It was called River Dell High and Bill was a member of the first class of students to attend. The construction of the new school would turn out to serve as a milestone in Bill Parcells's life, a catalyst for his continued development as an athlete and also the beginning of his predilection for coaching.

The River Dell athletic teams would play just a sophomore schedule in 1956–57. That way, the coaches would remain with them as they moved into their junior and senior varsity years as a way to build continuity at the new school. Tom Cahill was the football coach; he would later become the head coach at the United States Military Academy and hire former player Bill Parcells as one of his assistants. Cahill was a hard-nosed coach who didn't play favorites. Players had to earn his respect. While he taught future coach Bill many fine points of the game and showed him that a varying degree of toughness was necessary, he wasn't Bill's primary influence in high school

That honor went to Mickey Corcoran, River Dell's basketball coach, and a man Bill Parcells has called, "next to my father . . . the most important influence in my life."

Now in his late seventies, Corcoran remembers the high-school career of Bill Parcells very well, right from the first day he met him.

"I called the kids in during the summer before school started to get a look at them," Corcoran said. "As soon as we began running some basic layup drills I noticed [Bill]. He'd go in and make a layup, then get back in line. But instead of watching the other kids, he was staring at me, checking me out. It was as if he was looking to give me *his* approval, like he wanted to know who the hell this guy was who'd be coaching him in basketball. I just had the feeling that this kid was looking to see if he would have a good coach."

When Bill Parcells entered River Dell High he was already 6' 2" and weighed 180 pounds. Though he was one of the biggest kids in school, he didn't want to be a lineman in football. He wanted to be a quarterback. Control again. Not surprisingly, that's where he played, with occasional forays as a running back and tight end, and as a full-time linebacker on defense. Once football was over it was time for basketball and that's when Mickey Corcoran began to make a real difference. Even then, Bill said he could see immediately that his new coach was different from any coach he'd ever had before.

"It was always defense with Mickey," he explained. "He said that by playing defense you wouldn't win every game, but you would be in every game with a chance to win."

Winning was already the name of the game for Bill. When he didn't win, or when things didn't go his way, he became angry. In fact, he had a pretty quick temper on occasions. But Mickey Corcoran had a trump card from the beginning, one that he would have to play several times during the three years the two were together.

"Call it youthful exuberance," the veteran coach said. "But Bill was overly competitive and would lose control of his emotions from time to time. He had to learn to handle himself as an athlete. I knew I might have some problems with him, until his father paid me a visit.

"His dad was the best," Corcoran continued. "The first time he met me he said, 'Coach, sometimes Duane needs a kick in the ass. When he gets out of line, just give him a good kick in the ass.' After that, I had all the cards I needed to coach him. His father and I were on the same page. They were just a tremendous, wonderful family."

All through high school Bill Parcells had two strong influences working for him. His father constantly challenged him academically, telling him he needed good grades if he wanted to attend college, and also letting him know that if he didn't keep his grades up, there would be no more sports. On the court, Mickey Corcoran challenged him athletically, getting him to maximize his talent and teaching him some hard lessons about having the proper temperament for sports.

Bill was the best player on the team his sophomore year, but the coach made sure he got no preferential treatment. In a game against Park Ridge River Dell had a seventeen-point lead by the second quarter. Suddenly, the whistle blew and a technical foul was called on Parcells for complaining a bit too vociferously to the official. Mickey Corcoran picks up the story from there.

"As soon as it happened I pointed to a kid on the bench and said, 'You're in for Parcells.' I sat him next to me and chewed him out, telling him you simply don't do things like that. I figured I'd sit him for awhile, then put him back in. Suddenly the lead goes from seventeen, to twelve, to eight, to six. Now he's got me by the short hairs. If I put him back in, we'd undoubtedly win. But he's also gonna think, 'The coach really needs me.' So I'm fighting with myself about what to do. The more I thought about it, the more I knew I couldn't put him back in. So I sat him and we lost the game in overtime.

"The next day at practice I ripped him a new asshole. Then I said, 'Get out. We don't need you and your lousy points.' Later, he came in and talked it over with me. It was a teacher and a student trying to do the right thing. I had to teach discipline and had to do it right then. That way, I'd have my ducks in line for the next two years. As it turned out, it was the right call. He was still a typical kid, would lose his temper and kick the ball up in the bleachers. I threw him out of practice three or four times, but he was always in my office at 7:30 the next morning to talk about it. All in all, he was a delight to coach."

Tom Godfrey remembers the incident and says Coach Corcoran's action was a lesson well learned. "Bill never forgot that the rest of his coaching career. It showed him that no one was too big for the team."

While Mickey Corcoran was always ready to read his star player the riot act, he also came to appreciate the qualities that Bill Parcells brought to the game, and to his career at River Dell.

"[Bill] worked harder at practice than any other kid I had," the veteran coach related. "He was always the first one there and the last to leave. Same with football and baseball. It was always one more jump shot, Coach; one more punt, Coach; just a few more swings, Coach; that type of thing. He was more competitive than anyone and worked very hard at acquiring skills. Plus he always prepared himself to play in order to maximize his talent. That quality was evident right from jump street."

If Mickey Corcoran wasn't sure about Bill's competitiveness, there was one incident that put it all into perspective. River Dell had lost a very close, hard-fought game during that first season. As usual, whenever the team lost Bill was the last one out of the locker room. The coach saw how badly he was taking the defeat and decided to console him a bit.

"He had played his ass off that night," Corcoran remembers, "and did a wonderful job, as he usually did. So I said to him, 'Pal, you did a great job out there. Look at it as a kind of moral victory.' He looked at me, very seriously, and said, 'Coach, there are no moral victories. You either win or you lose, and we lost.' Now that's a pretty astute statement, especially coming from a fifteen-year-old. He had it all figured out, even then."

The losses were always very difficult for Bill to swallow. Don Parcells remembers his brother sitting tight-lipped and silent at the family dinner table following a defeat. In the winter, when he was unhappy with the way a basketball game turned out, he would often go behind his house and shoot hoops for hours at the homemade backboard, sometimes despite numbingly cold weather.

There was something else about his young star that Mickey Corcoran noticed in those early years. The coach would often take members of the team to nearby universities—Fordham, Columbia, or West Point—on weekends to watch college teams play. While most of the kids just relaxed and enjoyed the game as spectators, Bill Parcells sat and watched very intently. He seemed to be taking everything in. Afterward, he always wanted to discuss what he had seen with his coach.

"He would ask me all kinds of technical questions," Mickey Corcoran said. "It was always 'Why does [Coach] Johnny Bach do that?' or 'Why does [Coach] Lou Rossini do this? Why are they attacking a zone like that?' He was very observant and inquisitive, a student of the game, even then. It was something not many high-school kids do and, although we never discussed it, I thought he might make a coach some day. It was, I thought, certainly an avenue he might travel later in his life."

On the football field, Bill also exhibited the take-charge qualities that had been in evidence since Babe Ruth League days. Tom Godfrey remembers a game in which River Dell had driven within a couple of yards from the end zone with a first down. Two running plays failed and now the team had a third and goal.

"After the two running plays didn't get it done, [quarterback] Bill went over and talked to coach Cahill," Godfrey said. "He came back in, switched positions with the running back, took a handoff, and busted over the goal line himself for the score. He was the kind of player who was always going to figure out how to get it done, a leader. There was no doubt about it and everybody, all his teammates, knew it."

Yet there were times when he wasn't so heroic. No one can be successful all the time. If he messed up, the coach was always ready to read him the riot act. During the Thanksgiving game his senior year River Dell was again near the goal line. This time quarterback Parcells changed the coach's call with an audible, but the team failed to score. Afterward, Coach Cahill put his arm around his quarterback and said, quietly,

"Parcells, you s.o.b, the next time you make a call like that, your fat ass is going to be on the bench for the rest of your career, which fortunately isn't too much longer."

As much as the coach's words might have hurt, losing hurt Bill even more. Still, he was always willing to put himself on the line, take the last shot, try to get over the goal line, come to bat with two out in the final inning with the winning runs in scoring position. He was simply an outstanding all-around high-school athlete.

"He was great at all three sports," Mickey Corcoran said. "I always thought he was a tremendous baseball prospect. In fact, if he was coming out of high school today I'm sure he would be offered a nice contract from one of the major-league teams. As with basketball and football, he understood the game [of baseball], and worked hard at all the skills. He could hit and throw. Maybe he didn't have great speed, but he was quick. If you pinned me down, I'd say that basketball was his third-best sport. But he had toughness and tenacity, and that great competitiveness every time he played."

While sports and his studies occupied almost all of his time, Bill found one other source of enjoyment during his final high school years—his

1956 Ford. It was something he earned, working in the summers to buy the car. In fact, he said that his dad didn't give him a dime toward it. He bought it, worked to pay the insurance, and also paid for the repairs. If he didn't have the money, the car sat until he earned enough to have it fixed.

"He loved that car," his friend Walter Bartlett said. "He was always polishing it, keeping it spotless, and doing some of his own engine work."

One of the popular pastimes in those days was cruising. Bill and his friends would make the two- or three-mile ride to Hackensack where they would cruise up and down Main Street, a scene reminiscent of the film *American Graffiti*, east coast style. The boys would sometimes catch a movie at the Oritani or Fox theaters, then hang out for a while at Munn's Ice Cream Shop. After that it was back on the road, checking out the other Fords, Chevys, Mercs, and older coupes that were chopped and channeled in the early years of hot-rodding.

"We'd put our varsity jackets on and just go out and drive," Tom Godfrey said. "But Bill was so into sports that he didn't do it that often. I think I can say that he really had no other main interests, just sports and more sports."

By his senior year colleges were beginning to show interest. Bill was a big kid, weighing close to two-hundred pounds his final year at River Dell, and still filling out. Plus he was versatile. He was both a center and power forward on Mickey Corcoran's basketball teams; played quarterback, sometimes tight end and linebacker in football; and was a catcher, sometimes pitcher, and occasional first baseman on the baseball team. Recruiters from some of the local schools, such as Seton Hall and Fordham, talked to him about playing basketball for them. Back then, colleges didn't offer that many baseball scholarships. He might have hooked on with a big-league organization, but he definitely wanted to go to college. So he began to think more about football as his primary sport while he continued his education and decided what he ultimately wanted to do.

There were subsequent scholarship offers from schools with big-time football programs, such as Auburn and Clemson. He considered both but, as he would later acknowledge, thanks to his father's influence his grades were excellent and he began gravitating toward schools that stressed academics more than athletics. After scrutinizing some of the Ivy League schools, he finally settled on Colgate University. But before leaving for Hamilton, New York, in the fall of 1959, he decided to get some more practical experience. Bill and Walter Bartlett spent the summer playing semiprofessional baseball, and that's when he got to know Larry Ennis.

Ennis was the player/coach of a couple of local semipro teams, the Oradell Raymonds and Clifton Giants. He was fine pitcher who, like many other young baseball junkies of that era, had professional aspirations. A big-league career was almost every kid's dream then. By 1959, Ennis knew the dream would never be. His arm had gone dead, an archaic diagnosis that today usually means a damaged rotator cuff or other such medical problem. Though he could no longer throw high heat, Larry Ennis was still good enough to play semipro ball, a very popular pastime in Jersey at the time.

"Semipro baseball flourished here after the war," Ennis said. "We played at twilight and on weekends, occasionally at night if a field had lights. We'd travel locally, also to South Jersey, and made some New York stops. Most of the players were in their late twenties or early thirties. When Bill came to me and said he wanted to play, I took him on right away since I had already seen him in high school.

"I knew he could handle himself behind the plate because I had watched him at River Dell. Plus I also remembered a game he pitched against Teaneck High in a tournament. Teaneck was a county power, but they only beat River Dell by a 1–0 score, and had scored that run on a fluke. Bill pitched a tremendous game."

Both Bill and his friend Walter Bartlett were watching Ennis's team take batting practice one day when they decided to ask in. Bill's confidence was something else that impressed Larry Ennis.

"Most high-school players would normally have doubts about stepping up and playing with older guys," he said, "but not Bill. He was always wanting to move up, play with older guys. It would have been easy for him to just look for games against younger kids coming up behind him, but he wasn't interested in dominating players not as good as he was. He wanted a challenge, and he related to the older guys real well. We were all pretty good ballplayers, guys who weren't quite good enough for the majors or guys still hoping to make it. So the quality of play was high. Yet Bill wasn't bashful, wasn't hesitant about taking charge behind the plate, even if it meant setting up the infield or outfield. He wasn't mouthy, but knew that the catcher ran the team and that he would have to earn the respect that came with the position. While he was one of the youngest players on the birth certificate, it wasn't that way on the field.

"Maybe the best way I can describe him is to say he could never spell the word intimidation," Ennis said. "His confidence seemed to come naturally, as if he had it all inside him"

Obviously, Larry Ennis was extremely impressed by the young catcher. As big as he was then, Ennis saw that Bill set up well behind the plate and obviously knew what he was doing.

"He had quick hands and called an intelligent game. In fact, he took it personally if you shook him off," Ennis said. "He had a quick release and strong throwing arm, and was very agile for a man his size. I remember the first game he played with us. I put him in the seventh slot in the batting order and he didn't like that. He shook his head, as if to say I'm better than that. Before long, we had him batting fourth."

Ennis recalls another game when the opposing team intentionally walked the batter ahead of Bill to load the bases. The object was to set up a force play at any base, but it still didn't sit well with Bill Parcells.

"I remember the guy sitting next to me on the bench saying that they made a mistake. I just nodded my head in agreement and, sure enough, Bill hit a bases-clearing double. Walking the guy in front of him had stirred up his pride, and he was the kind of kid who was always able to turn it up a notch when he had to."

Bill continued to play semipro ball with Larry Ennis right up until the time he left for Colgate in the fall. While he said he felt football had become his best sport by the time he was a high-school senior, he never claimed he liked it best. He seemed to enjoy them all. It was competition and winning that were number one. That was everything. He appreciated and respected coaches like Mickey Corcoran and Tom Cahill because they worked him and then worked him some more.

"Everybody who ever coached me was on me, coaching me hard," Parcells said, in later years. "So whatever I give as a coach, I took as a player."

He especially admired coach Corcoran for the way he prepared for situations, any and all situations—"Mickey was always a step ahead," he said. "He could see things coming before they happened."—and for the way he emphasized defense. Always defense. "From the time I was fourteen, Mickey talked about defense. So much of what I learned from him in basketball influenced the way I coach football."

Bill Parcells had certainly made his mark in high school. Mickey Corcoran called him the best athlete in the two towns (Oradell and River

Edge) that made up River Dell High. Bill, however, was keeping his options open. He still had not talked openly to his friends or coaches about the possibility of becoming a coach himself one day. In choosing Colgate, he certainly wasn't putting all his eggs in one basket. It wasn't pro football or bust. No, Charles Parcells's insistence that his son keep his grades up and study hard seems to have made an impact equal to that of sports, even though Bill himself said the thing he remembered most about high school was practicing, practicing nearly all the time.

On thing, however, was certain. As Bill Parcells prepared to embark on the next phase of his life, he was ready. He was competitive and hard-working, and he always wanted to win. It was a formula for success in whatever field he would eventually choose. His role models—namely, his father and Mickey Corcoran—had done their jobs well. The kid from Jersey was well-prepared for whatever would come next.

CHAPTER TWO

A Player Evolves

B Y DECIDING TO ATTEND COLGATE UNIVERSITY, IT SEEMED THAT
Bill Parcells had made a conscious, well thought-out choice. The
small school nestled at the northern end of the Chenango Valley
in central New York State was less than a day's drive from his New Jersey
home. It had an outstanding academic reputation and, with an enrollment
of just over two thousand students, was certainly not a football factory.
The picturesque, fourteen-hundred-acre campus in the tiny town of Hamilton was in a rural setting and surrounded by green, rolling hills. It was
an atmosphere conducive to introspective study with minimal distractions,
a place where the serious student could thrive.

At the same time, the athletic program was no Punch and Judy show:
Colgate played a Division I schedule in the major sports. While the Red
Raider gridders didn't go up against the Alabamas and Ohio States of the
world, they nevertheless played a competitive slate of games, facing some
Ivy League schools, Army, and teams the caliber of Duke. The Red Raider
roster over the years shows an impressive number of players who went on
to play in the NFL, beginning back in the 1930s.

Colgate provided the Oakland Raiders with two successive outstanding
fullbacks—Marv Hubbard and Mark van Eeghen—from 1967 to 1981.
Mark Murphy was an All-Pro safety for the Washington Redskins from
1977 to 1984, while safety Eugene Robinson went from Colgate to the
Seattle Seahawks in 1985, played there for ten years before joining the

Green Bay Packers 1996 Super Bowl champions, then moved on the Atlanta Falcons in 1998, where he played in yet another Super Bowl. So no
one could say that a good football player *couldn't* go from the rolling hills
of Hamilton, New York, to the grass and turf of the NFL.

Bill Parcells, however, didn't see it that way. Before long, he began to
feel that something was lacking. He played football in the fall and baseball
in the spring, and he studied hard, as always. Yet when the year ended,
the big freshman found himself the equivalent of the perennial unhappy
camper.

"I hated the place," he would say, later, admitting that the problem
came more from within himself than from the University or its athletic programs. At the crux of young Bill's dilemma was his already developing philosophy of competition. As he told Mickey Corcoran when he was at River
Dell High: *There are no moral victories. You either win or you lose.* Therein
was the problem, or at least the problem as Bill Parcells perceived it.

At Colgate he didn't sense enough of the absolute single-mindedness
he had already developed when it came to the end result of a ball game.
In other words, he didn't think enough of his teammates wanted to win as
badly as he did, a situation he found increasingly unacceptable. Though
he would later say that this assessment didn't apply to every single player
on the team, there was enough of it to begin souring him on Colgate. The
level of competition just wasn't high enough for a guy who wanted to win
more than anything else. It didn't help, either, when the team finished the
season at 2–7.

That summer, he returned home agonizing over whether he should return to Colgate for his sophomore year. He knew what education meant
to his father and, in truth, to himself as well. Charles Parcells had been
pleased by his son's careful selection process when choosing a college.
Bill could have opted for a scholarship to Auburn or Clemson, but chose
Colgate instead. Now, after a year, he thought about throwing in the towel,
but in one sense that would be quitting. He decided to give it one more
try. When it was time for the football players to report in the fall of 1960,
Bill was once again back in Hamilton.

This time, however, it took just two days for him to realize nothing had
changed. After two practice sessions he quit the team. With the prospect
of no football for the first time in years, he also decided to exit Colgate.
He was soon back home in New Jersey with no clue as to what he would
do next.

"He came to me the day after he left Colgate," said Mickey Corcoran. "He said he was looking for a more competitive atmosphere where there was a greater commitment toward winning. Everything he had done in his early life was geared toward competing. He just didn't find what he wanted there."

What next? Loafing and drifting weren't options. That wasn't Bill, and even if it were, Charles Parcells wouldn't have let that happen. He told his son in no uncertain terms that if Bill wasn't back in school somewhere the following year he would receive no financial help from him, even if he decided to return to school at a later date. Once again, it was Mickey Corcoran to the rescue: the River Dell coach starting making phone calls. Finally, he talked to one of the football coaches at Wichita State University, describing Bill as a guy who can play a little if the team was willing to let him have a chance. The Kansas school agreed to give Bill books and tuition for one semester while he tried out for the football team. That had to be good enough.

In the fall of 1961 Bill left his Jersey roots behind, driving halfway across the country to enroll at Wichita State. This time, there would be no turning back. Bill knew he couldn't walk out again. The Shockers played a solid brand of football in the Missouri Valley Conference, meeting the likes of Arizona State, Louisville, Boston College, New Mexico State, and Tulsa—a big-time schedule. If he made the team, Bill would be competing against some of the best players in the country, players fully capable of going on to the NFL.

South-central Kansas was about as far from New Jersey as an Easterner can get. Toward the western part of the state lay the Great Plains, a huge expanse of flatland rife with the wheat and other crops that form the staple of the country's agricultural production. To the south was Oklahoma, where protrusive oil rigs once shared space with herds of cattle. Wichita was located at the confluence of the Arkansas and Little Arkansas Rivers, and was the largest city in the state. The university was tucked into the city's northeast section, with plenty of activities in town when the students had free time.

Bill Parcells would spend three years at Wichita, playing football, studying, and wondering what the future held. He would later call it a stroke of luck that he landed there, for he soon met Judy Goss, a secretary in the school's Sports Information Office. It wasn't long before they married, and they had their first child, Suzy, even before Bill graduated. That was surely a turn he couldn't have predicted but one that would influence the decisions he made in the ensuing years, and undoubtedly one that gave him even more determination to succeed.

As always, Bill immediately began to play hard and study hard. He decided to major in physical education with a minor in history. Again, he was leaving himself with options. Once he took to the gridiron, the coaches knew immediately that the 6' 2", 225-pound sophomore could indeed— as Mickey Corcoran had told them—play a little. At a time when two-way football was still commonplace, he was both an offensive and defensive tackle, and even saw some time at linebacker.

In the 1961 season Bill didn't start but did see considerable action. The team finished 8–2 in the regular season (3–0 in the conference) with sophomore Parcells showing his versatility, even filling in at tight end and catching two passes for a total of forty-eight yards, one of them for a touchdown. That year, he and his teammates won the Missouri Valley Conference championship and earned a bid to the Sun Bowl in El Paso, Texas. Though they lost to Villanova 17–9, Bill Parcells now knew he was getting the taste of big-time college football that he had wanted.

The next year he became a starter and from that point on would answer the bell for every game over the next two seasons. In 1962, however, the team did something that was difficult for Bill to handle: They had a losing season. The Shockers would finish the year with a less-than-mediocre 3–7 record, and that including tasting the short end of all three Missouri Valley Conference games. Difficult as it was, Bill continued to play hard, going out there with the idea of helping his team to win. He knew no other way.

That year, he played defensive tackle alongside Len Clark. In an era when players were not nearly as big as they are today, 225-pound Bill was the team's biggest guy. Clark weighed in at 185, yet did battle in the trenches without complaint. It wasn't long before he began to notice some unique qualities about the New Jersey kid playing next to him.

"Bill always had a maturity about him," Clark said, "a drive, an instinct, a knowledge and sense of football that others didn't possess. I guess I could describe it as a kind of awareness of the game that was several steps above his peers. Even during that difficult 1962 season Bill was always focused on winning and never stopped trying to get his teammates focused in the same way. He was the kind of player who was always willing to turn it up a notch, knew that he could turn it up a notch, and would get others to turn it up a notch or two in order to win. That's why it was such a difficult year for him."

Despite the Shockers' losing record, it was the combination of Bill Parcells and Len Clark who produced perhaps the most exciting play of the year. Wichita State was facing West Texas State, a team led by a prolific passer aptly named "Pistol" Pete Pedro. According to Clark, Pedro was leading the nation in several passing categories at the time. During one series in the game he had the Buffaloes driving when he dropped back to throw once again.

"When we saw it was another pass play, Bill put the rush on and I dropped back looking for the screen [pass]," Clark said. "He beat his man and was almost to Pedro when he tried to throw. Bill batted the pass in the air, I grabbed it and ran forty-five yards for a touchdown. I was lucky to be in the right place, but Bill made the play. He had size and had pretty darn good speed as well. And he always wanted to win."

The overwhelming desire to win and the constant striving for a competitive edge sometimes made Bill testy, especially in 1962.

"Bill wasn't always the easiest guy to get along with," Clark recalled. "Because he wanted to win so badly he was always trying to encourage other guys to hit someone, then hit them harder. It was his competitive drive that led him to motivate others in his own way. I don't think everyone perceived it that way at the time, not when he was in their midst. It was something you realized later on."

By 1963 the Shockers had rebuilt, were healthy, and returned to their winning ways. Bill was named one of the team captains, along with a player named Larry Beckish, who would later coach at the college level, and quarterback Henry Schichtle, who would be drafted by the New York Giants. Wichita State would compile a 7–2 record that year, going 3–1 in the conference to earn a share of the Missouri Valley title. This was also the year that Bill Parcells proved to one and all that he was more than ready to play big-time college football.

During the season, Bill and his teammates went up against some very good teams and a number of outstanding players. Running back Charley Taylor of Arizona State went on to a great pro career as a runner/receiver with the Washington Redskins. Brig Owens, who played quarterback for the University of Cincinnati, would become an All-Pro defensive back with those same Redskins. Tulsa quarterback Jerry Rhome and receiver

Howard Twilley were both collegiate All-Americans who went on to fine NFL careers. As Bill himself said, "It was a brand of football I wouldn't have seen at Colgate."

Perhaps Wichita State's biggest rival back then was Tulsa. The year before, Bill and Len Clark had produced that exciting tip-and-intercept that led to a touchdown against the Golden Hurricanes. That was nothing, however, compared to what Bill did in 1964. Talk about raising the level of your game. Against Tulsa that year, he must have raised it about ten notches. Fortunately, the stadium didn't have a roof.

With Rhome and Twilley the Golden Hurricanes were favored, but no one counted on the one-man wrecking crew that was Bill Parcells. He not only clogged up the middle and brought the Tulsa running game to a halt, but he also chased and harassed Rhome whenever the QB dropped back to pass. It was old-fashioned, smash-mouth, in-your-face football. When it ended, the Shockers had a 26–15 victory and Bill Parcells had an incredible twenty tackles and six quarterback sacks. It was one of the great individual performances in all of collegiate football that season.

"You can hit someone hard on every play," Len Clark said. "But there's a difference between hitting someone hard and punishing them. Bill punished Tulsa that day, he really did."

There was little doubt in 1964 that Bill had arrived as a player. He was named to the All-Missouri Valley Conference team, and was invited to play in the postseason Blue–Gray game—one of the showcase events for the best collegiate players whose teams weren't going to a bowl game, players most likely to be scouted and subsequently drafted by the NFL.

With pro football now a possible option, he also knew he would soon have to make a decision. If, indeed, he were drafted by an NFL team, there was no guarantee he would make it. In fact, the odds were pretty much against him. There are many players who can compete successfully at the college level, but only a relative few make that successful transition to the pros. In addition, Bill was already married and had a young daughter, giving him responsibilities that extended beyond the NFL draft. Continuing his education was one option, getting a job was another, and coaching was a third. In fact, looking back, Len Clark feels that Bill was already beginning to gravitate in a definite direction.

"As a student and an athlete, he seemed to make a conscious effort to become even more familiar with the game," Clark said. "There's a difference between knowing what *you* do on a particular play and knowing what everyone else does as well as understanding the philosophy behind the play and what it's intended to accomplish. I think Bill was beginning to move in that direction.

"Looking back at his efforts to motivate and encourage his teammates, I think we were getting a preview of his coaching career. So I really think that at some point during his stay at Wichita State he had figured out what to do with his life in terms of athletics, or at least had a strong view of what he wanted."

Bill himself admits that his decision to coach came while he was in college, though at that time he felt it was something he would do "down the road." He also says at that time he wasn't even sure how to break in and where to start, but confirms that sports, especially football, was thick in his blood.

"I wouldn't have known what to do with myself without some kind of practice once school let out," he said.

Not playing anymore was a point in the road that many athletes reach. Some get there sooner than others, but for all of them it is tantamount to having a piece of their world removed. Whether it's the rush of competition, the camaraderie of being part of a team, or the adulation of a starstruck public, having it taken away—bang!—just like that, is like a junkie suddenly going cold turkey. It ain't easy. Some, like Larry Ennis, eased away from it by playing semipro ball, then continuing locally at the recreation level. Sports was still fun, albeit on a decidedly lesser stage. Others, however, never find anything to replace the thrill of the game and the rewards that go with it.

Not surprisingly, coaching isn't an option for everyone. In fact, it has been said that superstar players rarely make it as coaches or managers because they demand the same kind of perfection from their players that they always demanded of themselves, and not all players are capable of that. In fact, there is no way to tell whether a young coach will remain a low-echelon assistant or will finally become a head coach. And even when the head coaching position is attained, the name of the game becomes winning, with job security often tenuous and sometimes riding on the outcome of one big game.

Had Bill not been drafted, his decision would have been easy. But in the 1964 NFL draft, Bill Parcells was the seventh-round pick of the Detroit Lions. Like most athletes, he apparently couldn't resist the challenge. That spring, he graduated from Wichita State, continued to train, and in August played in the now-defunct College All-Star Game. That was the game in which the drafted college stars played the defending NFL champion. Bill got a taste of action as the powerful Chicago Bears whipped the All-Stars 28–17, in the annual game that was discontinued after 1976. He then reported to the Lions training camp.

In a nutshell, his professional playing career lasted just two weeks before the Lions cut him. It was probably a matter of the basic physical tools. Players were getting bigger, stronger, and faster. Despite his determination and competitive fires, the pro game was just a notch above his abilities. Even confidant and close friend Mickey Corcoran wasn't sure about Bill's feelings.

"He was a pretty darn good football player," Corcoran said, "but he never discussed his aborted pro career."

By this time, Judy Parcells was expecting their second child and Bill knew he needed a job. He also knew he had to be around football. The obvious transition was to coaching. After he was drafted by the Lions, he'd had a talk with Dean Pryor, who had been the backfield coach at Wichita State. Pryor had just been hired as the head coach at tiny Hastings College in Nebraska. If things didn't work out in the pros, Pryor told Bill, he'd love to have him on staff at Hastings. Once again, Bill had an available option. When the Lions cut him, he called Pryor to let him know he was on the way. By the end of August Bill and his family arrived at Hastings, Nebraska, to begin the next phase of his life. He was now officially a coach.

Although he was also about as far from the big time as a coach could get, it was a starting point. The Jersey guy arrived in Hastings, Nebraska, once again in the country's heartland, some one-hundred-fifty miles from Omaha. Hastings was a small college affiliated with the Presbyterian church, with an enrollment of about a thousand students. The football team played in A. H. Jones Stadium, built back in 1925, which would be bursting at the seams if two thousand fans showed up. There were high-school stadiums with larger capacities all over the country. The team, known as the Broncos, played in the Nebraska College Conference under the National Association of Intercollegiate Athletics (NAIA) banner, the organization that directed very small schools. Hastings met the likes of Chadron State, Nebraska Wesleyan, Doane College, Kearney State, and Colorado School of Mines. None of those teams was about to receive a bid to the Rose Bowl.

Still, that didn't completely answer the question, "How small is small?"

Bill, Judy, and their daughter took a one-bedroom apartment under a dentist's office with an affordable rent of $62.50 per month. The apartment didn't have a window and it was tough hanging pictures on the cinder-block walls. Bill described it aptly as "living in a tomb." But it was a necessity, since his salary as part of the four-man coaching staff was about $1,750 a year. To earn that, he had to do considerably more than coach the defense.

There isn't really a game plan for cutting the grass, lining the field, washing the uniforms, and building additional lockers. All those chores were written into the job description at a place where Bill said the two big events of the fall were the opening of the football season and the start of the pheasant-hunting season. Despite these perceived hardships, however, the young college graduate wasn't complaining.

"I was a coach and I loved it," he said.

Bill jumped into his new job with freshness and zeal. Coach Pryor described him as a "young man with the whole world to conquer." He had learned a great deal about football over the years and had mentors such as Mickey Corcoran to give him direction and set an example, but no one becomes a great coach overnight. Part of Bill's problem that first year was trying to do too much too soon. He admitted that he was attempting to tell his players everything he knew about football all at once. It didn't work.

"Football players forget things under pressure," he said.

He recalled a game against Nebraska Wesleyan in which he had drilled his defense about a play in which the Plainsmen's quarterback started to bootleg, then would throw on the run. They did it so well that it became their favorite scoring maneuver. Bill assigned his fullback/safety Jack Giddings the primary responsibility of stopping the bootleg. Not only was Giddings the Broncos' most talented player, but he was also extremely easy to coach. All week prior to the game Bill geared the defense to stopping that one play.

Then, on game day, Nebraska Wesleyan drove down near the Broncos' goal line. Here it comes, Bill thought. Sure enough, the Plainsmen began to run the bootleg. Neither Giddings nor the Hastings defense reacted quickly enough and Nebraska Wesleyan scored. On the sidelines the twenty-three-year-old coach was all over his twenty-year-old safety (Giddings) like bees on honey. He ranted, raved, and accused the player of not learning something they had practiced for a week. Finally, it took Coach Pryor to tell him to knock it off, to leave Giddings alone.

Bill protested, telling his head coach that he was angry because they had practiced the play all week long. Pryor's immediate retort was, "Well, you didn't work on it enough, because they scored."

It was one of Bill's early lessons, that the coach always had to take part of the responsibility for breakdowns on the field. You can't simply place blame on the player and let yourself off the hook. Even when, as a coach, you feel you know how to stop an offense or a particular play, if you don't break it down just right for your defense, they may still screw it up. Knowing and teaching are two different things. Learning to apply your knowledge is a lesson that can't be learned overnight.

Hastings had a solid 7–2 record in 1964. So Bill Parcells had begun his coaching career with a winning team, which certainly made his debut more of a feel-good situation. In addition, he also participated in another local custom—going pheasant hunting for the first time. He accompanied Coach Pryor in wading through a thigh-high creek looking for birds. When they rousted some, Bill aimed and fired. His target fluttered down, but wasn't dead. For the New Jersey boy, this was something new. He didn't have the heart, or stomach, to finish the task. One of the local boys accompanying them came up to wring the bird's neck. Hunting would never become one of Parcells's favorite pastimes.

Neither would coaching at Hastings. With a valuable year of experience, Bill and his family piled their possessions into a U-Haul and drove back to Wichita, where Judy Parcells's family lived. Once again, there were big decisions to be made. Bill knew he couldn't return to Hastings, not for the same anemic salary. He thought briefly about following in his father's footsteps and applying to law school. Ultimately, however, the answer was right on his own doorstep.

Wichita State had undergone a coaching change prior to the 1965 season. The new coach, George Karras, was still looking to fill out his staff when he heard that Bill was back in town. Because of Bill's outstanding playing career there, a host of Shockers supporters recommended him for Karras's staff. When the new coach offered Bill the chance to be defensive line coach in addition to working with the linebackers, he took it. It was a staircase up from Hastings and a chance to be a bona fide assistant coach at the major college level. Law school went on permanent hold. Once again, Bill Parcells would be putting his charges through their paces during the week and working the sidelines on Saturdays. The evolution from player to coach was almost complete.

CHAPTER THREE

Coach Pretty

F OR ASSISTANT COACHES AT THE COLLEGE LEVEL, THE PHRASE "JOB security" is not part of the lexicon. Even those who are satisfied as assistants and have no head coaching aspirations can't be sure if they will have a job from one year to the next. In many cases, if the head coach is fired the assistants go as well. Those who move from program to program, looking for a better spot, often find they have made a mistake and should have stayed put. Call it a crapshoot, because snake-eyes come up as often as lucky seven.

Head coaches can face a similar situation. With the exception of a few elite programs such as Florida State, Nebraska, Penn State, and Florida, football is generally a cyclical sport. If a coach takes over a program that is already successful and in an "up" period, oftentimes the only place it can go is down. Conversely, if a coach takes over a program that is down, he has to build it up. If he isn't successful, he's gone. If he builds it up but can't sustain it, he's gone. If he builds it up and feels he's taken it as far as he can, he leaves.

So for many coaches, the antennae are always in the air, searching the horizon, probing for a better spot, a more secure job, a higher-paying situation. Each move they make also uproots the family, moves the kids into a new school, forces the family to make new friends, and often leaves the extended family (parents, grandparents, aunts, uncles) wondering if they will ever come home. So it takes a strong man with a love for the game and the support of a resilient family to embark on a coaching career at an early age. This is exactly what Bill Parcells did in 1965. The Jersey guy was back in Wichita with wife Judy, daughter Suzy, and now a second daughter, Dallas. The decision was a no-brainer, at least at first. He was totally familiar with the school and its football program. The breaking-in period would be minimal. In addition, Judy's family lived right in town. What more could they ask for? The entire family felt it was a good place to be and, still new to the lifestyle that accompanied the profession, probably weren't too concerned about what would happen next.

It didn't take long, however, for Bill Parcells the coach to realize that Wichita State wasn't really the best situation for him. For one thing, his timing was bad. Since he had played there just two short years previously, he suddenly found himself coaching some of the same guys who had formerly been his teammates. All Bill would say about it was that he never felt comfortable coaching at Wichita State, that there just wasn't enough distance between him and the college. He wound up staying for two years, until Coach Karras and the entire staff were fired following the 1966 season. The perils of being an assistant were already becoming apparent.

There was a legacy, however, from the two years Bill spent as an assistant at Wichita State, only its affects were felt half a continent away—at River Dell High School. During a summer visit home the Wichita assistant returned to his old high school, talked with the coaches, and installed a defense that would be used at River Dell for almost twenty years.

"It was called the 52 Invert Defense," said Tom Godfrey, Bill's old friend from earlier years, who was then part of the River Dell program. "Most schools played with three defensive backs sitting in a zone. We had two guys who would come up or go back, depending on which way the ball went. So you always had run support on one corner and always had the deep middle covered. Our opposition could never figure out what made the backs come up or go back.

"It was a defense that dictated to the offense, not a traditional sit-and-read defense. When the ball was snapped we were moving, and that caught people off guard. All five linemen were always moving one way or the other, and the secondary moved opposite to them. Instead of using what was then a prototype safety—tall and fast—we tended to use 130-pound kids who were wrestlers. They were tough and rugged, and could support the run. So we were able to use kids at that position who normally wouldn't have played. They were, in effect, a combination linebacker and defensive back.

"Bill's head coach at Wichita State used that defense. He came back and gave it to us, so Bill's influence on the River Dell football team remained strong here for almost twenty years."

It was an early example of Bill Parcells remembering his roots and showing extreme loyalty to old friends and, in this case, his high school. He was also beginning to learn his craft. Defenses that moved and attacked would become one of his coaching trademarks. In addition, he would soon begin using his linebackers in a different and unique way, the genesis of which began when he learned about the invert defense from George Karras at Wichita State.

That, of course, didn't solve Bill's immediate problem. After the 1966 season he was again out of work. This time, however, he knew he wanted to continue coaching and once again, things happened quickly. He would say later that his career path was dotted with breaks that always came at the right time. The Parcells luck, he called it. Again Jersey days rose up in the form of the River Dell High gang. Tom Cahill had been Bill's football coach at River Dell and, of course, Mickey Corcoran had followed his former star player's travels very closely. Now Cahill was the head coach at Army and Corcoran told him Bill was available. Bill was offered the position of defensive line coach.

So it was pack-up-the-family-time again, this time for the trip back east to the United States Military Academy at West Point. Back in New York he was close to parents, siblings, and friends in New Jersey, and looking forward to yet another new coaching experience. There was a time that the service academies, notably Army and Navy, fielded football teams that could match up with anyone, but by the 1970s the top players weren't as attracted to military schools and the five-year active-military commitment demanded after graduation. A player with professional aspirations certainly wasn't going to go there, and many others who wanted to play big-time collegiate football didn't want to balance it with military training. That didn't mean Army's program itself wasn't first-rate. Once Bill arrived there he quickly saw that Tom Cahill had put together a tremendous coaching staff.

Among Cahill's assistants were future college and pro coaches such as Al Groh, John Mackovic, Bill Battle, Ken Hatfield, and Ray Handley. In addition, Bill met another coach at Army who would become a lifelong friend, basketball coach Bobby Knight. Knight would go on to a long, successful, and often controversial career at the University of Indiana. While he would have many detractors in later years, Knight always had a loyal friend and admirer in Bill Parcells. Bill has always said that he learned many things by watching Bobby Knight coach basketball that he would later transfer to football.

For instance, many basketball and football coaches run standard drills in practice all the time. They run them, Bill said, because their coaches ran them and they were taught that you simply *had* to run them. Bobby Knight, however, didn't run drills unless they had a purpose. He never ran them just for the sake of it. That, Knight felt, was a waste of time. Bill said he always applied that theory to his football teams, as well. He also felt that Knight was a tremendous teacher of the game, something else he admired. In addition, Coach Knight always showed tremendous respect and admiration for the men who preceded him in the coaching profession. He always wanted to meet and talk with the various legends of the game, hear about earlier times, and learn from their vast experience. That was another Bobby Knight trait that Bill Parcells admired. It didn't hurt, either, that the two men hit it off personally from the first. They have remained friends over the years, no matter where their paths have taken them.

Bill has always maintained that his tenure at Army was his version of basic training when it came to coaching football. Mickey Corcoran, however, who made many trips to the Point to see his former protégé in action, felt that Bill already had what it took.

"The first time I went to the Academy to watch practice I wasn't there five minutes before I just knew what a tremendous coach [Bill] was going to be," Corcoran explained. "He was a great teacher of technique and skills. He would get down in the dirt with his players and demonstrate the things he wanted them to do. And he had the kind of inflection in his voice that you need to command attention."

Bill remained at West Point for three years, learning from the other coaches and learning on his own. Then it was time to move on again. He would call the next eight years the "gypsy years, the blur years." The reason was simple. Like many college assistants he began to move around, always looking for a better situation, the right head coach to learn from, the increased opportunity to get himself noticed and make the A-list of assistants considered to be solid head coaching candidates. At each stop, he observed, learned, worked to improve himself . . . and found himself increasingly dissatisfied. There always seemed to be something that, if not blatantly wrong, could be better than it was.

His first stop was Florida State University, where he spent three seasons (1970–72) under two head coaches, Bill Peterson and Larry Jones, receiving more responsibility, designing the defense and calling defensive signals. While there, he celebrated his thirtieth birthday and felt his ambition growing. As he put it, he was getting "caught up in the rat race" and always looking around. On the positive side, his coaching skills were improving and he met Dan Henning, another Florida State assistant, who would later coach in the NFL as both a head man and longtime assistant. Like Bobby Knight, Henning would become one of Bill's closest and most loyal friends.

On the negative side was Florida State itself. While he never went into details, Bill said he simply didn't much like living in the South. He also found something about the college game that he not only disliked, but literally hated. In fact, it was probably the one thing that would help write his eventual ticket to the pros, since it was the name of the game in college football: *Recruiting*. It was the one thing he could never get past, no matter how much he tried.

"I hated the rap you had to give to high-school kids," he said. "I hated the rap you had to give to their parents. I didn't cheat but I would have to be blind not to see cheating go on at other schools, and I hated losing good prospects to the cheaters."

After three years, Bill decided it was time to move on again. By this time he and Judy had a third daughter, Jill, and now had to consider other things, such as their daughters having to change schools and make new friends every few years. That isn't easy but has always been part of a coaching life. You either accept it or you don't. To this point, both Bill and Judy had agreed to accept it.

The first year Bill was at Florida State, one of the offensive assistants was Steve Sloan. Sloan had been part of a lineage of great quarterbacks at the University of Alabama in the 1960s, coming after Joe Namath and before Ken Stabler. Now, like so many young assistants, Sloan was bent on moving up the coaching ladder. In 1971, when Bill returned to Florida State, Sloan had moved on to become an assistant at Georgia Tech.

"Bill and I became friends at Florida State," Sloan said. "He was already an exceptional coach with a knowledge of the X's and O's and had a good way with the players. In fact, he had a kind of extraordinary per-

sonality, bright and well-spoken, and always with a dry wit about him. He
was also very knowledgeable at the time about defensive football."

Two years after Sloan left Florida State and in Bill's third year there,
coaching fraternity rumors began to circulate that Sloan was in line to get
the head coaching job at Vanderbilt. That's when Bill Parcells made a
phone call.

"He called me while I was still at Georgia Tech," recalled Sloan, "and
said flat-out that if I got the Vanderbilt job he would be interested in
coming with me. Funny part was I already had him penciled in as my
number-one choice for defensive coordinator if I got the job. We had
become friends in the short time we were together at Florida State and
always talked back and forth. I liked him as a coach and a person, and
knew he was dedicated. Football was what he did and what was important
to him. He just had a real feel for the game."

Heading to Nashville, Tennessee, in the summer of 1973, the Parcells
family might well have been listening to country music star Willie Nelson
singing "On The Road Again." It could well have become the anthem for
their life, maybe for every coach's life. It was the quest for the right job,
the right place, the chance to get more recognition and hopefully a top
job. You are constantly wondering if you made the right choice with the
right head coach, and whether you picked the program that will showcase
your talents and abilities. There are only so many openings at Notre Dame,
Southern Cal, Alabama, Texas, Penn State, or one of the other high-profile
perennial football powers. Everyone else is scrambling.

Thus, in 1973 Bill Parcells cast his lot with Steve Sloan. Many felt
Sloan was an up-and-coming star at that time, a coach on the rise who
would soon land one of the plum jobs that were always opening up. It also
helped that the two liked each other and got along well. Bill could always
be himself around Sloan.

Vanderbilt played in the tough Southeastern Conference, cracking
heads with the likes of Alabama, Auburn, Tennessee, Mississippi, Florida,
and Georgia. It wasn't an easy mix, and the Commodores often found
themselves on the bottom looking up. They brought in Sloan to change all
that, and the coach responded to the challenge. By 1974, the Commodores
had a winning record and had earned a trip to the Peach Bowl, where the
team played to a 6–6 tie with Texas Tech. According to coach Sloan, one
of the team's strengths was the defense orchestrated by Bill Parcells.

"If I recall, we ran pretty much standard defenses at Vandy," Sloan said, "but the defensive team was highly motivated and played very hard. The '74 team, that defense would knock you out. They didn't have a lot of talent, but they would play hard and hit hard. Back then they didn't blitz as much, though Bill had them mix a few in. He would get a little more creative after that, but he still did a real good job for me.

"He was also very popular among the players at Vandy, relating to them well. He knew how to balance his sarcasm with humor, yet was very tough. He didn't want to use anyone unless he trusted them to play hard. He simply didn't tolerate a lack of effort and, as such, a guy who didn't try hard wouldn't get in the game. Like I said, he was fun to be around because he had a lot of one-liners, a neat sense of humor. And believe me, he could fire them off one after the other, using the humor to soften his sarcasm and his criticism. He was just an excellent coach."

Several weeks after the Peach Bowl, Sloan announced he was leaving Vanderbilt. Ironically, he had been offered the head coaching job at Texas Tech, the team that had played the Commodores at the Peach Bowl. Now Bill Parcells had a dilemma. Sloan told him he would love to have him at Texas Tech as his defensive coordinator. At the same time, he had also told Vanderbilt officials that Bill was the best man to succeed him. Sure enough, at the age of thirty-four Bill found himself being offered his first head-coaching job. The question was: Should he take it?

While it might have sounded like an easy decision—a chance to head up your own program—there were nevertheless a number of possibilities that had to be considered. After all, if a coach flops badly in his first try as top dog, he might not be thrown the same bone a second time. When Bill sat back and weighed the pros and cons, he came to these conclusions. There were two ways a coach could be successful. The first was to come in and put a stumbling program back on its feet, which is what Steve Sloan had done at Vanderbilt. The second was to come in and turn a program around, then keep it functioning at a high level.

Bill thought about what it would take to keep the Vanderbilt program on the high road and came to the conclusion that it was nearly impossible. "I thought the only place for me to go was down," he would say. His reasoning was based on the fact that Vandy always had to meet such Southeastern Conference powerhouses as Alabama and Tennessee. There was no way, he felt, that the Commodores could recruit the top players and compete with these schools on a regular basis. Sloan had caught the program at the right time and produced a winning season. That, perhaps,

was an anomaly. Bill felt the norm would be something in the neighborhood of 3–8 or 4–7. Maybe things would come together every now and
then, with the team winning seven games or so as it had in 1974 with
Steve Sloan, but he simply didn't feel that would happen on a regular
basis. Sloan was the perfect example. He had a small taste of success,
then immediately decided to leave.

After considering the options, Bill made his decision. He put in a call
to Sloan and said, "Count me in." Then he informed Judy and the girls
that they would be packing up again, this time going from Nashville to
Lubbock, Texas, where he would become the Texas Tech defensive coordinator, once again under Steve Sloan.

Texas Tech played in the Southwest Conference against such formidable foes as Texas, Texas A&M, Arkansas, Baylor, Texas Christian,
Houston, and Rice. The school had an enrollment of more than twenty
thousand students and the Red Raiders played at Jones Stadium, with a
capacity of 50,500 fans. In 1973 Tech had an 11–1 record and was ranked
as the 11th-best team in the country by the Associated Press. That year,
Texas Tech capped its season by topping Tennessee in the Gator Bowl,
28–19. It was big-time college football, all right, maybe a notch below the
highest level.

In a sense, it would seem that this could be the final stage of Bill
Parcells's apprenticeship. He had already been offered one head-coaching
job. If he could build a successful defense and the team continued to win,
it seemed as if it would be simply a matter of time before another offer
came along. With all this in mind, he came to another conclusion during
his three-year tenure at Texas Tech, deciding that the next head-coaching
offer he got, he would accept.

What he didn't realize when he arrived in Lubbock was that his knowledge of football wouldn't be enough, at least not at first. He was about to
experience a kind of culture clash that not even a confident Jersey guy
would expect. As had always been the case, Bill Parcells had his own
blueprint for success. That meant being the kind of coach he had always
been. But from the first-year defensive coordinator at Texas Tech, the
players just weren't buying into it.

As the years went by, Bill would show an increasing tendency to reveal
less and less about himself, especially that which was separate from his
football teams. In his 1986 autobiography, *The Biggest Giant of Them All*,
he had this to say about his three-year stay at Texas Tech:

"The next thing I knew, I was in the middle of nowhere—Lubbock, Texas, is the state capitol of nowhere—watching the wind blow and wondering just where the next city was exactly."

There was, however, much more happening than that. He brought his loud, almost frenetic style to the Red Raider locker room and practice field, including his ever-sharpening tongue, biting wit, and thinly veiled sarcasm. It was the style that had been evolving since his first coaching job at Hastings. The veteran players on the Texas Tech defense were used to an entirely different style of coaching. For one of the first times in his coaching career, Bill Parcells found players teetering on the brink of open rebellion.

"We didn't understand much about him when he first arrived," said Greg Frazier, a free safety who would be a starter in both 1976 and '77. "He was very brash, what we would define as a Yankee. He really didn't quite understand how to get the most of boys from Texas. His idea of motivating was to embarrass you, try to goad you into doing better.

"We just didn't know how to take him that first year, didn't know what to expect. He was very vocal and his idea of motivation was a lot different from anything we had ever been around. I guess we didn't like the way he was coaching. Our previous coaches were a little more soft-spoken, not as intense. We felt he had to prove himself to us."

Richard Arledge, who would become an All-Conference defensive end under Bill, had an even more adverse first impression. "His first year he hated us and in our view he was a New York asshole," Arledge said. "He was a grab-you-by-the-face-mask-and-degrade-you type."

Arledge also provided a partial explanation for the incipient problem, something perhaps not even the wily Parcells fully understood then. "When you're recruited to go to a certain school a lot of it is because of the coaching staff," he said. "When a coach quits and a whole new staff comes in you feel kind of abandoned. So I think it would have been an adjustment for us no matter who came in that year. On top of that, he came in from the east and we were just West Texas boys. It took a whole year for us to get used to him and him to get used to us."

The early problems continued beyond first impressions. At one practice session the defense just wasn't playing well, wasn't into it, and tough-guy Parcells decided he had to do something to shake them up.

"The offense was at one end of the field working their butts off," Arledge remembered. "We're at the other end having a bad practice. All of a sudden he yells out, 'You guys make me sick. Just get the hell off the field!' I think he was expecting all of us to say something like, 'Coach, come on, we'll do better. Give us another chance.' Well, you never saw about eighty guys disappear so fast in your life. He just kind of stood there gasping. We were gone. It was terrible."

It was just a matter of coach and players not connecting on the same wavelength. One player that first year took a real exception to the Parcells style. The team was set for its first spring game, with the players in the locker room ready to take the field. Greg Frazier remembers what happened next.

"None of us really liked [Parcells] yet and still weren't sure what to expect," Frazier said. "We're all sitting by our lockers and Parcells began walking down the line, kind of pushing and shoving everyone, yelling 'All right, are you ready?' He was even hitting some guys on their pads. It was his way, but we didn't know that. Anyway, we had a defensive tackle named Billy Bouthwell who liked to sit quietly by himself and psyche himself up. Parcells goes by and pushes him, and Bouthwell jumps up and hits him, just punched him and knocked him down!

"Without missing a beat, our defensive line coach says to Parcells, 'I think he's ready, coach.' Funny thing was, though, he just got up and continued. I don't even think he was angry because if nothing else, he knew Bouthwell was ready to play."

Because this kind of situation hadn't happened at Vanderbilt, Coach Sloan knew he had a problem on his hands. Bill Parcells was the best defensive coordinator he knew, but if he didn't have the respect of the players, all his talents as a coach could disappear into the Texas sky.

"Part of the problem was one of philosophy," Sloan said. "Bill was a lot tougher than they were accustomed to the first year he was there. That was a big change for the players, and when the team began struggling just to play .500 ball, he was even less happy, because Bill doesn't like to lose. His practices were hard and he made a lot of demands on the players. When the defense began to struggle that first year, it exacerbated the problem. I had to hold a few meetings, especially with the seniors. And I think Bill realized he had to get closer to the players the next year."

Another part of the problem was Bill's feeling of alienation in Lubbock, a sense that he did fit and didn't belong. For one of the few times in his life he found it difficult to assimilate and come to terms with his new surroundings and its people.

"Bill was something of a loner when we came to Texas Tech," Coach Sloan remembered. "He didn't go to staff parties or things like that, and he was probably trying to figure what direction to take as a coach. West Texas was still mostly cowboys then, and it was a different kind of life than he was used to."

The Red Raiders struggled home with a 6–5 record in 1975. The juniors and seniors who had been part of the 11–1 team in 1973 were undoubtedly disappointed, and the younger players were still wondering if this coaching staff could bring the team back to the point where it was among the conference elite. Bill Parcells, the alienated easterner with his sharp, often insulting, often sarcastic tongue may have been the targeted symbol of what was wrong with the new coaching staff. It would be up to him to find a way to make the situation better.

In looking for ways to ameliorate the situation, Bill looked within himself. As a kid, he'd liked nothing better than to play ball, hang around the gym, look for another game, another challenge. Even Mickey Corcoran called him a typical gym rat. As a coach, he enjoyed being around the players, but knew there would be times when he would have to come down hard on them. Perhaps that had made him back off a bit, retreat from interacting with them on several levels. He needed a balance, something to counteract his sharpness and his sarcasm. Things had worked out fine at Vanderbilt, but the rocky start at Texas Tech demanded attention.

During the off-season, gym rat Parcells began taking to the basketball court, jumping into pickup games with some of his players. He was able to compete with them on an equal level, joke with them, and get to know them better. In addition, he called many of his returning players into his office for one-on-one meetings, talking football and his defensive philosophy, and, perhaps more importantly, asking for their suggestions and input.

"He talked to me about the defensive alignments he was planning to use in the next season," Richard Arledge said. "He asked my opinion about some things and we talked some serious football. After that, he would always talk to us when he was thinking about making some defensive changes and he listened to our suggestions. Like many of the other players, I began to see how much he knew and realized he was a good football coach."

Greg Frazier said, "Once we got to know him better we had to help the younger guys coming onto the team to get used to him. Otherwise, they might have the same reaction we had at first. Bill was hard on the players because he never minced words. If you messed up, he told you so."

By the start of the 1976 season Bill had a defense willing to go to war for him, while Sloan was busy cultivating a solid offensive unit. The result was an outstanding Red Raider team that once again challenged for the Southwest Conference title and for a place in the national rankings. Texas Tech won its first eight games that year, opening up with a 24–7 win over Colorado. Along the way they trampled Arizona 52–27, and whipped arch-rivals Texas A&M and Texas, 27–16 and 31–28. The team was doing it on both ends of the ball, and by this time all the defensive players as well as the other coaches knew just who they could thank.

"Bill overcame the problems he had the first year and from that point on did a great job," Steve Sloan said. "He took a lot of castoff offensive players and converted them to play on his defense. He had a knack for putting the right guy in the right place. . . . In a way the players both respected and feared him. The respect came from his productivity on the field; the fear from his toughness and sarcasm. "Sometimes," Sloan laughed, "I had to try not to be afraid of him myself. He had a commanding personality and during those years I worked with him, nobody could have done it better.

"In 1976 he became more creative. He went to an even front, something not many college teams were doing then. He ran a lot of slants and gave the offense different looks. And he really had the players in the palm of his hand."

Greg Frazier was one of those converted offensive players. He had been a quarterback before breaking his hand, and Bill suggested he become a safety. He then proceeded to give Frazier the full treatment, designed to make him Bill's kind of player and the best player he could be.

"We were working on our goal-line defense one day when a wide receiver cracked back on me, clipped me. Parcells comes over and kicks me in the butt. I kind of jumped up to see who did it, then started walking back to the huddle. 'If that ever happens again,' he growled in that voice of his, 'and you don't get up and kick that guy in the mouth, you'll never play for me again.'

"After that, I had an attitude adjustment. When I went out onto the field I didn't have any friends. I tried to become a defensive player, the defensive player he wanted me to be. He used to say whoever has the ball is the enemy."

Richard Arledge remembers his coach's ability to make adjustments. "If you watch games," he said, "the good football teams are better second-half teams. They make adjustments at halftime and nobody was better than Bill at that. That's why I always said we were in the right defense most of the time. He knew what the other team was going to do and we would work on that in practice. We were always prepared, but if the unexpected happened, he'd take us in at halftime and always make great adjustments."

However, the respect that Arledge cultivated with his coach didn't come without a price. Bill pushed him as hard as anyone else, and on one occasion Arledge pushed back. Literally.

"We were having a Saturday scrimmage," he said, "and I was playing defensive end. The offense ran a draw play up the middle. I mean, that's not my play and it went for about thirty yards. Well, Bill ran the whole thirty yards down the field hollering at me. Then he grabbed my face mask and I pushed him. I was angry and the push was real. But I think that's what he was trying to do, get me mad. He must have gotten the reaction he wanted because he didn't yell at me or punish me or make a big deal about it. He just ignored it."

Bill's unique defensive strategy also surprised the players. Though this kind of defense had been evolving in his mind since Wichita State days, it went against much of which they had been taught before.

"Ever since I had been playing football, defensive ends were always taught to turn in the play to the linebackers," Arledge said. "Parcells's theory was that the defensive end should force the back outside and then the cornerback would take over and force it to the sideline. His entire defense was set around the linebackers, a scheme I had never seen before. Everyone else was supposed to string it out, keep them going sideways until the linebackers would catch up inside-out. Plus the free and strong safeties were almost like linebackers and also supposed to make a lot of tackles. If you've got the linebackers, which we did, you've got a great defense.

"He took that theory right to New York, when the Giants had that great defense and great group of linebackers. He loves team speed and sets the defense up for the linebackers to make eighty percent of the tackles."

Greg Frazier saw the same thing from his safety position. "We were always taught to contain, to turn everything inside. He wanted us to get the running back to bounce to the outside, and to use team speed to make the tackle before he could turn upfield. So you forced them to go east or west and stopped them before they could go north or south. Once we learned it, it worked very well."

Another Parcells trait was to keep his team on the field. He had an expression that everyone heard every year: *You can't make the club in the tub.*

"He was hard on people who were hurt," Greg Frazier remembered. "He felt you needed to be out there, practicing and playing. He always used to say to the young guys, 'Potential means you ain't done nothing yet.' "

As would be the case later in the pros, there were always a few players who never did get used to the Parcells tongue, the needling and the sarcasm.

"We had a young cornerback that he nicknamed 'Toast,' " Greg Frazier recalled, "because the kid kept getting burned. This kid didn't take to it kindly and after about the third game, he just quit the team."

After winning their first eight games in 1976, Texas Tech lost a tough one to Houston, 27–19. The team bounced back to win its final pair and finish the regular season at 10–1. In eleven games, the offense had scored 312 points while Bill Parcells's defense yielded just 179, an average of just over sixteen points a game. Solid stuff. A tough 27–24 loss to seventh-ranked Nebraska in the now-defunct Bluebonnet Bowl ended the season on a low note. Still, the team was ranked 13th in both the Associated Press and United Press International final polls. The coaching staff on the whole, and Bill Parcells in particular, had certainly proved they could make the Red Raiders a big winner.

There were more high hopes in 1977, maybe this time for a top-ten finish. In three years Bill had gone from someone who was viewed with suspicion and distrust to a beloved, revered, and respected coach. He had taken a potentially perilous career situation and turned it completely around. Steve Sloan always loved Bill as a defensive coach and coordinator. Now, he felt Bill was ready to be a head coach . . . if . . .

"There was no doubt he was ready as far as his coaching ability and knowledge of the game," Sloan said. "He was bright, had a way with words—both good and bad—and had a lot of leadership qualities. I just sometimes wondered, though, if the tough side wouldn't drag him down. Sometimes people get a picture of a tough guy and back off. I guess it was a matter of him becoming diplomatic enough.

"But I also thought then that he was more ideally suited to the NFL. He didn't like to recruit; everyone knew that. In the pros you don't recruit, you acquire. He also wasn't that easy to get to know because he was basically a loner. He wasn't a big personality off the field. He didn't like to speak before groups back then and, as an assistant, he didn't have to. If he became a head coach at the college level, he would eventually have to do some of that. But I think he knew he could do the things a head coach had to do."

His players also saw something of a change by 1977. "He reached a point where he would also get on the other coaches if they were doing something he thought wasn't right," Richard Arledge said. "I mean, he would really jump their ass. But looking back, I believe it was because he was smarter than everyone else. He used to even get mad at Coach Sloan when the offense messed up.

"He always spoke his mind, no matter what—but he also backed it up. We were always prepared, always in the right defense. We might have gotten beat, but we were prepared. I can never once remember our defense being outcoached."

The coach also showed respect for his seniors, players who had been through the wars with him for three years. "The seniors always got a little preferential treatment," Arledge said. "You didn't have to do the grunt drills you had been doing your whole life. If you were a senior, you kind of earned some time off. That's why I always thought Bill was a player's coach. He was a guy you felt would stand up for you if there was a problem."

Greg Frazier was another player who had come full circle in his regard for the coach he called a "damned Yankee" when he first arrived. "We believed in what he was doing and had a lot of success. Success breeds confidence. He believed in the philosophy that if the other team does not score, you can't lose. And you still see interviews today with players who say they don't necessarily like him. But did he get me to play? Yes!"

The Texas Tech team got off to a 5–1 start in 1977 and looked as if it was in a position to at least duplicate its great 1976 season. Unfortunately, they had already suffered a crippling blow when the team's star quarterback, Rodney Allison, went down with an injury in Game Three against Texas A&M.

"Rodney's injury really killed us," Richard Arledge said. "We felt, as a defense, that no one could do anything on us. Rodney was being touted as a possible Heisman Trophy candidate. I remember in the fourth quarter of that A&M game our defense held them to negative-16 yards, but they still scored sixteen points. They got three long field goals and recovered a kickoff in the end zone. They beat us 33–17."

The team was still good enough to beat the weaker teams, but after a 5–1 start they lost three of their next five, including the final pair, to finish the regular season at 7–4. Nevertheless, they received an invitation to the Florida Citrus Bowl, where they were beaten 40–17 by a very good Florida State team.

Despite Allison's injury and the late-season slump, it seemed as if Steve Sloan and his staff had the Texas Tech program operating at a high level. Bill had established himself as a top-flight defensive coordinator who had earned the players' respect. In fact, they had given him a rather incongruous nickname that year, one that they rarely called him to his face.

"We nicknamed him 'Pretty,' " Greg Frazier said. "Sometimes it was Coach Pretty, or Pretty Person Parcells. It was the neat way he combed his hair and some of his other mannerisms. But it was also a name out of respect. We weren't making fun of him."

Just when it appeared that the marriage between Coach Sloan and his staff and the Texas Tech program no longer needed counseling, the realities of the collegiate coaching world interceded and brought about a quickie divorce. Steve Sloan decided the grass was greener elsewhere and took over the head-coaching spot at the University of Mississippi. Only this time Bill Parcells wouldn't be following him. Coach Pretty was about to strike out on his own. He was offered the head-coaching job at the Air Force Academy in Colorado. This time he wouldn't say no. He was thirty-seven years old and it was time to test the waters. Since 1964, he had been a Bronco, a Shocker, a Cadet, a Seminole, a Commodore, and a Red Raider. Now he was about to become a Falcon.

CHAPTER FOUR

Grounded

M UCH OF WHAT BILL PARCELLS WOULD ULTIMATELY BECOME AS A
coach had its genesis during his three years at Texas Tech. He
was learning to put a balance to his highly critical, often sarcastic style. The mini-revolt he had experienced in 1975, his first year in
Lubbock, had shown him that he needed to achieve a degree of closeness
to his players in order to coach them in the style he had chosen, the one
he felt made him most effective. If you made a player feel two inches tall
one day, you had to make him think he was ten feet tall the next day.
Otherwise, you could lose him permanently.

He was also beginning to learn which players he could ride and push,
and which ones he more or less had to leave alone. There was one thing
he did in this regard at Texas Tech that didn't sit well with Richard
Arledge.

"I always thought his biggest flaw in terms of hurting the morale of the
team was that he would always take one player under his wing," Arledge
said. "That player, it seemed, could do no wrong. If it was the team's best
player—which one year it was—then you don't have any problem with it.
I'm referring to Thomas Howard, an All-American linebacker who went
on to play in the pros. But when [Parcells] took a young guy who's screwing
up all the time and wasn't very good, and he's yelling at you and not ever
yelling at him, well, I always thought that was the biggest flaw he had."

Arledge also saw the transient nature of college coaching as sometimes a detriment to the entire program at a particular school, in this case Texas Tech.

"The thing that kind of hacked me off about that entire staff was the recruiting situation. I was in the last class recruited by Coach [Jim] Carlen, who was there before Coach Sloan took over. We had twenty-eight or thirty kids and almost everyone of us started. There was a lot of talent within that group. Tech had won eleven games when I was a senior in high school, 1973. Then in my junior year at Lubbock we won ten games. When you have a program that is winning, you try to keep it going. Other good players want to come in. But [Coach Sloan and his staff] just killed it. They didn't recruit anybody.

"I just didn't see too much recruiting activity. I'm sure some of them tried, but there just wasn't any talent coming in. We were an all-senior team in 1977, and even with the injuries to Rodney Allison and others we were 7–5. After that, there wasn't much left and it hurt. They worked with talent that was already there and didn't leave the program in real good shape."

In truth, Texas Tech was 7–4 the year after Sloan left. But in the two following years they were a losing team, at 3–6–2 and 5–6, so the incoming coach did have some rebuilding to do. It was a situation similar to the one at Vanderbilt when Bill had turned down the head-coaching job in 1975. He felt the program could only deteriorate. When there are frequent coaching changes, that's often what happens. The Joe Paternos (Penn State), Bobby Bowdens (Florida State), and Steve Spurriers (Florida)— coaches who stay at the same school for many years—have the leverage and history to get the most talented kids and keep the program at a consistently high level. That, however, is the nature of the sport.

As for Bill, he might have hated recruiting but he appreciated intelligent football players who used their heads. He apparently felt that Richard Arledge was one of these, because when he left for Air Force he wanted Arledge to come with him.

"He offered me a job," Arledge recalled, "not as a full-time assistant but a grade above a graduate assistant. It was a way of getting me started. He told me he thought I would make a good coach. I thought about it, but I was planning to get married right after I graduated and had a family business waiting. So I turned him down."

Perhaps Arledge had seen enough of the coaching life not to want any part of it. But Bill Parcells had already chosen. Though Air Force seemed a strange fit, certainly presenting no more opportunity for the big stage than Vanderbilt had, he felt it was time to roll the dice. The word was out that longtime Air Force coach Ben Martin was retiring, leaving a program that he had built up in the 1960s but one that now suffered from four straight losing seasons with few prospects for improvement.

Bill was one of a number of coaches who applied for the job. Another was Jimmy Johnson, the same Jimmy Johnson who would later win a national championship at the University of Miami, then a pair of Super Bowls with the Dallas Cowboys. At this point, however, it was Bill Parcells who had the more solid credentials. The three years spent at Army probably gave him the edge, due to his prior knowledge of the workings of a service academy.

"Bill had a fine recommendation from Tom Cahill, who was the Army head coach when Bill was there, and also his high school coach at River Dell," said Jim Bowman, the current assistant athletic director at Air Force and one who has been at the Academy for more than thirty-five years. "Coach Cahill told us we couldn't get a better coach. He said Bill was a competitor and a winner, a guy who always plays to win."

That combinations of factors—the strong recommendations and service academy background—resulted in Bill being offered the job. Once again the Parcells family hit the road, traveling from Lubbock to the rarified air of Colorado Springs, which is situated at the end of the Great Plains and at the foot of the Rocky Mountains. It was a place that Judy Parcells and her three daughters would quickly grow to love.

As for Head Coach Parcells, his hiring at the Air Force Academy would lead to a strange and enigmatic year, contradictory in some ways, successful in others, and open to several different interpretations. One thing, however, was certain. Bill's arrival in Colorado would mark the beginning of perhaps the oddest and most difficult two years of his life, where the decisions he made would be questioned on several fronts and result in a crisis of conscience that would affect his entire family as well as his coaching future.

Bill admitted that he came to Colorado "filled with the proverbial piss and vinegar." Hell, it was his first head-coaching gig and there probably isn't a football coach alive at any level who wouldn't leap into his first top job ready to lick the world, drive his team, and produce a big winner. That's exactly how Bill said he felt, but with one big caveat. He was going into his first head-coaching spot with a secondary thought, one that reached beyond the obvious desire to create a winning team. He knew that recruiting and Bill Parcells would never mix. They were oil and water, an anathema that he could not overcome. Thus he viewed the job at Air Force not as a stepping-stone to a major collegiate program but rather as his ticket to the NFL, the pro ranks. He was hoping to fly there on the wings of the Falcons, a team he would shape to win, a program he would work to revive.

He started like a house afire. First, he brought in some top-flight assistants. His offensive coordinator was Ken Hatfield, whom he had met at Army and who had been currently working as an assistant at Florida. The defensive coordinator was Al Groh, another cohort from Army days. A third assistant was Ray Handley, yet another old friend from West Point. Besides being excellent coaches, all three were familiar with service academy programs and players.

"It was a great staff, one of the best I've ever been around," said Jim Bowman. "Parcells was this very young, very dynamic, very upbeat guy with this great positive attitude. He was aggressive and a disciplinarian. He was just what we needed at the time."

Bill immediately had the team begin a weight and strength program, something that had been sorely lacking at the academy. He upgraded the facilities and got all the players into a routine. Ken Hatfield saw the enthusiasm that Bill brought to the job and felt he was just the man to get the program rolling again.

"I think the academy was content to go 6–5 or 5–6 every year," Hatfield said. "There was a feeling, I think, that [anything better] couldn't be done, and that as long as the team didn't embarrass itself, it was okay. Bill wasn't going to have that. He was too competitive for that. He was too much of a winner."

There's little doubt that the enthusiasm was genuine, the goals lofty and ambitious. Yet under the surface there was an ominous churning, a volcanic action that came from something more than a meal full of spicy foods. Witness this statement Bill would make about Air Force years later.

"It took me only three months to know that I'd made a mistake. Again. All the things that were wrong with the Vanderbilt job were wrong with the Air Force job. Plus, I had an extra monkey on my back with the military."

Once more, Bill Parcells wasn't happy. He seemed to have nearly the same complaints at every stop along the way. The job wasn't what he expected. Maybe the next one would be better. Another disappointment. It was okay in one way, bad in another. The wrong program again, one that could only go down. And, oh, did he ever hate recruiting.

With that kind of attitude how in the world could he ever do a good job? As an assistant he always ended up working his defensive magic. This time, though, he must have had a hard time not bringing his feelings home with him. It seems his wife and daughters had quickly fallen in love with Colorado. They had a nice house, the kids loved their new schools and their friends, and Bill was making $40,000 a year, more than he had ever made before in his life. The female side of the family were probably hoping that this was the place where they would finally settle for a long run. No wonder Bill would say later that "I feel like I'm trapped."

For a football coach, however, the show must go on. Bill knew only one way to do things—all out. It was more than a decade since he had been an assistant at Army, and in that time big-time college football had grown rapidly. There was more at stake for the big schools and they went after the best players with an intensity and an urgency not seen before. Winning was the goal, as always, but the by-product now, with television contracts and more sponsorships available, was money. More for the universities, more for the coach. In addition, the best collegiate players were being seduced by the increasing salaries of the ever-expanding NFL. So it was becoming harder and harder to compete, and Bill began to see the restrictions of the military as a roadblock to his success.

He said that he felt his players could handle the combination of athletics and academics, but throw in the time-consuming responsibilities of military training and the burden on the kids becomes a source of additional stress. To ameliorate the situation somewhat, he felt the academy should try to decrease the academic pressures slightly during the season. It was promised, he said, but never happened, and the on-field effectiveness of many of his players decreased as the season wore on.

There was a wide receiver named Cormac Carney that Bill said was one of the best freshman in the country. But Carney simply found he couldn't handle the trifecta (football, academics, and military training) that was thrown at him and the next year transferred to UCLA. The forward-looking Parcells said he saw that happening over and over again, even if he was lucky enough to recruit that caliber of player. In his mind, he had visions of 4–7, 3–8, even 2–9 seasons, which he called "a dead-end road."

All this prompted him to say, "I had finally become a head coach and I was just . . . goddam . . . miserable."

Oddly enough, the perceptions of those around him weren't quite the same. It was either a matter of Bill covering up his true feelings, or others remembering it the way they hoped it would be. Ken Hatfield couldn't say enough good things about the job Bill did. When asked to comment in January 1999, Hatfield expressed these thoughts.

"It was an amazing year, a year I'll never forget. Bill made an unbelievable impact at Air Force. . . . I think it's fair to say Air Force wouldn't have had the success it's had over the past twenty years or so if it wasn't for Bill Parcells. His goal was to get Air Force up to speed with the things other major programs were doing. There's no question in my mind he's the one who got the ball rolling there."

In reality, Bill's 1978 Air Force team won just three games, beating Boston College, Texas–El Paso, and Kent State. They lost eight others. It was that old 3–8 record, the one he felt he would always have. That year, however, he was playing the hand that was dealt him: holdover players only; none that he had recruited. Perhaps he felt that his longtime aversion to recruiting would prevent the situation from ever getting much better. Jim Bowman basically agreed.

"He hated losing," Bowman said. "But he didn't get down on the kids. I think he knew they were here for a different reason. They were going to be cadets. Knowing that, he also realized he didn't have the same control over kids at a military academy that he would have elsewhere. They weren't there to be athletes. And things he can't control bother him.

"He was always firm, but fair; but a no-nonsense guy like Bill wants control. Yet he always had a positive sense of humor. I think he realized these weren't big-time players. After that, he got impatient. I don't think he really gave the school or himself a chance."

Then came the phone call Bill thought would change his life. While he was still at Texas Tech, Bill had met Ray Perkins, who knew Steve Sloan from Alabama days. Perkins was an All-American wide receiver for the Crimson Tide and was an assistant coach with the New England Patriots when Bill first met him. He had come to Texas Tech to visit old friend Sloan and scout some players.

The phone call came soon after Bill had returned from a hated recruiting trip to California. With no options available, he was beginning to plan for his second season at Air Force. But the phone call changed everything. Within seconds, Ray Perkins said the magic words: *New York Giants!*

Bill had known that Perkins had been hired as Giants coach prior to the 1979 season, but never expected a call from a man he barely knew. Yet here was Perkins, calling New York to Colorado and wasting no time asking Bill if he was interested in flying to New York to talk about becoming the Giants' linebackers coach. It was like a bolt from the blue, a gift from heaven, a final, successful roll of the dice—any superlative you could create. *The New York Giants.* Give Bill Parcells the choice of any football team in the land, college or pro, that he would most love to join and the answer would roll off his tongue faster than a quarterback sneak. *The New York Giants.* Talk about the Parcells luck. Coming off a despised recruiting trip and not looking forward to a second season at Air Force, he suddenly gets an offer to talk about coaching for the Giants.

If he could have beamed himself to New York, a la *Star Trek*, he probably would have done so. That's how eager he was to get the job. He liked Perkins, and when they talked in New York, he liked him even more. Both were straightforward guys who spoke their minds, didn't eschew hard work, and would do whatever it took to produce a winner. Philosophically, in a football sense, they were on the same wavelength.

It must have felt like a blast from the past when Bill checked into the Sheraton Hotel in Hasbrouck Heights, New Jersey. He was, in effect, home again. It had been a long time. With seven jobs in fourteen years, he had only been east once—his three-year stint at Army. Now he saw familiar sights, spent time with his family, traveled the roads from his past, got to see Mickey, and then got the job offer he always wanted. Perkins wanted to change the Giants' defense from the traditional 4–3 to the more mobile and flexible 3–4. That meant building a strong linebacking corps, something that Bill considered his specialty. When Perkins asked Bill what he thought, Bill said, simply, "When do we start?"

Bill called his family to tell them the news, then flew home on an airplane that closely resembled cloud nine. As soon as he returned, he submitted his resignation at the Air Force Academy, recommending friend and Assistant Coach Ken Hatfield for the position. Hatfield got the job and Parcells was criticized in some quarters for walking away after only a single season. Ken Hatfield didn't see it that way.

"Bill made an unbelievable impact at Air Force for only being there one year," Hatfield said, in a 1999 interview in the *Rocky Mountain News*.

"I think it's fair to say Air Force wouldn't have had the success it's had over the past twenty years or so if it wasn't for Bill Parcells.

"There's no question in my mind he's the one who got the ball rolling there. I learned a lot from him, and in a lot of ways, he made my job easier when I took over."

With the Academy making more of an effort to upgrade its program and with Ken Hatfield at the helm, Air Force turned things around and began a strong lineage. Two years after Bill left, Hatfield brought in a new assistant from tiny Appalachian State to install a wishbone offense. He was Fisher DeBerry, who would eventually succeed Hatfield and was still coaching the Falcons in 1999. Air Force began winning under Hatfield, however, who was voted Coach of the Year by the American Football Coaches Association in 1983. Hatfield would go on to coach at Clemson and then Rice, where he was still active in 1999.

"You can make the argument that without Parcells, there's no Kenny Hatfield, and with no Hatfield, there's no DeBerry," Jim Bowman said. "So who knows where we'd be today if it weren't for Bill Parcells? He's the guy who got it all started. Even though he wasn't here long, he was the catalyst."

He was also a professional coach in waiting. Whereas a Ken Hatfield thrived and succeeded at the collegiate level, that would never have been Bill's bailiwick. His style was better suited to the pros and acquiring players. Recruiting them never worked for him—it simply became more objectionable with each passing year. Yet his one year at Air Force did benefit the program because it led to Hatfield and then DeBerry.

Now, however, Bill hoped there would be no looking back. A dream job had come knocking at his door and he welcomed it without hesitation. Bill was so high with anticipation that he failed to notice that the rest of his family didn't exactly share his jubilation. He soon realized that Judy wasn't very excited about the idea at all. She told him she didn't like the east, her only previous experience living there being their time at West Point. She was now extremely happy in Colorado and had been hoping to stay for a long time. She and the girls had made a lot of friends and, to put it bluntly, they were very tired of moving.

Bill apparently couldn't shake his euphoria long enough to listen to them. Even when his wife said she wasn't sure if she could move again, he kept talking about his dream job, how he had to take it, how it was the opportunity of a lifetime. He figured that Judy would eventually understand. Finally, he left the family in Colorado in the summer of 1979, checked back into the Sheraton, and went to work with the Giants, who were already preparing for the upcoming season and getting ready for the team's first mini-camp. He would revel in being part of the Giants during the day, then call home at night only to find that things weren't changing. The family wanted to remain in Colorado. It didn't take Bill long to realize that his family was not going to come east. Now he had a huge decision to make, but he made it quickly because of what was at stake.

"I decided [my family] needed me more than [Ray] Perkins did," he said.

He explained things to Perkins, telling him he had to resign. The coach understood and asked him to stay for a short time longer, until the mini-camp ended. Bill agreed, finished out the mini-camp, then left for Colorado. His professional coaching career had lasted just two months and he was convinced he would never again receive a pro offer. As he described it, "I cried all the way back to Colorado."

One Giants player who would later play a key role on Parcells's first Super Bowl team, tackle Brad Benson, has one lasting image from Bill's short stay with the team in 1979. Benson said he was in the training room one day as Bill sat in the whirlpool. One of the other players asked him what to do in practice that day. According to Benson, Bill answered without missing a beat.

"How the hell should I know?" he said. "I have as much say around here as a fart in a whirlwind."

The Parcells tongue was a sharp as ever, but he probably already had part of himself back in Colorado. Giving up the Giants job was bad enough. However, his sudden resignation automatically opened up question number two. Where would he go from there? If not coaching, what would he do to make a living? In fact, what in hell would he do with the rest of his life?

As hard as it was to leave the Giants, Bill felt he owed Judy. After all, she was the one making the sacrifices all those years, traveling from place to place, setting up yet another home, registering the kids for yet another school, saying goodbye to old friends and then making new ones. As the wife of an itinerant football coach, she didn't have much choice. He knew it wasn't an easy life. She had always done it without knowing what was waiting at the end of the rainbow. There were simply no guarantees that the pot of gold would finally be there.

Bill's friends supported him, telling him that it took real character to walk away as he did. Some coaches don't care enough about their families to make that decision. If the wife and kids don't follow, well, tough. On the other hand, Bill was going on thirty-nine years of age, and unlike Jack Benny, he wouldn't remain in a holding pattern. The years were passing and as a traveling assistant coach he hadn't saved much money. He figured they could survive maybe six months without him working, but didn't want to wait that long. He tried to think of a profession that had some similarities to coaching. The only thing he could come up with was sales. As a coach, he was always trying to convince his players to buy into a system, e.g., he was selling them on it. Maybe he would have luck selling something other than football.

Fortunately, he had met a number of people in Colorado Springs during his short coaching tenure at Air Force. He asked around and wound up working for the Gates Land Company, which was a subsidiary of Gates Rubber, a big tire and rubber company in Denver. Gates Land was developing some five-thousand acres in the immediate area, with plans to build residential homes, all of them situated around The Country Club of Colorado and none of them very far from the Air Force Academy.

"At the beginning, Bill stated that he and his family needed to settle down and have a home somewhere," said David Sunderland, who was then president of Gates Land. "That was one element of why he elected to stop coaching and try something else."

If Sunderland and Bill's other new associates were skeptical at first, wondering if a guy who had done nothing but coach football for fifteen years could function in a new and foreign (to him) environment, he soon convinced them he was serious. He took a real-estate course three hours a day for seven weeks and passed easily.

"Bill was an effective salesman," Sunderland said. "He was fully committed to the real-estate business. He didn't sit around with a long face, saying he wished he was back on the football field. He wasn't in a blue funk. He was focused and energetic and committed to results."

As a salesman, Bill's life changed in many ways. Suddenly, he was a 9-to-5 guy who ate breakfast and dinner with the family, went for rides on the weekend, and did many of the other things regular dads do. He also had a side job as athletic director at The Country Club of Colorado, where he set up independent programs in swimming and tennis for club members and their children. Everything seemed to be falling into place.

But guess what? He hated every minute of it. He was miserable. He even thought about calling Perkins and begging for his job back, though he knew the position had already been filled. Ironically, however, as a salesman he was earning a little *more* money than he had as the head coach of Air Force the season before.

Then came the chill of fall and the scent of football in the air. That might have been the toughest time. His internal clock was still being regulated by football, and he couldn't help thinking about what he would be doing as a coach—at a particular time of day, or at any given point during the week. His mind would drift and he would begin to think about defenses, dealing with injuries, motivating his players, trying his damnedest to win the next game. To try to quench his thirst he began to follow a different kind of football regimen. He and Judy got season tickets to watch the Denver Broncos, sitting in the end zone at Mile High Stadium on the Sundays that the Broncos were home. He even found himself going back to the Academy to watch Air Force play, a situation that made him feel a bit uncomfortable. After all, he had resigned to take a pro job and suddenly he was back in town working real estate. He knew there were probably whispers, but it was football and he couldn't seem to stay away. To complete the package, he did color commentary on Friday nights for a Denver radio station that broadcast the high-school Game of the Week. In effect, he was suffering withdrawal symptoms, trying to fill a void and finding that it wasn't working.

In his mind he knew he was a real-estate salesman. But in his heart he was still a football coach. He would always be a football coach. That would never change. Yet despite his longing for the smell of the locker room, the banter with the players, the intensity of practice, and the excitement of the sidelines on weekends, Bill did learn something about himself while he worked for Gates Land.

"Sometimes, when you're locked into a profession," he would say, years later, "what's out there scares you, because you don't know if you could make your way in this world in another profession. But then when you're out there, you find out that you can. The routine of life is different. Getting used to that was probably my biggest acclimation. Having, like, a regular job."

But deep into the fall and the football season, everyone in the Parcells family was edgy and restless. Both Bill and Judy knew why. Someone just had to admit it. It was Judy who finally told her husband he was driving her crazy. When he asked why, she told him she thought it was time he made an effort to return to football. Her words were tantamount to turning a key and unlocking a very large door. He had tried to do it another way; now they both knew it had to be football. For better or worse, it was the only life for Bill, and for his family. Ken Hatfield, coaching Air Force that year, must have sensed his friend's frustration. Looking back, he assessed the situation this way.

"After six or seven months, Judy knew [selling real estate] wasn't him. But I give the guy credit. He tried and did what he had to do, made a great commitment to his wife and family to do what he thought was right. I always questioned how long it would last, but I wasn't going to tell him that. I knew what he was, first and foremost. It was just a matter of time before his family said, 'Now, Dad, get your butt back and do what you like doing.' "

Up to the moment when he resigned from the Giants and joined Gates Land, Bill's life had been geared around sports and football: pickup games, practices, competition, winning and losing, learning all he could, looking forward to the next season, to a better job, to a winning team. Football had become his time clock, set his schedule, dictated the rules, regulated his life. It was that way from one season to the next. As Bill himself admitted, "I wasn't built for breakfast with the family at eight-thirty."

He had opted out just when he got his biggest chance. Now he was about to get back in.

CHAPTER FIVE

The Dream Becomes Real

O NCE BILL PARCELLS MADE THE DECISION TO RETURN TO COACHING he began to worry whether anyone would want him. After all, he resigned from the Air Force Academy after just one year as head coach. The reason he quit was to take a job that lasted just a few months before he resigned once again. Now he wasn't sure just how the coaching fraternity would view him. A knowledgeable and effective coach, sure. But a flake, a quitter, a guy who couldn't seem to make up his mind where he wanted to be and how long he wanted to be there. Is that the Bill Parcells people would see when they considered him for a job? It was a concern. At the same time, he knew enough about the profession to be certain that there was always a place for a good coach.

What he didn't want, however, was to take his family on another cross-country odyssey, being an assistant here, an assistant there for a year or two, or maybe three. The pros were what he really wanted. He knew that now. But would they want him? His pro coaching career had lasted all of two months. That didn't make for an impressive NFL résumé.

The only way to find what was out there for him was to test the waters, to let people know that he was available and that he was ready to make a total commitment. The first person he called was Ray Perkins. When he told his former short-time boss that he wanted back in, Perkins said he wasn't surprised. The 1979 season was still in full swing and the two friends met for breakfast in Kansas City, where the Giants were playing. Though Bill ached to return to the Giants, Perkins didn't have any openings. He said he wasn't sure about the next season, but he would keep in touch. Apparently, he held no ill will because of Bill's swift exit a year earlier. Now fully committed to getting a football job, Bill and Judy put their house in Colorado Springs up for sale. They sold it in December and were supposed to be out by January 10, 1980. The clock was ticking.

Next, Bill called old friend Steve Sloan, who was still coaching at Mississippi, and told him he was rededicating himself to coaching. Sloan put the word out and Bill soon received a call from Rod Dowhower, who was then head coach at Stanford University. Dowhower met with Bill in Colorado and told him flat-out he wanted him to coach the Stanford defense. Still having mixed feelings about returning to the college game, Bill flew to Palo Alto, loved the campus, knew his family would love it, and made one of those preliminary agree-to-agree commitments to Dowhower. Then just a day later, the coaching pigeons came home to roost. Dowhower flew the coop, taking a job as offensive coordinator with the Denver Broncos. Just like that, Palo Alto was out.

Fortunately, the Parcells luck was still running strong. Steve Sloan called him back and offered him a job as defensive coordinator at Mississippi. Sloan had apparently never forgotten the job Bill had done for him at Vanderbilt and Texas Tech. But Bill had reservations. In his heart, he still wanted to go to the NFL. He also remembered from past experience that he didn't particularly enjoy living in the south. Mississippi was the Deep South and he was probably reluctant to take the family there. But if nothing else came up, well . . .

Then Ray Perkins called him back. While Perkins still didn't have an opening with the Giants, he suggested Bill call Ron Erhardt, the head coach of the New England Patriots. The Patriots, it seemed, needed a linebackers coach. When Bill told Sloan about the possibility, his old friend suggested he look into it. Seems as if everyone knew he was more suited to the pros. Bill flew to Boston immediately and met with Erhardt, telling the Patriots coach that he needed an immediate decision because he felt it only fair to give Steve Sloan the quickest answer he could. Erhardt called him later the same day and said the job was his. When Bill told Steve Sloan of his decision, the Mississippi coach accepted it with grace, bestowed his blessing on Bill with a terse, but heartfelt: "Give 'em hell. You've always belonged in pro football anyway."

Bill spent one year in New England. He and Ron Erhardt hit it off to the point where Erhardt would later become his offensive coordinator with both the Giants and later the Jets. The Patriots still had a solid nucleus that year, with quarterback Steve Grogan, wide receivers Stanley Morgan and Harold Jackson, tight end Russ Francis, guard John Hannah, and linebacker Steve Nelson among the top players. Erhardt had brought the team in at 9–7 the season before, and in 1980 the Patriots were 10–6, finishing one game behind the Buffalo Bills in the AFC East. Unfortunately, the Pats just missed making the playoffs. Bill, however, felt Erhardt had the team on an upswing and thought there was a good chance he would settle in and be there for quite some time.

But again fate—or the Parcells luck—intervened. Soon after the season ended, there was that old telephone ringing again. Bill must have had a hard time believing his ears when he learned it was Ray Perkins, saying he wanted him back, only this time as the Giants defensive coordinator. No interviews, no question about whether he would stay this time. The job was his, period, if he wanted it.

It was an incredible turn of events. The dream that had turned into a nightmare in 1979 had suddenly become a dream again just two years later. Now Bill not only had a second chance to join his beloved Giants, he was also being offered an even better position, that of defensive coordinator. He gave Perkins his answer as fast as the word "Yes" could roll off his tongue. Then he called Ron Erhardt and told him that he would be leaving the Patriots. Erhardt, a veteran of the coaching wars, understood and wished him well. Ironically, it was a stroke of luck. The following year the Patriots crashed, bottoming out to a horrendous 2–14 record, and Erhardt was gone.

Bill has always felt that coaches such as Ron Erhardt and Dan Henning were fired from situations much too soon. Owners seemed to want such instant results that they didn't consider the intangibles, such as injuries, players just having poor seasons, guys being unhappy with their contracts. Perhaps that's one reason he always wanted as much control over his own destiny as possible. Had he remained in New England another year, he too would have been out of a job. Ray Perkins's phone call had changed all that. Now, Bill not only would be working with a head coach he liked and respected, he would also have a chance to construct an NFL defense and turn it loose on the rest of the league.

The New York Giants had a long and glorious NFL history, having joined the league in 1925, just five years after the NFL got its start. The team lost its first-ever home game to the Frankford Yellow Jackets, an indication that pro football was barely out of the Stone Age. In fact, one reason the league wanted a team in New York was to dispel the myth of the league being a small-town endeavor. The league had only one division that year and began the season with a cumbersome twenty teams, some of which not even the most ardent trivia buff would remember. Try these teams on for size: the Pottsville Maroons, Akron Indians, Rock Island Independents, Canton Bulldogs, Hammond Pros, Duluth Kelleys, Dayton Triangles, and Columbus Tigers.

The Chicago Bears were already operating, as were the Green Bay Packers. There were also teams in Cleveland and Detroit, but in those days the smaller franchises came and went like rabbits in a hat. In a one-division league the team with the best record was declared champion, the Giants achieving that distinction in 1927 when they finished at 11–1–1. When the league finally split into two divisions in 1933 there were just 10 teams left. In the first-ever championship game between the Eastern and Western Division winners, the Giants lost to the Chicago Bears 23–21.

A year later, the 8–5 Eastern Division champion Giants were huge underdogs to an unbeaten, 13–0 Bears team. The game was played in windy, frigid weather at the Polo Grounds in New York on December 9, 1934. The field was frozen rock-hard and slippery. In the first half the Bears had a 10–3 lead, with the lone touchdown scored by the legendary Bronko Nagurski. At halftime, Giants coach Steve Owen remembered something that his All-Pro end, Ray Flaherty, had said during warmups. Flaherty recalled a similar field condition from college days and remarked that the players got better traction with basketball shoes as opposed to the traditional cleats. Owen mentioned this to trainer Gus Mauch, who made a call to a friend at Manhattan College and was told they had a supply of sneakers available.

The sneakers arrived at the beginning of the fourth quarter with the Bears now having a 13–3 margin. Giants players dove into the pile of shoes, looking for the right sizes. When they came back on the field the players suddenly seemed to be gliding on air, moving easily around, past, and through the Chicago defenders. The shoes had done the trick. First there was a twenty-eight-yard touchdown pass from Eddie Danowski to Ike Franklin. Then halfback Ken Strong busted loose for a forty-two-yard touchdown run, giving the Giants the lead at 17–13. When the carnage ended, the New Yorkers had their first NFL championship, their twenty-seven-point fourth quarter giving them a 30–13 victory. That win is still remembered in NFL folklore as the "Sneakers Game," and it helped make the Giants an early NFL power.

The team was in three more title games in the 1930s, winning one, then made it another three times in the 1940s. Unfortunately, they were beaten each time, but that didn't prevent a strong winning tradition from growing during the league's first three decades. By 1956 the Giants were back, beating the Chicago Bears 47–7 for the championship at Yankee Stadium. These were the Giants of Sam Huff, Charley Conerly, Frank Gifford, Kyle Rote, Rosey Brown, and Jim Patton. And for the first time, chants of *"Defense! Defense! Defense!"* rang down from the three tiers of Yankee Stadium whenever middle linebacker Sam Huff and his teammates took the field.

In 1958, the Giants met the Baltimore Colts at the Stadium in a title game now dubbed "The Greatest Game Ever Played." The Colts would win it in sudden-death overtime 23–17, as quarterback John Unitas began putting his own personal stamp on his position. Though the Giants lost, they were part of a game that today is earmarked as the one that really put the NFL on the map. The team lost to Baltimore again in 1959, then with veteran Y. A. Tittle at quarterback won three straight Eastern Division titles from 1961 to 1963. Unfortunately, they met Vince Lombardi's Green Bay Packers in the first two championship games, then lost to a tough Chicago Bears team 14–10 in 1963.

Despite the five championship losses, the Giants had reached the championship game six times in eight years. For the thrills they provided, and the great players who represented them, these were still considered the team's glory years. Age and injuries took a toll in 1964 and the team plummeted from 11–3 in '63 to a basement 2–10–2 mark the next year. Through the rest of the 1960s and '70s the Giants failed to reach the playoffs and had just two winning seasons.

When Bill Parcells joined Ray Perkins's staff in 1981, the team had suffered through eight straight losing seasons, winning just thirty-one games over that period, an average of less than four victories a year. In Perkins's two previous seasons, the team had been 6–10 and 4–12, putting the coach somewhat on the hot seat. Though team owner Wellington Mara was considered one of the league's best, a fine gentleman with a reputation for being patient with his coaches, Perkins knew he had to turn the team around. In addition, the long-suffering loyal fans, many whom remembered those glory years, were now starving for a winner.

The 4–12 Giants of 1980 impressed no one. The team was especially vulnerable on defense, allowing 425 points and finishing as the twenty-fifth-ranked defense in a twenty-six–team league. That's the reason Perkins wanted Bill Parcells so badly. One of the first things he said to Bill was, "Build me a linebacking corps that I can build a defense on,"

That's how it began. Though it was Bill's ultimate coaching challenge rolled into his dream job, it wasn't going to be an easy "he came, he saw, he conquered" situation. It would be a process for both Bill and the team. Finally, though, everything was in place. The Parcells family was now living in New Jersey. While it was new to Judy and the girls, it was old hat for Bill. In reality, however, it was the first time he had lived in his home state since he had left for Wichita back in 1960. He was a long time in coming home.

The 1981 Giants were a combination of veteran players and young talent, a group that still hadn't put it all together. Quarterback Phil Simms, out of tiny Morehead State, had shown some ability but still had a penchant for throwing more interceptions than touchdowns. Scott Brunner, a second-year QB from Delaware, didn't have Simms's arm strength but showed definite leadership qualities. Whether either of these small-college quarterbacks would emerge as an NFL star was still open to conjecture.

There were really no standout players at either running back or wide receiver. Billy Taylor had led the team's rushers in 1980 with just 580 yards, while Earnest Gray was the top receiver with fifty-two catches for 777 yards. With an offensive line that still needed shoring up, the Giants' offense seemed sorely lacking. It was a unit that produced only 249 points in 1980, while the defense yielded 425. That does not translate to a winning team. The offense was averaging about 15.5 points a game, while the defense was allowing 26.5.

This had to change if the Giants were to become winners. Bill Parcells couldn't do anything about the offense, but the defense was going to be his baby, and he'd be damned if he was going to coach a defense that gave up more than four-hundred points. When he went to work assessing the situation he saw there was already some solid talent on the roster. This included three fine linebackers—middle linebacker Harry Carson, who had been with the team since 1976; and veteran outside backers Brian Kelley and Brad Van Pelt. Kelley and Van Pelt had joined the Giants in 1973.

Defensive ends George Martin and Gary Jeter were both considered fine players. Because he was switching from the 4–3 to the 3–4, Bill had to find a nose tackle, and there were several candidates from which to choose. The secondary was led by veterans Terry Jackson and Beasley Reece, but wasn't considered an elite group. Into this defense walked Bill Parcells not prepared for the x-factor that would greet him. That x-factor was a rookie linebacker out of North Carolina named Lawrence Taylor. As Bill would later say, "[Lawrence and I] came riding in to clean up the town, a couple of guys from an old Western."

That's because Taylor was one of those once-in-a-lifetime players, an immense natural talent with a burning desire to wreak havoc on an offense and win games. It became apparent not long after he arrived at the Giants training facility at Pleasantville, New York, that Coach Parcells had a player around whom to build not only a great linebacking corps but also an entire defense. Taylor had been the team's number-one pick, the second player chosen in the draft that year. Only Heisman Trophy–winning running back George Rogers was picked before him, going to the New Orleans Saints.

Working with a group that he had to shape and mold quickly, Bill would have to make a solid first impression. Some of the veterans were used to other coaches, a situation Bill had experienced at Texas Tech when he had problems getting the players into his camp his first year. He didn't want that to happen now, but he also knew only one way to coach. He just hoped he would get that chance. Harry Carson, for one, said that Bill would have to prove himself because of his quick exit two years earlier.

"I didn't know what to expect at first," Carson said. "Here we were going through another transition. Bill had come in two years earlier, then left. Ralph Hawkins replaced him that year and stayed through 1980. Now Bill was back. We had a group of veteran players, especially the linebackers, and Bill had to deal with guys who were set in their ways. That was the first challenge for him, I think, coaching guys who were pretty good but might have had some bad habits."

George Martin, the defensive end who had been with the club since 1975, had seen a bevy of coaches come and go. Considered a team leader and fine player, Martin was soon won over not only by Bill's knowledge of defense but also by his willingness to take the veterans aside and explain things to them.

"He was making major changes that first year," Martin said. "He converted the defense from a 4–3 to a 3–4. That was earth-shattering for guys like myself and the other veterans. We were very comfortable playing the 4–3, the traditional four-man front. At first, the change wasn't well received by us and we put up some resistance. Players . . . were pretty much subservient in those days, but there was some grumbling. We always had small groups discussing and disapproving what he was doing. He was coming in and changing tradition, so we looked at him as someone who was upsetting the apple cart."

Had the new coach come in and said, "Do it this way. Why? Because I said so," he might have had serious problems. Tough as he was, Bill was too smart to come on like a totalitarian coach, a my-way-or-the-highway guy, without explaining things. It was his willingness to interpret and define that quickly won over George Martin and other veterans.

"This was the very first time we had a coach who was explicit," Martin recalled. "He would always tell you the reasons he was doing something different as well as what the cause and effect would be. I'd say he was the first educational coach I had in my career. That made a tremendous difference because we were able to see the logic behind what he was doing.

"For instance, he explained the conversion to the 3–4 by telling us that it would allow us to play to our strength. Because we had a host of good linebackers, he was going to use their talents to the max. He happened to be right, because that was the beginning of a long run of outstanding Giants linebackers. In 1981, Harry Carson was already one of the best middle linebackers in the game. Brian Kelly was very solid and Brad Van Pelt was an All-Pro. Then along came Lawrence and the rest, as they say, is history."

Veteran punter Dave Jennings, who had been with the team since 1974, noticed something else about the team's new defensive coordinator.

"He had a real good relationship with his players almost from the first," Jennings said. "I could see that he really knew how to gets players to respond to him in a positive way on the field. They wanted to play for him and please him. In addition, his knowledge of defense was tremendous. He could also recognize the type of player who could respond best to him and those who wouldn't. He had that [ability] right from the start."

Once Bill saw the talent he had in Taylor, he told Perkins he had to have the rookie in the lineup. The head coach agreed. Bill was astounded by the fact that one-third of Taylor's tackles his senior year at North Carolina were made *behind* the line of scrimmage. In the Giants' first training-camp scrimmage, the rookie linebacker had four or five quarterback sacks and was close several other times. He had strength and quickness, and was extremely aggressive. In a nutshell, the guy was a superstar from day one. But even a natural talent like Taylor still had a lot to learn.

"He didn't know a thing about pass defense or coverages," Bill wrote in his autobiography, "but he was willing to learn. More importantly, he was willing to listen. . . . Lawrence had been so damn good at Carolina that I think he was used to intimidating people. I made it clear from the start that intimidating me was just out of the question, and we've gotten along fine ever since. My basic position with him has always been, 'I'm going to say what's on my mind. I won't b.s. you, don't try to b.s. me.' "

By the time the preseason games rolled around, Bill was putting the puzzle together. Taylor was the fourth linebacker, and another big rookie, Byron Hunt from SMU, began spelling veterans Kelley and Van Pelt. Rookie Bill Neill from Pittsburgh was the nose tackle, backed up by another rookie, Jim Burt of Miami. Burt would later become an integral part of the team's defense. This group of front-seven players was what made the switch to the 3–4 successful. For Bill's part, even though he was working with them as a group every day, he still made sure he treated his players as individuals.

"Bill was great at what I call having fireside chatter," George Martin said. "He would pull you aside and have these little conversations with you. He didn't have to do it, but for the first time he gave you a behind-the-scenes look at what he was doing. With those of us considered leaders, he did that almost daily. *Here's what I'm trying to accomplish. This guy has strength, this guy has quickness. Here's where we stand collectively.* It made you look at what we were doing in a whole different light, at least for me. He would say, for instance, 'Listen, if we can get three or four games early, it puts us in a good position at that point in the season and gives us a chance to win.' We had never looked at it like that before. We just used to go out there and play one game at a time."

That doesn't mean the Giants were dealing with Saint Bill that first year. Though he took the time to explain his concepts to the players, he also drove them hard, and sometimes punished them with his sharp words.

"Even in that first year he reacted to each player differently," Dave Jennings said. "He knew which players he could put the needle to and which ones were more sensitive and couldn't be dealt with like that. With those guys he would work in a more positive way, but I think he always liked the guys he could needle, and get them to play a little harder by needling them in his way.

"I'll give you a good example. Lawrence was so good that it was tough to needle him in the usual way. So [Bill] always used Hugh Green, an outstanding linebacker with Tampa Bay, who came in the same year Lawrence did. He was always pumping Green up to Lawrence, saying how good he was and sometimes adding, 'That's the kind of linebacker I'd want on my team.' And, of course, that would get Lawrence to step it up just a little more."

There was a noticeable difference in the Giants' defense as soon as the 1981 season began. After losing the opener to Philadelphia 24–10, the defense gave up just seven points in each of the next two games as the team whipped Washington and New Orleans. Two more losses followed before the team bounced back to win three straight, including a 32–0 whitewash of Seattle, the first shutout by the defense in three years. The Giants had a 5–3 record and were still in the playoff hunt, a far cry from a season earlier when after eight games they were 1–7 and out of it. One of the biggest improvements from a year earlier was the defense.

Then there was another important change before the sixth game. The team made a trade with Houston, acquiring running back Rob Carpenter. Carpenter wasn't a real breakaway threat, and was a cut below the league's elite runners, but he was tough and durable, capable of wearing a defense down in the fourth quarter. His acquisition finally made the team's ground game respectable. Just when it looked as if the Giants were headed in the right direction, however, they suddenly reverted to old ways and lost three straight: to the Jets, Packers, and Redskins. In those three games the defense yielded eighty-two points. Not great. The game against the 'Skins was a double loss. Quarterback Phil Simms suffered a shoulder separation and was lost for the remainder of the season.

It was then that Parcells rallied his troops, urging his defense to pick it up, especially with Simms gone. Scott Brunner filled in more than adequately at quarterback, and the defense responded to their coach. The team won four of its final five games, including a 13–10 overtime victory over Dallas the final week that put the Giants in the playoffs at 9–7. In those five games, the Giants' defense gave up only ten, seventeen, seven, ten, and ten points. For the season, the D yielded just 257 points, compared with 425 the year before.

Bill was extremely pleased with the way his players had responded. He felt as if they had improved steadily as a unit all season long. By the end of the year, he was confident that if the opposing teams were offensively even, the Giants would win it because of their defense. That helped complete a great turnaround, from 4–12 to 9–7 and a wild-card playoff berth. The first opponent would be division rival Philadelphia, against whom the Giants had split two games during the regular season.

In this one, the Giants looked like a real up-and-coming team. Three Scott Brunner TD passes and a Mark Haynes fumble recovery in the end zone gave the New Yorkers a 27–7 halftime lead. With Rob Carpenter helping control the clock with his rushing, the Giants held on for a 27–21 victory. Carpenter gained 161 yards and the defense came up big in key situations. Now the team had to meet Joe Montana and the powerful San Francisco 49ers. The winner would go to the NFC championship game, a step away from a trip to the Super Bowl. The Niners, though, were 13–3 in the regular season and wouldn't be easy to beat.

It was a game in which the Giants definitely belonged. They scored early on a seventy-two-yard touchdown pass from Brunner to Earnest Gray to tie the game at 7–7. By halftime, San Francisco had moved out to a 24–10 lead. But early in the third period Brunner hit Johnny Perkins from fifty-nine yards out to bring the score to 24–17. Only this time the defense couldn't stop Montana and company. The Niners made it 31–17 early in the fourth, then a Ronnie Lott interception return for a score upped the lead to 38–17. A late Giants TD made it 38–24, and that's the way it ended. San Francisco would go on to win the Super Bowl that year. The Giants, however, certainly had no reason to hang their heads in shame.

The team had come a lot farther than anyone could have predicted. With a mix of youngsters and vets, and a superstar like Lawrence Taylor, there was no reason to believe the Giants wouldn't continue to improve, as a playoff team and beyond. Perkins was doing the job as head coach, and new defensive coordinator Bill Parcells had certainly made an impact in his first year. He had also finally proved something to himself.

"I knew I could pull my load in the NFL," he said.

Knowing you can do the job, however, doesn't always guarantee success. In coaching, unlike most professions, situations can change very rapidly. In the course of a single game, you can go from supreme elation to utter devastation, just in the time it takes to complete a long pass or run a kickoff back for a touchdown. From one season to the next fortunes rise and fall, coaches are hired and fired, teams crest and regress. The causes vary. A few key injuries with no adequate backups can decimate an offense or a defense. A group of veterans aging at once and suddenly playing a notch below their previous level can make a world of difference in a short time. Defections due to free agency can leave a team with gaps it cannot adequately fill. Conversely, a team can suddenly play several levels above the previous seasons for similar but inverted reasons. Young players suddenly mature; a couple of great rookies contribute beyond expectation; free-agent acquisitions upgrade the team at several key positions. Who can predict? It can sometimes be a guessing game from year to year.

The Giants had gone from 4–12 to 9–7 and the playoffs in one short year. The sun finally seemed to be rising on the team known as Big Blue. It was assumed that Ray Perkins was ensconced for a long run as head coach, while defensive coordinator Bill Parcells had finally found his dream job with the team he had loved from early childhood. In his first year he had made a huge difference. The players had responded to him and he was putting together his kind of defense. He couldn't know it then, but things were about to change, the unstable and often fickle nature of the profession hitting both the Giants and Bill Parcells in a variety of unexpected ways. The next two seasons would be filled with a series of events that would test Bill's mettle and resolve, and ultimately reshape the future of his football and personal life.

The first two rounds of the 1982 draft produced a pair of potentially fine running backs. The first choice was Butch Woolfolk, a big back out of Michigan, and the second selection was Joe Morris of Syracuse, a 5' 7" dynamo who had broken the collegiate rushing records of distinguished Syracuse alumni Jim Brown, Ernie Davis, Floyd Little, and Larry Csonka. Despite his credentials, however, some thought Morris was too small to be as effective in the NFL. Besides Woolfolk and Morris, the draft for the Giants was rather thin, but the nucleus from 1981 was still intact so everyone anticipated another winning season.

Then things began going sour. Rob Carpenter, who had played so well after coming over from Houston the year before, was holding out for a new contract and had yet to report. In the third game of the preseason, quarterback Simms went down with the knee injury that would require surgery and finish him for the season. Scott Brunner was again the first-string QB. Then, to top off the preseason injury list, Lawrence Taylor was hurt and would not be available for maybe a month or more. So the team was starting the season without its number-one quarterback, its top running back, and its best defender.

Not surprisingly, the Giants lost their first two games, to Atlanta 16–14 and to Green Bay 27–19. Considering the absentee players, the losses weren't that devastating, but starting the season at 0–2 is never anyone's first choice. What happened next, however, was even more upsetting. The NFL players voted to go out on strike. How long the Players' Association and owners would take to reach an agreement, no one could know.

It was as rough on the coaches as anyone. Because they didn't know when the strike might be settled, coaching staffs had to work every week preparing a game plan just in case there was football the following weekend. Bill called it the strangest time he ever spent in football, preparing game plans that were never used. He said it was like being a defensive coordinator in the Twilight Zone.

The strike would last two months. Players walked out after the games of September 20, and didn't return until Sunday, November 21. Seven games were canceled outright, and one was postponed. When the strike ended, the NFL decided on an abbreviated nine-game season, followed by a revamped playoff format which became known as the Super Bowl tournament. By the time the Giants were ready to play again, Carpenter had signed and Taylor was over his injury and ready to go. After losing its first game, the team then won its next three to even the season at 3–3, games in which the defense excelled, allowing just twenty-seven total points. The playoffs were still a possibility. Then the other shoe dropped.

Following the team's 27–7 victory over Philadelphia on December 11, Ray Perkins called a team meeting. That's when he shocked everyone— players and coaches—by announcing he would be resigning in order to become the head coach at his alma mater, the University of Alabama. Perkins had been chosen to replace the legendary Paul "Bear" Bryant, who was retiring after a lengthy tenure that had made him a collegiate coaching icon. Apparently, coaching at Alabama was what Perkins always considered his dream job. He told the team he wasn't sure whether owner Wellington Mara and General Manager George Young would want him to finish the season. When a coach resigns before season's end, management often wants him out immediately, figuring a lame-duck coach may lose the team. As it turned out, Young decided to let Perkins finish the year since the team was still in the playoff hunt.

The thing, however, that caused the eyebrows to be raised was when Perkins told his assistants, "I think one of you guys might be offered the job."

It wasn't long after Perkins's sudden announcement when George Young called Bill Parcells into his office. At that time Young was a rotund man, prematurely bald, and with a high-pitched voice that belied his size. As he sat across the desk, Bill's heart had to be pounding. He had to know, or at least have a very good idea, what was about to happen. When Young began talking about the importance of having continuity within the organization, that just about clinched it. The general manager told Bill that everyone was impressed by the way he had turned the defense around. After what must have seemed like an eternity, Young finally came to the point.

"Do you want the job?" he asked.

"Yes," Bill Parcells answered, without hesitation.

CHAPTER SIX

Head Coach, But For
How Long?

HEAD COACH OF THE NEW YORK GIANTS WASN'T A JOB THAT BILL Parcells had to think about. It was simply a too-good-to-be-true situation that he couldn't have imagined happening during all those years he when he drifted from one college job to another. Any immediate celebration had to wait or simply be a private matter, since there were three games to play and Ray Perkins was still the coach of record.

Perkins was genuinely happy that Bill was going to succeed him, and the two longtime friends talked about the changes in store for both of them. Bill was asking Perkins about the organization, things he wasn't yet familiar with; and Perkins, in turn, asked Parcells questions about the college game, where his successor had spent so many years. Bill also told his friend that he felt Ray would be back in the pros within five years, feeling that Perkins, like himself, was more suited to the NFL.

Both coaches were genuinely happy about the way things worked out. "Coaching at Alabama has been in the back of my mind for a long time," Perkins said. "Deep down, it's something I want to do more than anything else in the world." Hearing that, Bill embellished Perkins's thoughts this way: "Coaching the New York Giants for Bill Parcells is what Alabama is for Ray Perkins."

Parcells was happy; Perkins was happy; George Young was happy. "Continuity is important, but you want to get the best guy, too," the general manager said. "Bill Parcells was first on my list, and it was a short list.

Besides, if we waited until the season was over, somebody else was sure to be attracted to [Bill]."

Whether the sudden coaching change affected the team or not is difficult to say. The Giants wound up losing two of the final three games to finish at 4–5 in the strike-shortened 1982 season, missing the playoffs by one game. Because of the nature of the season, it was nearly impossible to draw conclusions about the team's overall performance. So Bill would be coming in fresh in 1983, but there was little doubt that expectations would be high. Though the team, as a whole, was shocked by the sudden turn of events, no one complained about Bill Parcells being their next head man.

"I thought the club made the right choice [when they appointed Bill]," said veteran punter Dave Jennings. "He had leadership qualities and he had certainly gotten his defense to play. In my mind, he was the logical choice."

Defensive end George Martin felt the same way, once he had time to think about it. He admitted he was upset at first, but for a very different reason. "We knew he was the right man for the job," Martin said, "but he had such an indelible impact on the defense that we were pissed off when he was named head coach. We simply didn't want to share him with everyone else. That's true. We did not want to share Bill Parcells. We felt he was ours and ours alone."

For tackle Brad Benson, it was Bill's directness with the veteran players that impressed him: Parcells had taken charge almost from the first.

"Our offensive line coach for the past four years had been Bill Austin, who had previous head coaching experience with the Steelers," Benson recalled. "When Perkins resigned, I think Austin thought he would get the job. I can even remember a few instances when Austin was tough and surly with Parcells. He was also on a campaign to get rid of me and a couple of other guys.

"After Parcells got the job he called each and every player in to talk with him. I remember him saying to me, 'Don't worry about what's going on around here. It's up to me to worry about it. You're staying here. Some people who have affected your situation, they'll be gone soon.' Sure enough, when the 1983 season rolled around we had a new line coach. Austin was gone. That's when I began to realize that Parcells always meant what he said."

The transition went smoothly and the 1983 draft proved a strong one.

Safety Terry Kinard of Clemson was the number-one pick. Next the team took defensive tackle Leonard Marshall of LSU. One of the two third-round picks was offensive tackle Karl Nelson of Iowa. Cornerback Perry Williams of North Carolina State was the seventh choice and linebacker Andy Headen of Clemson was eighth, while placekicker Ali Haji-Sheikh of Michigan was ninth. All would make major contributions to the team in upcoming years.

There were high hopes when the team came to training camp prior to the 1983 season. Everyone expected the rookie head coach to continue building on the 9–7 season of 1981. The strike of 1982 had made that season something of a wash, a kind of no-harm, no-foul situation. By 1983, it was felt, the young players had another year under their belts, the veterans were still solid, and the draft was a strong one. Harry Carson said that the veteran players were now relating to Bill differently, showing the respect a head coach should receive.

"We knew we had to change our approach in the way we talked to him," inside linebacker Carson said. "When he was defensive coordinator we talked to him as if he was one of us. Sometimes we would even curse at him if we got into an argument. But as head coach we knew we had to change our approach in the way we reacted to him and talked to him. We knew the younger players would take their cue from us. If we didn't show respect, the younger players wouldn't. So we had to alter the way we did things."

It seemed as if all the pieces were in place. Then, even before the season started, they began coming apart, one by one. First there was a quarterback controversy. Phil Simms was going into his fifth season and felt he should be starting. But Simms had been injured for the final five games as well as the playoffs in 1981, then missed the entire 1982 season. Scott Brunner had stepped in on both occasions and had acquitted himself well. Since Bill had only been with the team since '81, he had seen more of Brunner than Simms. When neither quarterback was able to lock up the job in the preseason, the rookie coach decided to go with Brunner.

That prompted a trade demand from Simms which, of course, the Giants would not honor. Bill tried to smooth the situation as best he could, but Simms went into the season a very unhappy player. Despite this, the team managed to split its first four games, including an impressive 27–3 victory over the Packers. The following week, however, the defense crumbled and the high-flying San Diego Chargers whipped the New Yorkers, 41–31.

Next came a pivotal game with arch-rival Philadelphia. A win would draw the team even and keep hopes alive for a solid season. A loss would drop them to 2–4 and make things infinitely tougher.

It was in this game that the rookie coach took a gamble and lost. The Giants were trailing midway through the game when Parcells suddenly yanked Brunner in favor of Simms. Simms promptly completed four of his first five passes, lifting the team, the crowd, and the coach. Then, Lady Luck vanished. Just a few series later Simms was injured again, this time with a compound fracture of the right thumb. He was once again finished for the season, the third year in a row an injury had put him on the shelf. Brunner returned to finish the game, which the Giants lost, 17–13. Bill would later write in his autobiography that his ill-thought out quarterback shuffle really hurt the team. "The end result was that I had really screwed up my offense. I had hurt Brunner's confidence by benching him early in the season in favor of Simms. Then with Simms out and Brunner back in, I had hurt [the team's] confidence in Brunner. He was only back in there because the other guy got a thumb. . . . It would be six weeks before we beat anybody."

After that, it all fell apart. Player after player began going down. Before the season ended the team would have twenty-five different players on injured reserve at one time or another. Among them were such key performers as Simms, Harry Carson, and Rob Carpenter. In addition, some of the veteran players Bill had inherited from the Perkins regime seemed to have lost something, playing that inevitable notch or two below their previous high levels.

The loss to the Eagles was just the beginning. The Giants were blown out by Kansas City the following week, then played to a lackluster 20–20 tie with the St. Louis Cardinals, a game Bill called "one of the ugliest of all time." Losses to Dallas, Detroit, and Washington followed. The team was self-destructing at 2–8–1. Bill Parcells's dream job was quickly turning into a nightmare. With the rash of injuries and just plain lousy play, there was little he could do to stop it.

"We had all kinds of injuries on the field that year," Dave Jennings remembered. "And I think Bill related to the players his first year as head coach much in the way he had when he was an assistant. That's tough to do. You can't be pals with the players, and that was something he learned that year. By the end of the year I think he knew he had to change."

The injuries weren't the only factor in a totally disastrous year. Bill also

A teenage Bill Parcells (50) was a star on the River Dell High basketball team in the late 1950s. While basketball may not have been his best sport in high school, he always said he learned more about winning from his coach, Mickey Corcoran (top row, far left), than from anyone else. Corcoran has remained a friend, mentor, and confidant ever since. (Photo Courtesy Mickey Corcoran)

As a high schooler, Bill already had the build of a football lineman. However, he was still agile enough to be a star on River Dell's basketball team, as evidenced by this uncontested lay-up during action against a rival school. (Photo Courtesy Mickey Corcoran)

A student-athlete at Wichita State University, Parcells sports the clean-cut look of the early 1960s. Though he was a fine collegiate player, he opted for coaching rather than fighting for a place in the NFL. (Courtesy Wichita State University)

As a young assistant coach at his alma mater, Wichita State, Parcells began to learn what the football business was all about. He would make numerous collegiate stops before realizing his future was in the NFL. (Courtesy Wichita State University)

As defensive coordinator under Steve Sloan at Texas Tech, Parcells's often loud style clashed with many of his Texas-born players. But he soon had their respect and built an outstanding defense. His mid-70s hairstyle caused some of the players to give him the unlikely nickname of "Coach Pretty." (Courtesy Texas Tech University)

Parcells's only head coaching job at the collegiate level was with the Air Force Academy in 1978. He seemed to enjoy posing with the mascot, Falcon, but stayed only one year before joining the Giants briefly, then taking his only sabbatical from coaching. (Courtesy United States Air Force Academy)

The changing of the guard. When Ray Perkins (r) resigned as head coach of the New York Giants in December 1982, assistant coach Bill Parcells was immediately chosen to succeed him. It was Parcells's first head coaching job in the NFL and the one he wanted more than any other. Coaching the Giants was simply his dream job. (UPI/Corbis-Bettmann)

Parcells was the first coach in the NFL to get a Gatorade shower after a victory, a tradition that has now spread around the league. This one was special. Linebacker Harry Carson douses the coach in the closing minutes of the Giants 39–20 victory over the Denver Broncos in Super Bowl XXI. (UPI/Bettmann Newsphotos)

It's the second time around for Parcells and the Giants. The team won Super Bowl XXV over the Buffalo Bills, 20–19, in perhaps the greatest title game ever. Here the victorious coach joins the game's MVP, running back Ottis Anderson, in raising the Vince Lombardi Trophy for everyone to see. (Corbis/Reuters Photo)

A smiling Bill Parcells, now coaching the New England Patriots, talks to reporters and a bevy of microphones on media day in New Orleans prior to Super Bowl XXXI in January 1997. Though the Pats would lose to the Green Bay Packers and Parcells would resign as the result of a feud with owner Bob Kraft, his coaching magic was more apparent than ever. Within a month he would be coaching the New York Jets. (Corbis/Agence France Presse)

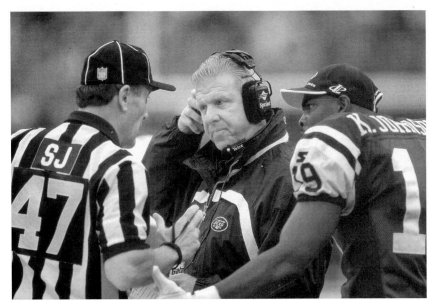

Always ready to go to war for his players, Parcells takes up the argument for star receiver Keyshawn Johnson (r) in a 1998 game against Miami. (Photo Bill Lenahan)

Practices under Parcells are legendary, a time when the coach rides his players mercilessly. That doesn't mean there aren't light moments when the disarming Parcells smile makes a sudden and sometimes unexpected appearance. (Photo Bill Lenahan)

In a long tradition, many former Parcells players love to visit their old coach. Here Phil Simms, Parcells's favorite quarterback from his Giants days, swaps stories with the coach on a sunny summer day at the Jets camp. (Photo Bill Lenahan)

The Parcells scowl, a look that has made even the biggest and toughest of players cringe with fear. (Photo Bill Lenahan)

Prowling the sidelines during games, Parcells is aware of everything, in control of everything, and coaching his team from the opening kickoff until the final gun. (Photo Bill Lenahan)

Fashion was never the coach's strong suit, especially at practice. Where did he get the "one sock high, one sock low" look? (Photo Bill Lenahan)

said that just a short time into the season he began to realize that some
of the players were using drugs, a problem that was not endemic to the
Giants, nor to the 1980s. In a biographical portrait aired on HBO, legendary quarterback John Unitas told a story about accepting a trade from
the Baltimore Colts to the San Diego Chargers in 1973. At age forty, Unitas
decided to play one more season. Like many athletes, he was loath to
admit his career was over, especially since at that time he was nearly
universally acclaimed as the greatest quarterback ever.

In an attempt to become closer with his younger teammates, Unitas
dropped in on a bunch of the players who were talking in a room. It took
a few minutes to dawn on him that they were passing around a single
"cigarette." In Johnny U's early days, many of the players were hard-
drinking men, some of whom undoubtedly drank too hard. This, however,
was new to him. When he realized what it was—a joint—he quickly
excused himself with a terse "I'm outta here." The world it was a-changing,
even for the professional football player.

Bill admitted he knew very little about drug use and abuse when he
realized some of his players were involved in 1983. Richard Arledge, who
played for Bill at Texas Tech, recalls an incident in 1977, the year before
Bill took the head coaching job at Air Force.

"We had a kick returner on the team who was using pot," Arledge said.
"About the third game that year we were on the road and the team was
staying at a hotel. Greg Frazier and I were walking past the guy's hotel
room and [the smell of] pot was pouring out of it. Couldn't miss it. When
the game came around the next day, the opening kickoff hits him in he
head and bounces up into the air. We lose the ball. Afterward, Greg
Frazier told him if he ever did that again he was gonna whip his ass.

"After the regular season, we go to the Tangerine Bowl in Orlando
against Florida State. Sure enough, we open the guy's door and out comes
the smoke. So Greg takes him in the back room and gives him a good
beating. Then he went to Coach Parcells and told him what happened.
We already knew Coach Sloan, Coach Parcells, and most of the staff were
leaving. Anyway, Parcells and another assistant talked it over and
benched Frazier for the last game. That still boggles my mind that they
didn't stand up for him. I thought that's what you'd want your players to
do.

"Greg told him why he did it, that it had happened earlier in the season
and he wanted [the kick returner] not to do it again, so this time he went

and gave him a few licks. To me, if I was a coach, I'd like my players doing that stuff."

Maybe Bill and his fellow coach didn't like the idea of Greg Frazier taking matters into his own hands. But was his offense, giving a few licks to a player who was using drugs and not being able to play one hundred percent, worse than that of the player using drugs? Maybe it was a tough call and maybe the two coaches didn't have a complete grasp of the problem. In 1983, Bill knew he would have to learn more about it.

Despite admittedly not having a complete knowledge of drugs and drug abuse, he nevertheless knew then that a player using drugs and refusing to get help couldn't continue to play for him. He was always willing to give a player more than one chance, but the player had to learn, had to make an effort to get himself clean, and then had to stay clean. It didn't take a genius to know that if drugs were affecting a team, they could also affect the coach's tenure with that team.

As the season wound down, the Giants continued their free fall. Only the tie with St. Louis and a surprise 23–0 victory over Philadelphia in Game Twelve prevented the opposition from running the table on a still-proud franchise. The Giants finished the season at 3–12–1. Three wins, twelve losses, and a tie. That was the beginning of Bill Parcells's head coaching résumé. He couldn't help wondering if it might also be the end.

The injuries were part, but not all of it. Downright sloppy play was also a major factor. The team simply did not take care of the football. New York led the entire league with fifty-eight turnovers in sixteen games. That included thirty-one interceptions and twenty-seven lost fumbles. Scott Brunner was the quarterback for the major part of the season, throwing just nine touchdown passes as opposed to twenty-two interceptions. His confidence was so shaken that Bill had veteran Jeff Rutledge play the final few games, with basically similar results. Rookie Butch Woolfolk ran for 857 yards and Earnest Gray caught seventy-eight passes for 1,139 yards. Linebackers Taylor and Carson, cornerback Mark Haynes, and place-kicker Haji-Sheikh made it to the Pro Bowl. That, however, meant next to nothing. The real statistic was 3–12–1, and not even that said it all.

So disastrous was the 1983 season for Bill Parcells that the team's dismal play on the field wasn't even the worst part of it. In fact, perhaps no rookie coach in the history of the NFL had a harder cross to bear than Bill did that year. Not only did he have to deal with a team going down the tubes, but he had to do it while enduring a succession of off-field tragedies that could have destroyed a lesser man. Besides trying to find a way to get the team out of its funk, he also had to deal with the following:

• In October, Giants backfield coach Bob Ledbetter died suddenly from a stroke. He had been Parcells's friend, as well as a talented and popular coach.

• In December, former Giants running back Doug Kotar died after a battle with brain cancer. Kotar, who played with the team from 1974 to 1981, was a hardworking overachiever whom Bill met his first year as defensive coordinator. The entire team attended Kotar's funeral in Pennsylvania.

• In October, Charles "Chubby" Parcells had open-heart surgery, his full recovery in doubt.

• In November, Ida Parcells was diagnosed with cancer. She would die within a month.

• In February 1984, Charles Parcells died of complications from heart problems.

In just a little over one football season, Bill Parcells had lost both of his parents, a fellow coach, and a former player. Any one of those deaths would have put a damper on the season and led him to coach with a heavy heart. But four deaths? Including both parents? It's amazing he didn't ask for a leave of absence. The season turned out to be a testimony to his toughness and resolve, something the players didn't fail to notice.

"Looking back now," George Martin said, "I wonder how he stood up under the pressure, especially the deaths of both parents in such a short period of time. I would look at Bill that year and it was like seeing a friend suffer and you being helpless to lend a hand. We gained such tremendous respect as a result of the ordeal we all went through, but particularly Bill. He weathered that storm like no one I ever saw before. We all felt that the only way we could tangibly do something for him was to go out and perform the following year."

But would there be a following year? Even before the season ended, Bill began hearing rumors and rumblings. With everything else, he also began to worry about his job. While the Giants were barely able to produce a victory in the second half of the season, the University of Miami was rolling over its collegiate opponents and appeared ticketed for a national championship. What in the world could that possibly have to do with the Giants? The answer was the Miami coach, Howard Schnellenberger. Years earlier, in 1973 and '74, Schnellenberger had been the head coach of the Baltimore Colts with current Giants GM George Young his offensive co-ordinator. Though Schnellenberger's tenure at Baltimore had not been especially successful, he and Young remained friends. Now Schnellenberger was tearing it up at Miami and Young was interested.

Bill insists to this day that reliable longtime confidantes told him bluntly that Young was courting Schnellenberger, that Young wanted Schnellenberger to coach the Giants. It was yet one more concern the struggling coach had to deal with as the season progressed. He soon heard that the two men were meeting, and quite frequently, something George Young always denied. To make matters worse, there were already some cries in the press for a new coach, several writers deducing that it was apparent Parcells couldn't cut it. After all, two years earlier the team was 9–7 and in the playoffs. This was supposed to be a better team. It stands to reason that George Young had to be thinking about a coaching change.

"When you're 1–12–1, and in the third-to-last game we had 51,000 no-shows, you have to think about those kind of things," Young would tell a writer several years later.

Parcells and Young never discussed the Schnellenberger situation directly. Before the season ended, coach and general manager had a meeting and Bill asked it he was coming back. Young countered by telling him that they would meet after the season. Bill voiced his concern to old friend Dan Henning, who was then coaching the Atlanta Falcons. Henning told him not to worry, that if the ax fell in New York he would have an immediate job in Atlanta.

To this day Bill feels that Young did make some kind of offer to Schnellenberger who, for reasons never discussed on either end, turned the Giants down. Again, George Young has never confirmed this. All he would say, a few years later, was that, "The season ended, I think, on a Sunday. By Friday management was totally committed to Bill for the following season."

So Bill had weathered the most difficult season of his life, a year he would say that was even more difficult than the one in which he sold real estate. For his part, he held no grudge against Young and said that the two of them had worked closely together ever since, always agreeing on all major personnel decisions. The trick now for Bill Parcells was to get his team turned around, and fast, To do that, he knew he would also have to change.

"I just decided, 'I don't give a damn, I'm gonna do things my way,'" he wrote in his autobiography. "I'd always been an aggressive person and I'd certainly been an aggressive coach almost from the start, but I thought I'd been straitjacketed some of that previous season. I wasn't going to make that mistake again. In the end, you've got to be yourself. . . . If you're not comfortable with yourself, don't even bother showing up."

Beginning in 1984, Bill Parcells was going to do it his way. The dream was still alive; the Giants were still his team. He never wanted to go 3–12–1 again. He would now become the Parcells people would get to know, but not always love.

CHAPTER SEVEN

The Parcells Way

T HINGS CHANGED IN A HURRY AFTER THE 1983 SEASON. PARCELLS has always felt that head coaches are often fired too quickly. No matter what the record, one season isn't enough to get a clear picture of a coach's ability to build a winner, despite the kind of hand he's dealt. He also knew he was working on a second one-year contract. If he didn't get things turned around this time, he probably would be gone.

The first thing he wanted to do was avoid a repetition of an overcrowded injured reserve list. There was no reason why twenty-five players, more than half the squad, should go down in the course of a season. He quickly hired Johnny Parker as the team's strength and conditioning coach. Parker had performed similar jobs at a number of major universities and got an A-one recommendation from Parcells's old friend Bobby Knight, who knew Parker from the University of Indiana.

Then came the draft, and for the Giants it turned into an extremely productive one. The top choice was linebacker Carl Banks of Michigan State. Banks was an inside linebacker who generated much of the same havoc as Lawrence Taylor and would quickly become an All-Pro. A second first-round choice that year produced offensive tackle William Roberts. Quarterback Jeff Hostetler was the third choice, and linebacker Gary Reasons one of two fourth-round picks. Wide receiver Lionel Manuel was chosen in the seventh round. All five of these players would make major contributions to the team's success.

With another solid draft, there were also a bevy of cuts. Parcells was convinced he had to make wholesale changes to turn the team around. Some of those released were marginal players, guys with limited roles who simply hadn't done them well. Others, however, were former standouts now approaching the end of their careers. Linebackers Brian Kelley and Brad Van Pelt had been outstanding players for a lot of years. While *Bill* Parcells liked both players personally, *Coach* Parcells felt they would never play for him the way he wanted them to play. So they were gone.

"Bill was a different coach right from the start in 1984," said Dave Jennings. "He put his foot down and was a lot tougher. You could notice the difference right away in training camp, and the guys reacted differently to him as well."

Harry Carson's first recollection of 1984 was that the coach was definitely committed to change. "He was now making the hard decisions that resulted in a lot of people being let go," Carson said. "He was changing the makeup of the ball club and that isn't easy. To do that, he had to exert his own personality on the team. So he wasn't adverse to cutting guys, even those he had been friendly with, like Kelley and Van Pelt. They had given their best *to* the team, but now it was at a point where Bill had to consider what was best *for* the team. It was nothing personal.

"As players get older and their skills begin to diminish, they simply are not going to help the team get to the next level. He had drafted Carl Banks and Gary Reasons, two linebackers with their best days ahead of them."

Carson said that the coach began to do little things, individual things that made each player know he was interested and he cared. But he also did it in a way that sometimes made you wonder at first.

"He was finding ways to get to each player. That often meant doing his homework, due diligence if you will, to learn about the guy, both the vets and new guys coming onto the team. It might mean talking to the players' friends or former coaches. He was always looking for a hook, something to throw out there.

"For instance, he found out what my nickname was as a kid. To this day, I don't know how he did it, but I know he must have worked at it. One day he comes up and whispers it to me, just like that. It was a nickname I didn't want him yelling out to the whole team. But it got my attention and for awhile he hung it over my head. But the funny thing was that it told me the guy cared enough to dig into who I was."

He was also a different coach in training camp. "He was always coaching, every minute," said Carson. "He was yelling screaming, chewing out some people, calling them names, making fun of them. Others he would pat on the butt and praise them. He knew exactly what he could do with each player, what makes that player tick. But when he chews you out, he always leaves it on the field. Whether it's praise or criticism, it's always constructive. The thing is, you can't be thin-skinned around him or your feelings will be hurt."

One newcomer to the Giants in 1984 was wide receiver/kick returner Phil McConkey, who was getting a real glimpse of Parcells at work for the first time. McConkey was an interesting study, having graduated from the Naval Academy in 1978. Always an outstanding football player, McConkey was too small in high school—145 pounds—to get offers from major colleges. Yet he excelled at Navy, participating in a winning effort against Bill Parcells and the Air Force Academy his senior year.

After that it was five years of active duty for McConkey, flying helicopters and leaving his football career behind. As his military tour began coming to an end, he found himself getting the itch again, asking himself *what if?* and wondering if there was a chance for him to make it in the NFL. Only former Dallas Cowboys quarterback Roger Staubach had made it big in pro ball after serving five years in the armed forces. Others tried, but the five-year layoff robbed them of precious years, and sometimes of finely honed skills. Add to the layoff the fact that he weighed just 162 pounds and McConkey knew he was bucking the odds.

He got a leave of absence to attend the Giants training camp in 1983, invited there after some excellent recommendations, including that of Bill Belichick's father. Belichick was an assistant coach with the Giants and his father had been an assistant coach at Navy for more than thirty years. McConkey came in and immediately began working his butt off. He remembers his first contact with Bill Parcells.

"The morning after the first practice Parcells calls me aside," McConkey said. "I had been like a crazy man, going a thousand miles per hour, because I knew there were going to be numerous cuts. He comes up to me after practice and says, 'Hey listen, kid, better slow your motor down. This is a long camp. Better take it easy.' I don't know if any head coach ever said that to a player."

At the end of camp Parcells decided to sign the dynamo, even though he wouldn't be discharged from the Navy until the following season. "He offered me a thirty-five-hundred-dollar signing bonus," McConkey recalls. "My dream team had always been the Buffalo Bills. I grew up there and had also written a letter to them. So when Parcells said he wanted to sign me, I didn't jump. I told him I wanted to see what Buffalo had to say. Then he says, 'How about I throw in another thousand?' I said, 'Done deal.' So back then he just waved $1,000 in front of my face and I jumped at it."

The Giants put McConkey on military reserve, allowing them to retain his rights for the following year. He returned to the Navy while the Giants blew out all their tires in that 3–12–1 season. McConkey saw the difference when he returned full-time in 1984.

"When I came to camp the next year Bill was in the process of cleaning house. He now wanted *his* guys, guys who only wanted to know where and when. Where the game was and when it was going to be played. He wanted guys who, if the game was going to be played on the Brooklyn Bridge at midnight against the Jersey City Destroyers, would show up ready to play."

McConkey soon proved to be one of Parcells's guys. He started training camp listed at number fourteen on the depth chart of wide receivers. But he fought like a tiger, making plays, scrapping at practice, and excelling in the preseason.

"I think it was my return ability that clinched it. Being able to catch punts and kickoffs was the key for me and for Parcells. We were getting ready to play the Steelers in the last preseason game and it was still iffy. I knew there were going to be a few more cuts. Four hours before the game, he walks over to me in the locker room, pulls up a stool, and says, 'Hey, kid, want you to know you made this team. You're a heckuva kid and you've done a great job. I just want you to go out there tonight, relax, and have a great game.' "

No one would have bet on Phil McConkey. He didn't have the size or skills to become a major star. Rather, it was a matter of attitude. Parcells knew he was a player who wouldn't allow himself to fail, a player who would sacrifice everything for the team, who would never give an ounce less than his best. Bill would come to love guys like Phil McConkey, but that didn't mean he was very easy on them. He continued to drive and push, even after the season began.

"Any time the ball was punted in practice he would stand there next to me," McConkey said. "Now you've got to understand something about Parcells. He never caught a punt in his life, but he is the absolute expert on catching punts. He critiques every catch and it's never good enough.

I got so I could put four balls on my body, under my arms, between my legs. I would do a drill where I would throw two balls in the air, catch the punt, then catch the two balls. Yet it was never good enough for him.

"But because he was like that, it made me focus. There were no excuses with him. I remember a day at practice in New Jersey when the wind was blowing at fifty or sixty miles per hour. You just couldn't catch the ball. There were still no excuses with him. But his attitude trained me to handle that sometimes wild weather at the Meadowlands."

McConkey saw the no-excuse philosophy from that first training camp. "You might see a game today when a player slips on the wet Astroturf," he says, "goes to the sidelines and says, 'I slipped, coach.' And the coach accepts it. Parcells might say, 'Get some shoes that work.' It means there is no excuse, so you force yourself to concentrate because you know that no excuse will be tolerated.

"Parcells makes you focus on yourself and not get caught up in everything else. It was as if the world didn't exist outside Bill Parcells's game. There are always distractions that can take away from preparation, but in a league that is so competitive you need every ounce, every iota of focus and concentration on your individual job."

This was the kind of attitude Parcells was trying to build, beginning in 1984. When the team was ready to open the season, the coach seemed satisfied that he had upgraded the personnel from the previous year. Simms was healthy, had played extremely well in the preseason, and was now the number-one quarterback. To eliminate any hint of the previous controversy, Scott Brunner had been cut. Veteran Jeff Rutledge was the backup. Woolfolk, Carpenter, Morris, and veteran Tony Galbreath, one of the best pass-catching backs ever, would handle the backfield work. Lionel Manuel, Bobby Johnson, and Earnest Gray were the wide receivers, with Zeke Mowatt, a free agent signed in 1983, emerging as a star at tight end. Chris Godfrey and Karl Nelson would make their mark on an improving offensive line.

The defense was also changing. Leonard Marshall and Jim Burt became starters alongside George Martin on the line. Rookies Banks and Reasons would join Carson, Taylor, Byron Hunt, and Andy Headen to form an outstanding linebacking corps, a group that could be physically punishing but also had outstanding speed. Terry Kinard, Perry Williams, and Kenny Hill joined Mark Haynes to form a solid defensive backfield. Role players like Phil McConkey contributed mightily. The team seemed ready to win.

In the opener against the Eagles, Simms threw for 409 yards in a 28–27 victory. According to his coach, Simms was playing as if he had something to prove. After all the injuries, he was determined to show everyone that he was not only a top-flight quarterback but also tough and durable, and that the injuries had just been a fluke. He would show that same quality all year long.

The following week the Giants met one of their longtime nemeses, the Dallas Cowboys. Along with the Redskins, Dallas was considered one of the elite teams in the NFC East. On this day, however, it was all Giants. Led by quarterback Simms, the Giants raced to a 21–0 lead by halftime. Then on the opening series of the second half, the Cowboys' Ron Fellows fumbled the kickoff. The Giants got it on the Dallas 18 and immediately went for the kill.

On first down, Simms dropped back and fired a bullet to the end zone where tight end Zeke Mowatt outjumped defender Dexter Clinkscale for the ball and the New Yorkers had a 28–0 lead. With Lawrence Taylor's three sacks spearheading the defense, the Giants won it 28–7, giving them their first 2–0 start in sixteen seasons. The developing offensive style impressed longtime Giant Harry Carson.

"In the old days a typical Giant series was run, run, pass, punt," Carson said. "It's different now, as you could well see." But Carson was also trying not to jump the gun. When someone asked about the team being first in the NFC East, the veteran linebacker quickly put up a hand.

"First place?" he repeated. "Throw first place back in my face with two games left in the season and I'll tell you," he said.

By the time the team won three of its first four games, it had already erased the debacle that was 1983. Next came a game against the Rams in Los Angeles. It was a contest the Giants would lose badly, 33–12. There was, however, a subplot going on that showed the developing motivational techniques that Bill Parcells was beginning to use with his players.

When Parcells joined the Giants as an assistant in 1981, Gary Jeter was a starter at defensive end and considered by many as one of the outstanding pass rushers in the league. But there was something about Jeter that the new defensive coordinator didn't like. The two clashed upon occasion, and when Parcells was elevated to head coach, Jeter was one of the first to go. Now he was playing for the Rams and still had his rep as a guy who, on a good day, could wreak havoc with opposing quarterbacks. This was the last thing Parcells wanted to see happen.

In the locker room before the game, the coach approached veteran tackle Brad Benson, who would be playing opposite Jeter that afternoon. "You've got to remember that Bill didn't like Jeter," Benson said. "Jeter challenged him on numerous occasions and Bill used to warn him, but Gary never heeded the call. Bill told him he was going to get rid of him, and he did.

"Now we're playing them for the first time since the trade. He begins talking to me in the locker room, very casually, about family, about Mickey [Corcoran]—always one of his favorite topics—until we were both completely relaxed. We must have talked for about a half-hour. Then I'm standing in the tunnel before the introductions and he walks past. Suddenly, he stops and says to me, 'Listen. Forget sacks. If Jeter even touches Simms today, you're ass is outta here.' And he turns and walks out onto the field.

"Well, from the line of scrimmage I had an almost picture-perfect day against Jeter. I relaxed a bit near the end and Jeter leaped over the top of the pile and blocked a kick. I knew I had let him in, but because I switched sides with Gordon King on kicks, Bill thought it was Gordon. I looked over and he's running up and down the sidelines like a madman, so I ran the other way and came to the sideline as far away from him as I could. Bill was so anxious to get to Gordon that he forgot to take off his headset and when the wire ran out the phones almost ripped his head off, and almost took him off his feet. I remember laughing at that one. But it also showed how he was a stickler for even the smallest of things."

The loss to the Rams showed that the team hadn't yet jelled, with the ups and downs continuing through eight games. The following week San Francisco did a number on the Giants, winning 31–10. Then, after beating Atlanta, the team lost to rival Philadelphia 24–10. With the schedule half over, the team was mired at 4–4, the season hanging in the balance. Parcells could have really gone off on everyone, screaming about underachievers, demanding more and more. While he certainly did his share of yelling and screaming in practice, and was often very emotional during games, he nevertheless was always a thinking man's coach.

"Bill is an extremely intelligent man," Phil McConkey said, "a quality that allows him to be aware of everything. He has the capacity to see everything and absorb everything. It's almost as if he has a sixth sense. Even though he pretty much had a system and fit the players into that system, he wasn't adverse to taking input from players.

"During the week after we lost to the Eagles to even our record at 4–4, I saw him having a conversation with Rob Carpenter at practice. Rob was a guy he had a lot of respect for because he was a tough, hard-nosed running back. The two of them must have talked for about twenty minutes. I was real close to Carpenter and asked him later what it was all about. Carpenter said, 'He asked my opinion and I told him he ought to play Joe Morris more and you more on third down.' That's when I took over the role as the third-down receiver. Joe also began to get more carries and was soon showing his immense talent. After that, things began to turn around. Here was Carpenter, a running back, telling him to use Joe Morris more. But that's why Bill listened. There were always certain guys he would listen to."

Of course, those few moves weren't the only reason the team turned the season around. Everyone began putting it together, the players learning to complement each other and the Parcells system taking hold. The Giants won five of their next six games, including big victories over Dallas, Washington, and the New York Jets. Suddenly the team was at 9–5 and appeared to be playoff bound. Though Carpenter was still the team's leading rusher, Morris was coming on strong. Simms was having a great year and the defense continued to improve. Parcells admitted, as he had with Simms, that he also misjudged Joe Morris.

"He wasn't too small," the coach said. "He was a lot of heart and skill and moves and speed and strength just stuffed inside a five-foot-seven package. It was toward the end of the season I realized Joe was going to be one of the best."

The 1984 season didn't quite have a fairy-tale ending. The team lost its final two games, to St. Louis and New Orleans, to finish at 9–7. That was, however, a far cry from 3–12–1 and, better yet, they still made the playoffs as a wild-card entry. The playoffs were almost identical to 1981. In the wild-card game, the Giants avenged their early season loss to the Rams, beating L.A. by a 16–13 count in a fine team effort. The next week, however, the season ended at Candlestick Park in San Francisco as the New Yorkers again fell to the 49ers. This time the score was 21–10 and, just as it was in 1981, the Niners went on to win another Super Bowl.

This time there was no talk of replacing Bill Parcells. Shortly after the season ended, he was rewarded with a new four-year contract. There was no longer any doubt that the Giants were his team. He was so pumped that he said he was ready to start the new season in February. But first things first. The draft brought more players who would help, including running back George Adams, wide receiver Stacy Robinson, tight end Mark Bavaro, running back Lee Rouson, and safety Herb Welch.

The team was becoming younger and more versatile. In 1984, Simms had set club records for attempts (533), completions (286), and yards (4,044). Add to that the fact that Joe Morris was about to explode on the scene as the full-time running back and the offense seemed better than ever. With another year's experience, the defense was moving closer to the league's elite units. As for Parcells, he was continuing to refine his coaching style, dealing with his players in a unique and different way, a way that was already making him very different from the majority of NFL coaches.

The Parcells needle was becoming sharper as he became involved in each and every facet of his team. He was able to rip a player from stem to stern one day, then walk off the field with his arm around him the next. Yeah, players needed a thick skin, as Harry Carson had said. Parcells himself confirmed this years later when he said, "If you're sensitive, you will have a hard time with me."

"He definitely ran everything," said Brad Benson. "His favorite drill was a one-on-one pass rush drill. When we were running it at practice he really performed. He performed for everyone—the linemen, the coaching staff, the people in the stands watching practice. He'd run it over and over, screaming at everyone, coaching everyone, taking over the entire drill.

"Even though he was known as a defensive coach he made a project of the offensive line. Before he got there the Giants hadn't had a solid offensive line for years. He put the line together, put a lot of effort into it, until it became a line he truly built. He worked with us because he figured he knew defensive ends better than anyone else. I remember he pulled me aside . . . on the Monday before we played [San Francisco] the following weekend.

" 'Don't walk around smiling like you just had a good game,' he said. 'I'm gonna tell you something. This guy [Niners defensive end Charles] Haley has more shit than what you think. I scouted him. He's good. He's got an inside move you won't believe. Take the film home and watch. This is a young guy who has more than anyone thinks.' "

Benson explained how the coach began devising for his linemen strategies not seen before in the NFL. "He always worked from the perspective of the defensive end," Benson continued, "and sometimes he had me do some very innovative and unorthodox stuff, things that hadn't been done before. For example, he had me split two yards away from [guard] Bill Ard on third and long. Most offensive tackles want to be real tight. He wanted me to attack the defensive end, rather than react to what he would do. He figured that kind of formation would bother the defensive end. It was his deal and it worked. Other offensive linemen would see how I played and ask, 'Why did you do that?'"

The attacking defense was an idea Bill had begun thinking about years earlier at Wichita State when he learned the Invert 52, which he then passed along to River Dell High. He began to refine it at Texas Tech, when he taught his defensive ends to force the play outside, string it out for the linebackers, rather than the traditional turning it back inside. Now he applied it to his offensive line and the way they dealt with opposing defensive ends. His football mind continued to grow and expand. As a coach, he was doing more than pushing the buttons. He was utilizing his talent in creative ways.

"Bill was also a stickler for conditioning," Harry Carson said. "He wanted his players working out, getting stronger, competing, and not getting hurt. But I think his greatest quality is that he can motivate. He knows the right buttons to push, and he has a way of touching everybody during the course of a week, whether it's in the locker room or on the field. He never lets you get comfortable. He's always finding something to keep you off balance and keep you motivated.

"Let's face it, Bill has a big mouth and he's always talking. We would never know how he was going to be from day to day. And yes, there is a fear factor. You don't want him picking on you and you know if you don't get the job done, you're gone. He will give you the opportunity to do it, but you've got to produce. Plus the guy is always coaching. If you're having a sandwich in the dining hall and he walks past you, he'll have something to say. It's all part of coaching. Everything he says and does has a purpose, with the end result being to win."

Then there were his ways of motivating. They varied somewhat, but were often rooted in some kind of sarcastic criticism that had a definite purpose." There were guys he knew he could use as scapegoats to send a message to the rest of the team," said Phil McConkey. "He knew they could handle it. Simms, me, Burt, Benson. I remember one time we were running patterns. He wanted the receivers to make an acute angle cut and make it perfectly. I ran the pattern and the ball was overthrown. He begins yelling at me about drifting upfield (out of the pattern). I knew I didn't drift and I was pissed. But it kept me focused and sent a message to the other guys on the team. But he wouldn't do the same thing to Mark Bavaro because he knew Mark couldn't handle it. So everything he did had a purpose.

"We could be having the greatest practice session. But if that happened to be the day he wanted to call it off early, tell us we were no good, and send us in, he would do it, no matter how good the practice. He simply had decided that was Message Day."

Others times, it almost seemed as if he would rile his players for his own amusement. McConkey remembers being the victim one day. "We were getting ready to play Philadelphia and were out on the field just walking through a few plays. No one had even stretched yet. I hadn't even warmed up. Suddenly, he wants me to sprint and catch punts. Now I'm really getting pissed. I'm wondering why is he making me sprint? Then he started screaming at me because I was walking for the ball.

"The next day I come in and he's drinking coffee. He just looks at me and says, 'Hey, you were really mad at me yesterday.' And he's smiling. By then I had calmed down and just old him, 'Yeah, and I get mad at my father sometimes, too.' But he loves it. He loves doing that kind of thing."

Tough and uncompromising? Of that, there was little doubt. A coach who would do anything to win? Absolutely. A guy who wanted his type of player around him? There was no other way.

"Yeah, there is such a thing as a Parcells guy," Harry Carson said. "It's a guy who wants to win and will do the small things in order to win—things for the team. He'll always put the team first, no matter what. Guys who have a tendency to be selfish and self-centered are not Parcells guys. If you're going to be a Parcells guy, you definitely have to check your ego at the door.

"You can be considered a great or potentially great player when you get here, but Bill will strip you down to the lowest point, then build you back up to where he wants you to be."

Carson also confirmed the long-held notion that Bill was always tougher on rookies and newcomers than on seasoned vets.

"He always talks about having stripes, or pelts," Carson said. "If you got stripes, then you've done it in the past and he'll go easier on you. If you don't have stripes, don't have pelts, then he's looking to see how much you can take. He might say something or yell at practice and it pisses some guys off. Maybe they weren't yelled at before. The question is, how do they handle it? Does it knock them off their game or do they persevere? That's what he wants to find out. If they persevere, then he's doing a good job because the results will happen out on the field."

Winning. That's what it all came down to. Winning. Now that Parcells had the Giants on the right track, he was intent on finishing the job, bringing his team to the top. Yet this hard man with an inexorable tunnel vision for victory also had a human side, if not a soft one. Prior to the 1985 season, the team signed a free agent punter from the then-rival United States Football League. Veteran Dave Jennings had been handling the Giants' punting chores since 1974, and was considered one of the best in the business. The newcomer, Sean Landeta, had a slightly stronger leg and was considerably younger, and the coach knew he had to make a very tough decision because Jennings was still a fine punter and not yet ready to retire.

"Bill and I had become friends," Jennings related. "We used to play racquetball together during the off-season. He was very talented, had great skills. I was a hustler, so we had some good pretty matches. Very competitive. I remember he'd call me at seven or eight on a Saturday morning and say, 'Come on, Jennings. Let's go play.' He'd pick me up and we'd play. It wasn't player and coach, but two guys playing racquetball, and that's how we really got to know each other.

"He was always totally up front with me. At the mini-camp prior to the 1985 season he told me he was looking for a younger punter, because he knew I couldn't go on forever. He just wanted me to know that and I was very appreciative. A lot of coaches wouldn't do that. He said he wasn't necessarily going to make a change, but if the right guy came along . . . When they signed Sean, I could see immediately he was a great punter and I knew pretty much how it would turn out. It wasn't easy for him or for me.

"But I totally appreciated his honesty. Finally, he had to make 10 cuts at the next-to-last countdown. I was going to be one of them. What he ended up doing was cut nine of the guys on Monday, which was countdown day. Then he released me the next day, on Tuesday. He just didn't want me being one of a group and that was nice. But he never let friendship get in the way of his coaching, which is something a lot of coaches can't do." Jennings would eventually sign with the crosstown

New York Jets and continue his fine career for a number of additional years.

Once the rosters were set, with the 1985 season looming, the Giants suffered a potentially crippling blow. Tight end Zeke Mowatt, who shared the team lead with forty-eight receptions in 1984, wrecked a knee. He underwent surgery and would be lost for the season. Only this time, coach and team must have had the right karma. Rookie tight end Mark Bavaro would step in and make the position his own, and everyone soon breathed a collective sigh of relief.

It was a season when the Giants almost came of age. *Almost*. In any sport, "almost" is a very big word. In fact, it's huge. It speaks volumes. It says you're not quite there. Unfortunately, when you're not quite there it doesn't matter if the difference is one inch or a thousand miles. You still didn't make it, didn't reach your goal. In the end, you lost. However, you can always learn from the bottom line. The Giants made a run, their best run in more than twenty years.

It began on an incredibly high note, a 21–0 whitewashing of Philadelphia, a team the Giants always loved to beat. After losing to Green Bay 23–20, the New Yorkers topped St. Louis and then Philadelphia a second time, this one in overtime. At 3–1, the team looked strong. Then there were two tough losses, 30–29 to Dallas and 35–30 to the Cincinnati Bengals. The Giants were now even at 3–3, with the trio of defeats coming by a combined margin of nine points. That's what it means when a team is *almost* there. A football team that has come full circle finds a way to win at least two of those contests.

The Bengals game, however, showed how far Phil Simms had progressed as a top-flight quarterback. Even though the bottom line was far from desirable, Simms set single-game club records by completing forty of sixty-two passes for an amazing 513 yards. Of course, you don't want your quarterback throwing sixty-two passes every week. In fact, you don't want him throwing that many ever. With a balanced offense, an early lead, and a solid defense, there's no way he would have to throw even half that much.

Week Seven saw the club facing another division arch-rival, the Washington Redskins. The Giants would win the game 17–3 with a very solid defensive effort. It was a game, however, that marked another kind of coming together, with an incident that became first a Giants tradition, then slowly spread throughout the league. For the New Yorkers, it showed just how close team and coach had become. It started the week before the game, between Parcells and nose tackle Jim Burt. Harry Carson relates what happened.

"Bill always liked to get on Burt. Jim was a solid player, but also a practical joker, and the two would often pull pranks on one another," Carson said. "The week of the Washington game Parcells came into the locker room and sought out Burt. He started giving him the needle. 'That Jeff Bostic is really playing well,' he said, referring to the Redskin guard Burt would be going up against. 'If you don't do the right stuff, he's gonna hand your ass to you.' Burt just laughed. 'Ah, Bill, I'll be okay. Don't worry.' He just kind of blew Bill off.

"Bill always wanted Burt to use dumbbells out of his stance in practice to improve his quickness off the ball. Burt didn't want to. Then in the locker room Bill would make little comments away from Burt, but always so Burt could hear them. For example, he would come over to me and say, 'You better be ready. I think Jeff Bostic is gonna eat Burt for lunch.' Things like that. Anyway, Jim goes out and has a great game. Near the end, when it was apparent we had it won, Jim comes over to me, I guess, because I was captain and one of Parcells's guys. He says, 'That cocksucker, I really want to get him.' Now we're all happy because we're winning the game. He suggests that we dump the barrel of Gatorade on him. Jim's smart. He knew if I did it, Bill probably wouldn't say anything.

"So we both grabbed the bucket, walked up behind Parcells, and when he took his headphone off, we drenched him. That's how the whole thing got started. It was the first time it was done to any coach and no one really noticed it then. The next year I started doing it independently of Burt and by 1986 it had taken on a life of its own."

Whether it was the Gatorade bath or just an up-and-coming team beginning to feel its oats, the Giants won four of the next five games to run its record to 8–4. The only loss was another squeaker, a 23–21 defeat by those same Redskins. The team then split its final four games, beating Houston and Pittsburgh and losing to Cleveland and Dallas. In the final game, which was against the Steelers, Joe Morris capped a great season by gaining 202 yards. Both losses were again close, by two to the Browns and seven to the Cowboys.

The Giants finished the season at 10–6, their best record since 1963. Both Dallas and Washington finished with identical marks, with the Cowboys awarded the division title because of their 4–0 mark in head-to-head games against the Giants and Redskins. Parcells's team, however, got the wild-card playoff berth over the Skins because of their 8–4 record within the conference. Washington had been 6–6 against other NFC teams.

Individually, Joe Morris had proved he was far from being too small, gaining a team record 1,336 yards on 294 carries and scoring an amazing twenty-one touchdowns, another team mark. Simms threw for 3,829 yards and twenty-two scores while rookie Bavaro caught thirty-seven passes, just twelve fewer than team leader Lionel Manuel, including a team-record twelve receptions against the Bengals. On the defensive side of the ball, Leonard Marshall set a team record with 15.5 quarterback sacks. He made the Pro Bowl along with Simms, Morris, Taylor, and Carson.

Perhaps the most telling statistic, however, was the one that came out of the six losses. The Giants had lost those games by a total of only twenty points. *Almost*, again. As Parcells wrote in his autobiography,

"Whatever those final qualities are that champions are supposed to have, we didn't have. It wasn't just the offense or the defense. If we needed to fumble a snap and lose, we'd do that. If the other team needed to drive down the field in the last minutes and beat us, they would."

The mark of a champion. It takes those little things, making a play in the final minute, stopping a drive on fourth-and-one, blocking a punt, intercepting a pass. That was the one thing still lacking. Yet the team was in the playoffs and if a few breaks went their way, if the ball took a Giants' bounce here and there. If . . .

In other words, everyone on the team from the coach on down thought they had a chance to surprise a lot of people.

CHAPTER EIGHT

Climbing That Final Mountain

T HIS WAS THE THIRD TIME THE GIANTS HAD MADE THE PLAYOFFS AS
a wild-card entry since Bill Parcells joined them in 1981. Each
time, the team had won its first game then been eliminated the
following week. Guess what? It happened again. The wild-card game was
against the San Francisco 49ers, the team that had whipped the New
Yorkers in both 1981 and '84. Those were Super Bowl–bound Niner
teams. This edition was 10–6, like the Giants. San Francisco, however,
still featured quarterback Joe Montana, running back Roger Craig, and
wide receiver Jerry Rice. With those three guys the Niners were good
enough to beat anyone.

With nearly seventy-six-thousand fans jamming Giants Stadium, the
New Yorkers were pumped, especially the defense. They began working
on Montana from the start, in fact, teeing off on whoever had the ball. The
linebacking corps Taylor, Carson, Banks, Hunt, Reasons, and Headen—
none of them weighing less than 234 pounds—was especially devastating.
Defensive coordinator Bill Belichick rotated them all afternoon, and they
were nearly unstoppable.

The Giants scored on a field goal in the first quarter, then on a Simms-
to-Bavaro eighteen-yard TD toss in the second, while the Niners could
only manage a field goal, for a 10–3 halftime score. Meanwhile, the defense continued to harass Montana, knocking him to the ground time and
again, sacking him, and taking away his running game when they got

101

Roger Craig out of the game with a bad knee. Because of the hard-hitting defense, the normally sure-handed Craig dropped five passes. Several other Niners also left the game with various injuries.

In the third period Simms hit reserve tight end Don Hasselbeck with a three-yard scoring toss. The extra point made it 17–3. In the fourth quarter the Giant defense teed off on the Niners, while first-year fullback Maurice Carthon helped open holes for the elusive but powerful Morris. The score held and the Giants had another wild-card victory. Montana was sacked four times, twice by Jim Burt, and ran for his life much of the rest of the time.

"He was rattled by the way we went after him," Leonard Marshall said, "by the way we went after his face."

It couldn't have gone better. Joe Morris controlled the ball and the clock by gaining 141 yards on twenty-eight carries. Later, he talked about the difference in the Giants' running game and how it made such a big difference in the New York offense.

"Last year you'd run a play once and that was it," he said. "They were concerned about protecting the passer. We had always been a fullback-oriented team, but in the off-season they started putting in halfback plays, more traps, some sprint draws, things to utilize my speed and get me into the secondary. The line had more room to work, and they did a great job blocking, plus we got [Maurice Carthon] from the USFL, and he's just been destroying people with his blocks."

It was a happy but realistic bunch of Giants afterward. Happy because they had beaten the team that eliminated them in both 1981 and '84; realistic because waiting for them the following week was the Chicago Bears, considered by nearly everyone to be the league's best team in 1985. The Bears had simply overpowered everyone, finishing the regular season as NFC Central Division champs with an eye-opening 15–1. They had scored an NFC-best 456 points, while their heralded "46" defense gave up a league-low 198.

It was a team reminiscent of the classic "Monsters of the Midway" Bears teams of the past. These were the Bears of Jim McMahon, Walter Payton, Willie Gault, Mike Singletary, Richard Dent, Wilbur Marshall, and a 300-pound-plus defensive tackle who sometimes played fullback named William "The Refrigerator" Perry. This was the team favored to win the Super Bowl and they would surely present a tall order for the upset-minded

Giants. It didn't help that the game would be played on cold, windswept Soldier Field in Chicago.

The defining moment in the game came early. In the first quarter Sean Landeta dropped back to punt near his own goal line. He grabbed the snap, but as he dropped the ball toward his foot, a huge gust of wind swept it just enough off-track that Landeta barely grazed it. It bounced just a few feet away where Chicago defensive back Shaun Gayle grabbed it at the five and waltzed into the end zone for a "gimme" touchdown. The kick made it 7–0 and the game and the Giants' season could have ended right then and there.

New York had a chance to tie when they moved to the Chicago two-yard line and had a first-and-goal with just thirty-one seconds left in the half. Instead of trying to run it in, Simms threw three times. All fell incomplete. Then kicker Eric Schubert missed a short field goal and the Giants had come up empty. On the sidelines, Bill Parcells must have died just a little. He didn't know it then, but his ball club would not threaten to score again.

In the third period Bears quarterback Jim McMahon threw a pair of TD passes to wide receiver Dennis McKinnon and that was the end of it. The Chicago defense did the rest, with the final score 21–0. The New Yorkers would be going home, while the Bears would continue their roll, shutting out the L.A. Rams 24–0 for the NFC Championship, then steamrolling the New England Patriots in Super Bowl XX 46–10.

As for the New Yorkers, they had been thoroughly dominated by the Bears. Joe Morris had just thirty yards on ten carries in the first half, before "Refrigerator" Perry gave him a slight concussion on a blindside hit. The team would wind up with just thirty-two yards on the ground. Simms completed just four of thirteen passes for forty-eight yards in the first half and wound up six out of twenty for eighty yards. Throw in six sacks, and the net passing yardage was an anemic thirty-five. At one point in the game, the team had five straight one-two-three-punt possessions. Thirty-six plays produced three first downs and the Giants were 0-for-9 on third-down conversions. They were a thoroughly beaten team.

Maybe the Bears were the better team, but Bill Parcells and his players had been hoping they were good enough to maybe jump on top early, get a few breaks along the way, make a big play or two, and win. Parcells admitted that if the two teams had played ten times, the Bears most likely would have won eight. He was just hoping that this would have been one of the Giants' two wins.

"I was upset; I was pissed," Bill would say. "But I knew once we got behind in the third quarter we were done. You just don't come back against that defense, not on a Sunday like that."

The coach felt bad for himself, but more so for his players. He sought out his most seasoned veterans, Harry Carson and George Martin, and promised them they would figure out a way to get it done the next year. He would also admit that he felt all along that this Giants team had a chance to go all the way. So there was certainly more than a fair chance the next year. Perhaps just another player or two, some fine-tuning here and there, and that innate ability of champions to make the big play when they need it most.

Most of the players also felt it could have been a Giants year. When asked if the players felt they were good enough in '85 to win it, George Martin said, "Absolutely." For that reason, everyone came back a year later determined to make that final climb to the top of the mountain.

"Bill really didn't change anything the next year," Martin said. "In fact, I think the players bought into [his philosophy and his system] more completely than they ever did before. The year before we felt we were one game away from the Super Bowl. Because Chicago beat everyone else soundly, we felt if we had gotten past then we would have been the champions. That, if nothing else, convinced us to stay the course and buy into what Bill was promoting, even more so than before."

During the off-season there were some minor roster adjustments. Carpenter was gone, Raul Allegre became the new kicker, Mowatt was back from his knee injury, and Pepper Johnson joined an already great linebacking corps. The draft produced defensive end Eric Dorsey, cornerback Mark Collins, and defensive tackle Erik Howard. But perhaps the biggest and most upsetting story of the off-season was that Lawrence Taylor was having problems with drugs.

Bill said he suspected something was wrong because LT wasn't the same man during the 1985 season. Because even a subpar Lawrence Taylor is better than most other players, the problem didn't become apparent immediately. As had become his policy, Bill never divulged too many details when players were involved with drugs. Suffice to say, Taylor was clean when he came to camp in 1986. He told members of the press that he stopped on his own, using a steady diet of off-season golf to occupy his time and his mind. Though he has had several well-publicized lapses since, especially after his career ended, there is little doubt that Taylor was not using drugs during the 1986 campaign.

When the team gathered at the beginning of training camp, the coach made it clear to everyone that there was just a single objective in the upcoming season.

"Everyone was at [camp]," Phil McConkey said. "I mean everyone. Not only the players and coaches, but everyone associated with the team down to the video guys, the equipment and security people—everyone who had anything to do with the team. And Bill told us right off that nothing less than the best would be tolerated. It was a strong message."

McConkey also talked about how devastating it had been to come so far and lose in a big playoff game. "The loss to Chicago was one of the worst defeats of my life," he said. "Losing in the playoffs like that is so difficult because you know the long road you will have to travel to get there again. You are three hours away from where you want to be and then you lose. So you come to the realization that to return you have to go through another twelve months—the whole off-season, training camp, the schedule, another playoff game. It's an unbelievably difficult task, one that takes insurmountable energy. Three hours earlier you are just where you want to be. And then you're not. I think that's why Bill wasn't going to settle for less the next year."

Phil McConkey almost didn't get to see whether the team could take that final step. He was shocked when Parcells told him that he would be part of the final cut.

"I didn't have a clue it was coming," McConkey said. "Bill said he didn't really want to do it, but he was caught in a numbers game. What can you do? Maybe I was disappointed, but life has to go on. I hooked up with Green Bay and joined the Packers for the first week of the season."

The euphemistic "numbers game" simply means that the team couldn't release any other player, probably because of their contract situations. Winning may be the name of the game, but football is also a bottom-line business that sometimes dictates coaching decisions. So the team would start the season without one of its most versatile and popular players, a Parcells guy through and through.

When the Giants lost their opening game to Dallas 31–28, it suddenly looked like more of the same. Some critics remembered the six losses in 1985 by a total of twenty points. Now, in 1986, the team opened the season by losing to a big divisional rival by a scant three points. Same ol', same ol', as they say. What, then, had they learned? Would it be another year of not winning the big one, not making the crucial play, not finding a way to become real champions? Those questions could only be answered on the field, and that's what the team started doing the very next week.

First they beat San Diego 20–7, then toppled the L.A. Raiders 14–9. Next came a 20–17 victory over New Orleans and a 13–6 win at St. Louis. Suddenly, they had a four-game winning streak, the last three all decided by a touchdown or less—close games, and all games the Giants managed to win. A damn good sign. The win over New Orleans, however, had been costly. Wideout Lionel Manuel suffered a knee injury and would sit out the remainder of the regular season. In less than four games he had caught eleven passes for 181 yards and three scores. Now the team needed another receiver. Coach Parcells reached into the grab bag and found that an old friend was available.

"Forrest Gregg was coach of the Packers then," said Phil McConkey. "After the fourth game he called me in and said he had good news. I was traded back to the Giants. I didn't jump for joy, but it felt pretty good. Gregg told me Bill was gonna call. So I waited and he finally calls and says, 'Hey, McConkey!' My reply was very simple: *'Hey, Bill. The grass is greener, my ass!'*

"He always finished all kinds of expressions with 'my ass.' He laughed and put it on the bulletin board, where it stayed the rest of the year. Chuck Knox once said it was the best quote he ever heard in pro ball. Anyway, Parcells says to me, 'Those Packers drive a hard bargain. I had to throw in a couple of clipboards and a tackling dummy to get you back.'"

So McConkey was back where he belonged and began contributing immediately. Another move was made after Game Five, against St. Louis. The Giants dealt a couple of future draft choices to the Cardinals in return for running back Ottis Anderson. Anderson had joined the Cards in 1979, gained 1,605 yards as a rookie, and immediately became one of the league's elite runners. He was over a thousand yards in five of his first six years, missing only in the strike-shortened season of 1982. The string ended in 1985 when Anderson ran for just 481 yards, missing seven games with a variety of injuries. At age twenty-nine, he would provide experience and insurance in the backfield.

The return of McConkey and the trade for Ottis Anderson provided an even closer look into the way Bill Parcells coached his football team.

Both players were able to see the Giants operation from another perspective.

"Not being on a winning team made me wonder what it was all about," said Anderson, who endured a series of losing seasons in St. Louis. "When I went to the Giants I thought if the Cards had a disciplinary problem, these guys were out of control. Some of the things that were done, I couldn't believe. For example, with [Cardinals coach] Gene Stallings we had to be in the meeting room five minutes before the meeting started. We couldn't chew gum, we couldn't have hats on, we had to sit at a desk. And we had to answer the roll, with someone calling your name like you were in high school.

"I go to the Giants and maybe one of the assistant coaches would come out about five minutes before and say, 'Let's meet.' You would think the guys would just rush in there. But they didn't They just took their time. The coaches would call the guys three or four times before they all went in there. But that was the way free-spirited Parcells allowed people to be. He let players be guys who played on Sunday, as long as they did what they were expected to do.

"He didn't trouble himself with the little things. If you were fifteen minutes late he would take notice. But if you walked in two minutes late it was no big deal. Parcells would just look to see who you were and make a mental note of it. He would look at you in a way that let you know you were late. He didn't have to go overboard. Some coaches would stop the meeting, make it a point to call you out and lecture you for not being on time. [Parcells] never bothered to address little trivial things like that. He would always say, 'I've got bigger fish to fry.' "

Anderson also appreciated Parcells's honesty when telling him what his role with the Giants would be. "He said he needed some production out of the fullback position, even though he knew I spent most of the career at tailback," Anderson explained. "He said that defenses were looking for [Joe] Morris to run to the side where [fullback] Maurice Carthon lined up. (Carthon was used almost exclusively as a blocker.) He wanted to take away tendencies. By bringing me in at fullback every now and then, he felt he would have more flexibility at the position. He also told me that it was Joe Morris's team and he wanted to be sure I understood that even before I came here.

"I told him I just wanted to be productive and that I wasn't here to disrupt what they had been doing. They were 4–1 when I arrived, and I had just left a team that was 1–4. I had never been part of a winning environment in the NFL before, and Parcells made it easy for me to fit in. It was the way every player wants to be treated."

When McConkey went to Green Bay, he soon noticed a difference in the way the players there looked at their coach. "My first team meeting and [Coach] Forrest Gregg is up there, a huge, imposing guy who was a great player. Then he begins ranting and raving. I'm sitting there ramrod-stiff, didn't dare take my eyes off him for fifteen or twenty minutes. Then I looked around a bit. The other guys are all relaxed, slouching in their seats, looking at their watches. They were used to it. His ranting just didn't catch the guys. Bill knows when to do it and when not to."

Knowing when to turn the heat up, when to tighten the screws, and when to let go is one of Parcells's keys to success. There is, however, no apparent formula for it, just the instinct of a coaching genius. That's why other coaches cannot be Parcells clones, and why so many of his former players remain amused and almost fascinated by his often contradictory actions.

"I remember coming into the locker room one time about three hours before a game," Brad Benson said. "Bobby Knight was there. Bill would always sit at this round table before a game. Well, he's sitting there with Bobby and they're talking about fly fishing. I joined them and, in typical fashion, within twenty minutes we're arguing, really going at it. How anyone can argue about fly fishing, I don't know. But Bill's ranting and raving, 'Don't tell me about this shit. You're not the only one who knows about fly fishing.'

"Beginning in 1984, I think he pulled away from the other assistant coaches and got closer to the players. He was very demanding of his assistants, just as he was with the players. Yet at the same time, he was able to endear himself to the players. Other coaches felt they had to keep their distance from the players to maintain discipline. Parcells was strong enough personality-wise where he could sit and argue with you about fly fishing before a game and still maintain discipline.

"In that regard, he would do whatever had to be done. There was a player whose wife was causing some problems in the wives' section about some decisions that had been made on the team. Right in the middle of a meeting Bill told this guy to tell his wife to keep her frigging mouth shut. Or he would make things easy for her in that she wouldn't have to worry about what was going on. I think that was after he called her. He would do that. He would call your wife. Nothing was off-limits if it was going to effect what was happening on the team."

As for the team, they were operating on all cylinders as midseason approached. After running their record to 5–1, they lost a tough 17–12 decision at Seattle. A week later they topped Washington 27–20, then beat Dallas 17–14. In both games, Joe Morris ran for an identical 181 yards. He was putting together an absolutely brilliant season. In fact, the Giants wouldn't lose another game all year. The scores, incidentally, proved that the team had learned something. After Dallas, they topped Philadelphia 17–14, Minnesota 22–20, Denver 19–16, and San Francisco 21–17—four straight victories by a total of twelve points. A year earlier they might have won two of them. Remember, championship teams find ways to win the close games.

The Minnesota game was one that could have gone either way. It was tight and close-to-the-vest all the way, a single play here or there capable of affecting the outcome.

Finally, it came down to this. The Vikings had a 20–19 lead with just seventy-two seconds remaining in the game. The Giants were at their own 48-yard line with a fourth down and seventeen yards to go for a first. It didn't look good. If they didn't convert, Minnesota could easily run out the clock.

The week before the game, Parcells had a talk with quarterback Simms. With Lionel Manuel hurt, tight end Bavaro had emerged as the team's most reliable receiver. The wideouts had been erratic and drops weren't all that uncommon. With his usual sense of instinct and time, Parcells told Simms he was a great quarterback and not to pay attention to things that had been written in the press. He reminded Simms how he had led the team to recent victories over the Cowboys, Redskins, and Eagles. But, he cautioned him, the only way he could be successful was to continue being "the daring player you've always been."

Apparently, the coach was concerned that Simms would become leery of the uneven play of his wide receivers and begin to hold back, play it too conservatively. If he did that, the coach knew, he wouldn't get the job done in the big games. Now, as Simms came to the line of scrimmage with a fourth-down play that could possibly decide the game, the coach's advice must have been lurking somewhere within his subconscious. He looked over the defense. The Vikings had eight men stacked in the secondary, knowing if they could stop the Giants here it was over.

Simms dropped back. As was his wont, he stayed in the pocket until the last second, spotted wide receiver Bobby Johnson, then released the ball as he was slammed to the ground. He got up to see Johnson also getting up . . . with the ball in hand. He had grabbed it for a twenty-two-yard gain to the Vikes' thirty and a first down. Parcells called it the "biggest single pass of our season." Seconds later Raul Allegre kicked his fifth field goal of the game and the Giants had a 22–20 victory.

With tensions running high throughout, the game also showed the extremes that could be reached between the coach and a player he truly respected. The incident occurred right before the end of the first half as the Giants were trying for a late score.

"I jumped offsides on a key play," Brad Benson remembered. "It was third-and-long, a crucial play, and possibly a turning point in the game. Well, he goes berserk. I could see his lips moving on the sideline. He called me one of his famous expressions and I got mad. Suddenly, we both wanted a piece of each other and had to be restrained. People were running everywhere because it's halftime and here we are, both trying to get at each other.

"After the game we got on the plane for the trip back to New York. We didn't talk. I walked past him and got a seat. A little while later he sends Ronnie Barnes, our trainer, back to get me. 'Bill wants to see you in first class,' he tells me. I figured, here we go again. I was a nervous flyer to begin with and didn't want an altercation on the plane. I really thought we were gonna get in another fight. So I go up to where he's sitting, kinda tense. Then he looks at me and says, 'Well, you know I love you. Just forget about the whole thing. Now go back and sit down.'

"It was in the heat of battle and then it was over. Ten minutes before, you're in a fit of rage, ready to take a punch at him. He can take that, say a few words, and make you feel so good about yourself, almost instantly. He has that kind of charisma and that's why I have a tremendous respect for him."

There was little doubt that Bill Parcells was the singular driving force behind a team that now seemed determined to erase all the doubts. Nothing would suffice except the ultimate success. They had seen firsthand what the Chicago Bears had done the season before. The Bears appeared to be almost as good as they were a year earlier, and the Washington Redskins were also rolling along right behind the Giants. So there was no time to relax. The feeling pretty much remained, however, that the road to the Super Bowl would still wind up going through Chicago.

The team continued to play at peak efficiency for the remainder of the regular season. Their next game after the Vikings was against the Denver Broncos. In this one, Simms did it again. With the game tied at sixteen in the final two minutes, the resolute Simms completed a third-and-twenty-one pass to Johnson for a first down. Without skipping a beat, he dropped back again and connected with McConkey for a forty-six-yard gain, allowing Allegre to come in and boot the winning field goal.

A week later the Giants had a Monday night date at San Francisco. It was more than a routine game because the Redskins had won the day before to run their record to 11–2, giving them a half-game lead in the NFC race. But after thirty minutes of football, Joe Montana and company had a 17–0 lead and things looked bleak. The team came into the locker room expecting their coach to read them the riot act. Always one to do the unexpected, the coach spoke quietly and purposefully.

"I was low-key," Parcells said. "The situation didn't need an explanation. The 49ers' intensity level had been about ten notches higher than ours. We just went over a couple of simple things and I told our guys they still had time to win the game if they got moving."

That showed the kind of confidence the coach had in this Giants team. It was tight end Mark Bavaro who set the tone for the second half. On the second offensive play of the half, Simms hit Bavaro with a short pass over the middle. The big tight end broke a tackle by All-Pro safety Ronnie Lott, then literally dragged five 49er defenders another eighteen yards before he went down. It was a thirty-one-yard gain and led to the Giants first score.

"Bavaro turned the game around," said Phil McConkey. "Six different 49ers hit him hard along the way. It took four men to finally bring him down. It was awesome. I'd never seen anything like it."

Two plays later, Simms hit Joe Morris for a seventeen-yard touchdown. Within nine minutes the New Yorkers scored three times to overcome the San Francisco lead and win 21–17. Suddenly the team could do no wrong.

"If we're going to succeed in January, we have to win games like this," Harry Carson said. "We can't use being on the road as an excuse. When we were behind 17–0 at the half, we stayed calm and kept our poise. We just believe that somebody is going to make the big play."

The team went on to run the table, including a 24–14 victory over Washington the following week to take the division lead. They finished with a 14–2 record, the best in club history and good enough for the NFC

Eastern Division title, the club's first in twenty-three years. They also put an exclamation point on the regular season by steamrolling Green Bay in the season finale, 55–24. Washington finished second with a 12–4 record, while the Bears equaled the Giants in the Central Division, winning it at 14–2. The fact that the Giants were the only unbeaten team at home gave them home-field advantage throughout the playoffs.

There were also some fine individual performances. Simms had thrown for 3,487 yards with twenty-one touchdowns. He didn't have to throw as much as he had the two previous seasons because Joe Morris had emerged as an elite NFL back, breaking his own team record with 1,516 yards on 341 carries. He scored fourteen touchdowns. Tight end Bavaro had also become a star in his second season, grabbing sixty-six passes for 1,001 yards and four scores. Once he caught the ball, the 250-pounder from Notre Dame was like a Mack truck and extremely difficult to bring down.

Defensively, the team gave up just 236 points in sixteen games, second in the entire league to the Bears' 187. It was a big-play defense, led by Lawrence Taylor's career-best 20.5 sacks. The team as a whole made twenty-four interceptions and, like the offense, came up big when the situation demanded it. They were now a defense that could take over and dominate a game.

As for the coach, it had to be the most satisfying season of his life. It also marked the beginning of the Parcells legacy as a coach with an innate ability to turn a franchise around. He had taken the Giants from an abysmal 3–12–1 in 1983 to 14–2 in 1986. To the team's long-suffering fans, he was tantamount to a savior, a guy who had come in and plugged the dyke, stopped the flood of losing that had been part of the team since 1964. Suddenly, with Bill Parcells at the helm, these had become the Giants of Conerly, Gifford, Rote, Grier, Robustelli, and Tittle all over again. The winning tradition of the past was back in the form of a modern-day juggernaut that was beginning to give the impression that it couldn't be stopped. Still, they had one last mountain looming ahead, the final summit: the playoffs.

Their first playoff game was against the same San Francisco 49ers that had almost beaten them a month earlier. It might have been against the same team, but it surely wasn't the same kind of game. This one showed just how good a team the Giants had become. It was one of those magical days when everything just clicked. The better team not only won, they embarrassed a formidable San Francisco ball club that had been Super

Bowl champions just two years earlier. From the opening quarter, when Simms connected with Bavaro for a twenty-four-yard touchdown, it was all Giants. In fact, it was probably as close to a perfect game as any team could play.

In the second quarter, Morris ran for a forty-five-yard touchdown, Simms hit Bobby Johnson from fifteen yards out, and Lawrence Taylor rambled thirty-four yards with an interception for the fourth score. On that play, just before the half, Jim Burt hit Niner quarterback Joe Montana so hard that it knocked the QB out of the game with a concussion. It also caused the pass to flutter into the hands of Taylor, who ran it in.

In the third quarter, Simms hit McConkey on a twenty-eight-yard scoring aerial, then connected with Zeke Mowatt from twenty-nine yards out; and Morris ran for another score, this time from the two. That made the score an incredible 49–3 after three. In the fourth period, the Giants simply controlled the ball and the clock with Morris running and the defense keeping the Niners from moving the ball. Morris wound up with 159 rushing yards. Simms completed just nine passes, but four of them were for scores, and the defense was again dominating.

"Shattered. We were simply shattered," said San Francisco coach Bill Walsh. "They played a perfect game. They destroyed our offense, shattered our blocking angles. We were dealt with."

If anyone doubted them before, that notion was out the window: these Giants were for real. Next came the NFL championship, the game many fans were waiting for, the big showdown with the Bears. But it didn't happen. The Redskins surprised the Chicagoans 27–13 to earn the right to face the Giants for a third time. Only this time the stakes were higher. The winner would be heading to the Rose Bowl in Pasadena, California, to play in Super Bowl XXI.

The NFC title game with the Redskins was played on a cold, windy January 11 at Giants Stadium. In fact, "windy" didn't begin to describe it. Gusts of up to thirty-five miles per hour were swirling around all afternoon. When the Giants won the toss they didn't take the ball, as most teams do. They took the wind, opting to have it at their backs in the first quarter. Using the wind, the Giants scored on a forty-seven-yard field goal by Allegre, and on an eleven-yard touchdown pass, Simms to Lionel Manuel, who had recovered from the injury that kept him out of the final twelve games of the regular season.

In the second quarter, Morris scored on a one-yard run, the extra point making it 17–0. Meanwhile, Washington quarterback Jay Schroeder couldn't deal with the wind, many of his passes going awry all afternoon. No one scored in the second half, the Giants' defense again dominating and the offense controlling the ball on the ground. Simms threw only two passes after intermission. The Giants had won it 17–0 and were heading to their first-ever Super Bowl.

To show how dominant the New York defense was, the Redskins— remember, this was an elite team—were 0 for 14 on third-down conversions, and 0 for 4 on fourth-down tries.

"Our defense didn't play a perfect game except in that department," Parcells said, the day after the game. "When you hold a team in that department to 0 for 18, it's not perfect, it's a miracle. . . . You get those three-downs-and-punt series, it's artistic."

There were many heroes. Simms was cool under pressure and played the wind a lot better than did Schroeder. Morris gained eighty-seven yards on twenty-nine tough carries. Offensive tackle Brad Benson shut down Washington's All-Pro defensive end Dexter Manley, holding him to just two tackles, no assists, and no sacks. Despite the cutting wind, Bill Parcells got his Gatorade shower from the combination of Burt and Carson. There were plenty of reasons to celebrate, including the fact that in two playoff games the defense had given up a total of just three points.

Now, there was one more game left, the biggest one, but the feeling was beginning to grow that this was a Giants team that simply could not be beaten.

CHAPTER NINE

Super Coach, Super Team

T HE ONLY THING NOW STANDING BETWEEN THE GIANTS AND THE
Lombardi Trophy was the Denver Broncos. Would the Giants take
home the prize from Pasadena on January 25, or would the strong
right arm of Denver quarterback John Elway shatter the dream of the east
coast team and its Jersey-guy coach? Though the Broncos had won the
AFC West with an 11–5 mark, they weren't considered in the Giants'
class. The Denver offense had scored seven more points than the New
Yorkers, but the Bronco defense yielded some ninety-one more points
than their Giants counterparts. During the regular season the Giants had
prevailed in a close game, 19–16.

There was one great equalizer, however, and that was the strength and
gambler's mentality of the Broncos' fourth-year quarterback. The words
"Elway" and "miracle finish" were already synonymous, and he had given
the football world an ample demonstration of his talent and his will just
two weeks earlier in the AFC championship contest. The Broncos had met
the Cleveland Browns in a tight, hard-fought game. Elway was operating
on a tender ankle, yet had the game even at thirteen in the fourth quarter.
Then, with just under six minutes left, Cleveland's Bernie Kosar connected with wideout Brian Brennan on a forty-eight-yard pass-run touchdown strike to give Cleveland the lead. The kick made it 20–13.

When the Broncos bobbled the ensuing kickoff, Elway found himself
facing an almost impossible situation. The ball was at his own two-yard

line. With just 5:32 left in the game, he had to take his team ninety-eight yards just to tie. Coming into the huddle, Elway told him teammates, "If you work hard, good things are going to happen."

Then he went to work—a short pass, an eleven-yard scramble, passes of twenty-two and twelve yards. Suddenly the Broncos were at the Cleveland 40 with 1:59 left. An incompletion and sack put the ball back on the 48 with a big third-down play. Elway calmly dropped back and hit Mark Jackson with a twenty-yard bullet for a first down at the 28. A fourteen-yard completion was next, and two plays later Elway ran it himself nine yards to the Cleveland five. On third-and-one, he fired a strike to Jackson in the end zone for a touchdown. The kick tied the game at 20–20, and the ninety-eight-yard march would become known forever in the annals of Denver Broncos football simply as *The Drive.*

The game wasn't over yet. Cleveland got the overtime kickoff, but their first drive stalled and Elway came on again. He wasted no time in taking the Broncos to the Cleveland 15, where Rich Karlis booted the winning field goal and Denver was in the Super Bowl.

Denver Coach Dan Reeves seemed very well-tuned to the possibilities when he said, "I hope the game is not one-sided," he said. "If it isn't, we have a chance to win it. I think one of the keys for the Giants is to stay on the field with their offense and keep John Elway off the field. You don't stop Lawrence Taylor; you hope you slow him down."

As for Elway, he dismissed the fact that the Giants were heavy favorites by restating an old football axiom. "It will be a zero-zero game when it starts," the quarterback said.

It wasn't zero-zero for long. Denver took the opening kickoff and went forty-five yards before Karlis booted a forty-eight-yard field goal to give the Broncos a 3–0 lead. Then the Giants came right back, marching down field and ending the drive with a six-yard TD pass from Simms to Zeke Mowatt. After that, however, the Broncos seemed to take over. Elway led another touchdown drive, scoring himself from the four and giving his team a 10–7 lead after one quarter. Denver had a chance to open it up, but Karlis missed a pair of field goals, one of them after a valiant goal-line stand by the New York defense. Before the half, George Martin sacked Elway in the end zone and the teams left the field with Denver ahead by one, at 10–9.

In the locker room, Parcells refrained from attacking his team. He told them he didn't mind losing, provided they didn't simply give the game away. From there, he basically told the team they weren't playing well, weren't playing together as a unit. He challenged the defense by telling them they weren't pressuring Elway enough and were taking stupid penalties. Then he told them they were goddamned lucky they were down by just a point. He wanted to see more discipline and more of a collective effort.

"You're lucky you're in it," he concluded. "Now go win it!"

The Giants took the second-half kickoff, and on the fourth play of the quarter, it was the gambler in Bill Parcells that might have turned the game around. The Giants had a fourth down with a foot to go for a first at their own 46-yard line. Parcells sent in the punting team with Sean Landeta. At the same time, he sent backup quarterback Jeff Rutledge into the game to line up at the blocking-back position. Rutledge normally did not play on the punting unit, but apparently the Broncos didn't notice. It was Rutledge who called the signals before the snap.

"Jeff could take a delay or run," Parcells said. "He looked over at me. I nodded my head and he went for it. We went for it because we're trying to win the game. This is for the world championship. I have a lot of confidence in our guys."

Just before the snap, Rutledge jumped behind center, took the snap, and sneaked two yards for a first down. Five plays later Simms hit Bavaro from the 13 and the Giants were in front to stay. Before the quarter ended, New York had seventeen unanswered points and a 26–10 lead. It was the Giants who had opened it up. Their second TD of the period came on a Morris one-yard plunge after Simms and McConkey connected on the old flea-flicker play. The Giants were on the Denver 45 when Simms handed the ball to Morris, who faked running into the line, then turned and pitched the ball back to Simms. The quarterback then hit McConkey at the 20 and the gritty receiver ran it to the one.

"We've run the flea-flicker in practice for I don't know how long," Simms said, later, "and we've never hit on the damn thing. When I hit McConkey down on the one, I thought, 'That's it. We've won it.'"

In the final period, McConkey caught a five-yard TD toss and Ottis Anderson scored on a plunge from the two. Karlis managed a field goal and Elway hit a late touchdown pass that meant nothing. Parcells got still another Gatorade shower as the Giants won the world championship going away, 39–20. Simms was the game's Most Valuable Player with an unforgettable performance. The much-maligned quarterback hit on twenty-two of twenty-five passes for 268 yards and three touchdowns. His eighty-eight-percent completion percentage set a Super Bowl mark that still stood as the 1990s ended.

Of course, the team went crazy. The coach thought about all the years at all the different colleges, about his family, his parents, Mickey—everyone who contributed to making him what he was. It had to be an extremely emotional moment for an intensely private man who generally keeps his innermost thoughts and feelings to himself. Immediately after the game, however, he said this to his team:

"No matter what anybody tells you the rest of your life, nobody can tell you you couldn't do it. Because you did it. They can't ever take that away from you."

There was little doubt that this Giants team—at least in 1986—was a great one. Bill Parcells had the biggest hand in molding them, keeping his kind of player on the field, then coaching them through the Super Bowl. It's difficult to say that one play turned a game around, especially when that game had a 39–20 final. But Parcells's decision to have Jeff Rutledge jump in and run the ball from punt formation to open the third quarter undoubtedly helped ignite the team. Don't forget, Denver still had a 10–9 lead at the time. Had Rutledge been stopped and had Elway taken his team downfield for a score, the Giants would have been looking at a 17–9 deficit instead of a 16–10 lead. Who knows? One thing, however, is certain. When the players see their coach willing to gamble, willing to put it all on the line, they are more likely to let it all hang out on the field as well.

The game, the score, the coaching moves, the Gatorade shower, the speech to the team, the interviews in the press—all these are out there for everyone to see. But with Bill Parcells, what you see isn't always all you get. Part of his personality and coaching idiosyncrasies happen behind the scenes, away from the glare of the cameras. In 1986, he was already a coach who did and said things his own way. Brad Benson remembers some Parcells images from Super Bowl XXI that have remained etched in his mind ever since.

"Bill didn't like to do anything different, ever," Benson recalled. "The pilot who had been flying the 737 stretches for us in 1986 was suddenly bumped up to 767s. Bill found this out before the Super Bowl and called the airline. 'This guy has to fly us,' he said. But they told him it wasn't possible. So he talked the Maras into taking the 767 so we could have the same pilot, same stewardesses, same everything. They had to buy the whole plane for that day and it probably cost them twenty or thirty grand just to make Bill happy."

Then, just before the game, Benson recalls that the coach was in rare form, pulling no punches with anyone, from NBC producer Sandy Grossman to music superstar Neil Diamond.

"All year long we had been going out on the field a certain way. Just before we took the field at the Rose Bowl, NBC decides they want to change it. Sandy Grossman, the producer, wanted to change the order. He explained to Bill what he wanted us to do and Bill just nodded. 'No problem,' he told him. But as soon as Grossman walked away, he turns to us and says, 'Fuck 'em, we're doing it our way.' And he screwed up the whole thing. They had commercial breaks planned and they went to commercial when our team went onto the field."

Finally, it was almost game time. Parcells and the Giants were standing on the sideline, ready to go. Neil Diamond was there to sing the national anthem. Diamond was a huge name in pop music then and somehow he wound up standing right alongside Parcells. Brad Benson, also standing there, remembers what happened next.

"The pregame stuff is still going on with the flag bearers and other people on the field. They're getting ready to announce Neil Diamond and he's standing there, looking nervous and very pale. Finally, Parcells asks him, 'What's wrong with you?'

" 'Hell, Bill,' Diamond says, 'I'm nervous.'

"Without missing a beat, Parcells says to him, 'What the fuck do you have to be nervous about? Want to trade places with me?'

"That's one of the images I'll always have of him. He would never say something like that to a player's father. He would never compromise a player's parents' integrity. But he would rip Neil Diamond on the 50-yard line. That's Bill."

When a team wins a championship, there is always one question that pops up immediately, usually asked right after the game by a broadcaster who doesn't know better. Instead of talking about the game and letting everyone enjoy the moment, the broadcaster will stick a microphone in a player or coach's face and ask, "*Can you do it again? Can you win it next year?*"

Who the hell is going to know the answer to that one? As a coach, you probably think, sure, we can win it again. We've got a great nucleus. As a realist, you know how many different things can happen to sabotage a team. So you don't know the answer. In Parcells's case, Brent Musburger asked the magic question in the locker room right after the game. As the coach said later, "I wanted to punch him in the face."

The coach was willing to answer all other questions, about the game and especially about his players. Simms had been magnificent and had plenty of support from the rest of the offense. The coached loved it when a guy like Phil McConkey, who had worked so hard just to have a place on the team, was able to catch a touchdown pass in the Super Bowl. He felt especially gratified that his veteran leaders, Harry Carson and George Martin, who had suffered through the losing years before he came, could finally sip the champagne. In addition, he embraced Lawrence Taylor who, despite his immense talent, had fought his own personal battle a year earlier. They, too, had done it together.

Mickey Corcoran was also there. It seemed that Mickey was always there in those days. The players all knew him, knew how much their coach loved and respected him. It wouldn't have been the same without Mickey. So it really wasn't the time to think about next year. There would be plenty of time for that. Maybe two days, if he was lucky. Standing in the locker room, soaking wet, was simply the greatest feeling in the world, the kind of satisfaction that only a head coach can have.

Unfortunately, the winner's high lasts only so long. Just as the losing player will soon bring himself back from a disappointing defeat, the winner also drifts back to earth. The satisfaction of the victory will always be there. If it slips away momentarily, there is The Ring to bring the memory back. For the coach, however, the time to celebrate is painfully short. Maybe a short vacation with wife and family, or a round of television appearances, interviews, and perhaps even some time to film a commercial or two. But by mid-February, it's back to work. Though he doesn't want to talk about it immediately after the game, the coach of the winning Super Bowl team knows he must soon step out front once more, his object to once again bring his team together and try to do it again.

It has been said that as difficult as it is to win a championship, it is even more difficult to repeat the next season. Seven times in the thirty-four-year history of the Super Bowl, through the 1999 season, there have been repeat winners. No team had ever won it three times in a row. Many felt, however, that the Giants team that Bill Parcells built had as good a chance as any to make it two straight in 1987.

The coach certainly didn't change his routine. He was soon back at

Giants Stadium, watching films of college games through February and March, as he and his staff got ready for the college draft. Soon the real scramble would begin. Teams not only have to decide on which players they would like to pick, but must also try to anticipate if that player will be available. That means assessing the needs of the teams that will be picking ahead of them and preparing contingencies, secondary choices in case the player they want is already gone.

For the Giants, the 1987 draft produced wide receiver Mark Ingram of Michigan State on the first round and safety Adrian White of Florida on the second. Two more wide receivers followed, Stephen Baker of Fresno State and Odessa Turner of Northwestern Louisiana. Tackle Doug Riesenberg of California was chosen on the sixth round. Primarily, Parcells and the Giants were trying to upgrade the wide-receiver position, where there was definitely a lack of big-play pass-catchers.

Now the coaches are working as hard as ever, planning for the next season, looking at free agents, thinking about possible trades, evaluating and re-evaluating the entire team, even one that rolled to a 17–2 Super Bowl-winning season. Everything they do now is pointing toward the start of training camp and the upcoming season. The past is done with, over, forgotten. John Elway's comment about every game starting at zero-zero also applies to the new season. Everyone starts with the same record— zero-zero.

There was, however, one rumor in the off-season that caused a real stir among the Giants' loyal fans, and probably even more trepidation among the players. A story broke that the Atlanta Falcons were eyeing Bill Parcells as their next head coach. It was surprising in that everyone who knew Parcells's history also knew that coaching the New York Giants was, plain and simply, his dream job. Why would he even consider going anywhere else? He *was* the New York Giants. Now that he had taken his team to the championship, it would seem he would remain a Giant for as long as he wished.

There was, however, some substance to the story. Because Parcells was still under contract to the Giants, he needed permission to speak to any other organization. His agent, Robert Fraley, asked the Giants for permission to speak with the Falcons. The Giants said no. Fraley then took it one step further. He went to Pete Rozelle, the NFL commissioner, and once again tried to secure permission for an exploratory meeting in Atlanta. Rozelle, however, followed the Giants' lead and denied the request.

Would Bill Parcells have considered leaving his dream job? Don't say no without thinking. Remember, by this time, football and sports in general had become big business. Teams were beginning to put out increasing amounts of money not only for free-agent players but for marquee coaches as well. It isn't inconceivable that Atlanta might have made Parcells an offer he couldn't refuse. As he himself said in his autobiography,

"Well, I've learned not to say never in this business. I've been too many places, seen too many things. Hell, it might have gone down to the wire with the Falcons, like that Jeff Rutledge sneak in the Super Bowl. I would have had to decide whether to duck my head and run with the ball, or punt it away at the last second."

Looking back, the brief and aborted courting of Parcells by the Atlanta Falcons could have been construed as a foreshadowing of events that would transpire in upcoming years. Once the Giants and the commissioner's office said no, it was back to the business of keeping his once and future team on top.

That task, however, was about to change dramatically, as events were about to unfold that would alter the beginning of the 1987 season not only for the Giants but also for every other team in the league. For the second time in five years, the Players' Association and the owners would reach an impasse in negotiations for a new contract. As is often the case during labor strife, the employees use the only real leverage they have—the threat of striking.

That cloud hung over the start of the 1987 season. Whether it affected any of the teams is hard to say. Parcells and the Giants wanted to get off quickly in defense of their title, but they were promptly shocked at Soldier Field when the still-powerful Bears beat them by a 34–19 count. A week later, the team lost a 16–14 squeaker to the Cowboys at the Meadowlands. It was shades of 1985, when they simply didn't win the close ones. For a defending champion to start at 0–2 is not a good sign.

"Bill tried to nip things in the bud," said Harry Carson. "He told us this was really about how you come to play. When you win a Super Bowl, you become a target. Everyone wants to knock you off and they play at a much higher level. As defending champions, you can't play a regular-season game like a normal game. You have to turn your game up to a higher level, as well. When a team comes in to play the defending champs, that becomes their Super Bowl. Bill tried to warn us, told us that was the reason teams had so much trouble repeating."

Unfortunately, the coach never had the chance to see if his players took his reasoning to heart. The labor deadlock continued, and after the second week of the season, the players went out on strike. Again. Not knowing how long the strike would last, the NFL powers that be didn't want to risk losing their season. What they did next was unprecedented in professional team sports. They canceled the games due to be played in the third week and directed all twenty-eight teams to sign "replacement" players. The season would resume in Week Four and would continue from that point on. If the regulars didn't return, the league would go on with a whole set of new players, the replacements.

Obviously, the level of NFL play was about to drop dramatically. Replacement players would come from many places—recent cuts, college players who didn't make it, a few guys who had been in the NFL some years earlier but weren't quite good enough to stay around long-term, and those playing in other, lesser leagues. The teams had almost no time to recruit and sign players, then get them ready to play. It was extremely difficult for the coaches and their staffs. It was especially troubling for Parcells, who was so close to so many of his players.

"The strike put Bill in a tough position," Brad Benson said. "I think deep down inside he knew the players were hurting themselves. In truth, we really didn't benefit from what we did. The present-day players may have benefited from our strike, but we lost significant amounts of money.

"In a way, I think Bill took it personally and held it against us somewhat. He thought he could have enough influence to get us back. I know that emotionally it was one of the most difficult things I went through. I felt very strongly toward him, toward the Maras and everything they had done for me. I liked them all. So I was torn hard, emotionally. But there was no way I could go back in. The same resolve that made me appreciate and admire Bill so much kept me out on strike."

Phil McConkey saw the same kind of situation between striking players and coach. "Bill felt as if we did it to him and, yes, the strike is one of my few regrets. But we were trained as a team to stick together. Bill always preached the us against them mentality. Suddenly, *them* became management. He took that whole thing as if we did it to him and it was extremely tough for him to deal with. He was forced to coach replacement players, which probably added insult to injury.

"I don't want to belittle the kids who were playing because I could have been one of them. But here's Bill Parcells, coming off a Super Bowl and used to coaching Lawrence Taylor, now having to coach a kid from down the street. It was just a bad situation. Painful as it was to everyone, I think it affected him in an awful way and it led to a wasted year."

The strike lasted twenty-four days before being settled, leaving three games to the replacement players. For some reason, the players signed by the Giants weren't up to the talent on some of the other teams. They lost badly to San Francisco, 41–21, and to Washington, 38–12. The following week the team began shaping up a bit, but still dropped a dull game to Buffalo, 6–3 in overtime. The announcement that the strike had been settled couldn't have been greeted with too much cheer in New York. By the time the regular players returned, the defending Super Bowl champs were already out of it at 0–5. Their chances to get to the playoffs were slim and none.

Under any circumstances it would have been difficult for a team like the Giants to regain the magic after the strike and an 0–5 start. The regulars returned to beat St. Louis in impressive style, 30–7, but then lost at Dallas before winning their next two. Another pair of losses followed before the team took three of its last four. They were 6–4 after the strike, but 6–9 overall. Even more embarrassing was that the defending champions finished dead last in the NFL East. To add insult to injury, the Denver Broncos, whom the Giants had beaten in Super Bowl XXI, reached the title game once again. Even though they lost to new champion Washington, the Broncos had battled their way back. The Giants had flopped miserably and gave Bill Parcells his first losing season since 1983.

More telling was the fact that the defense gave up more points (312) than the offense put on the board (280), not typical of recent Giants teams. The individual numbers were really meaningless. Only Mark Bavaro really stood out, grabbing fifty-five passes for 867 yards, a 15.8 yard-per-catch average, and eight touchdowns. He was now widely considered the best tight end in the game. Linebackers Taylor, Carson, and Banks joined Bavaro as Pro Bowl selections, but on the whole the team simply failed to put it together. They also had some eleven starters sidelined by injuries during the course of the year.

"Once we got back our problems continued," Phil McConkey said. "Both of our offensive tackles were hurting. Brad Benson left everything on the field in 1986. He had a Pro Bowl year, and had shut [Washington defensive end] Dexter Manley down twice, but in 1987 he was a physical wreck. Then Carl Nelson, our other tackle, was diagnosed with cancer.

That's forty percent of our offensive line. Things weren't the same on defense, either. Teams that couldn't run the ball on us for three years were suddenly eating up chunks on yardage. The defense just couldn't get it together."

Just one year after taking his team to the Super Bowl, Bill Parcells was faced with a new challenge: getting his team back among the NFL elite. The question was whether all it needed was some fine-tuning, or if the Giants had to be rebuilt once again.

CHAPTER TEN

Lessons That Never End

THE 1988 VERSION OF THE GIANTS WAS BASICALLY THE SAME TEAM as the one in '87. THE only major loss was the retirement of left tackle Brad Benson, who had been such a rock in the Super Bowl season of 1986. That gap was in the process of being filled. William Roberts, who had started on the right side in 1987, moved over to left tackle and young Doug Riesenberg took over on the right. On defense, young Eric Dorsey was the starter at end, with veteran George Martin appearing when the situation called for his talents. Otherwise, these were the Giants of 1986 and '87. Fans were wondering, however, which version of the team would show up. For the most part it was the '86 version, but there was just enough of the '87 team to upset the apple cart.

For the first six games the jury was still out. The club beat Washington twice, got blown out by the Rams 45–31, won a two-point squeaker against Dallas, lost a close one to the 49ers, and was beaten by a solid Philadelphia team 24–13. A 3–3 start is not optimum, but at least puts a team in a position to make a move. But a closer look at those first six games must have troubled Parcells and his staff.

The three wins came against Washington and Dallas, division rivals. But the Redskins were in a down year and would wind up at 7–9, while the Cowboys were even worse. They had crashed and would finish the season at 3–13. Yet the Giants just got past them by a 12–10 count. The three losses all came against very solid teams that were ticketed to the playoffs. In that respect, it appeared that the season could go either way. That wasn't a comforting thought for longtime Giants fans and probably had the coaching staff concerned as well.

There were, however, simply too many quality players for the team to remain a mediocrity. With the usual cast of characters (Simms, Morris, Bavaro, Taylor, Carson) leading the way, the team then won four straight and seven of its next nine. That gave the Giants a 10–5 record and sole possession of first place in the NFC East, a game ahead of the Eagles. Now there was one game left, against the crosstown New York Jets. Win it, and the Giants had another division crown and would be going to the playoffs.

This time it didn't happen. Remember, championship teams find a way win big games. The Jets, coming in at 7–7–1, upset the Giants 27–21 in a game that did more damage than first thought. It left the Giants with a 10–6 record, but in a kind of strange one-game swing, knocked them not only out of first place but also out of the entire playoff picture.

Both the Giants and Eagles finished the season at 10–6. In addition, there were three 10–6 teams in the NFC West that year, bringing the sometimes complex NFL tiebreaking system came into play. For starters, the Eagles were awarded the division title because they had won both of their games with the Giants. Next came the wild card. The Vikings, with an 11–5 mark in the NFC Central, secured one of the berths. The second was given to the L.A. Rams (after the 10–6 49ers won the division on a tie-break) on the basis of a better conference record (8–4) than the Giants (9–5) and the other 10–6 team, the New Orleans Saints (6–6). In one week the Giants had gone from potential division champs to the outside looking in. It wasn't a good feeling. Despite some fine individual seasons, the job simply didn't get done.

Though the season ended on a disappointing note, Parcells was the same coach—pushing, goading, screaming, motivating, and picking on his guys. Sometimes, it seems, he almost did it to humor himself as well as send a message.

"We were out there practicing at the Meadowlands on a cold day toward the end of the 1988 season," Phil McConkey remembered. "I was catching punts and returning them and he was watching me on every one, critiquing me, as usual. Some of the other guys were milling around, horsing around, whatever. Simms was standing on the sideline, his helmet on the ground, hands tucked in his pants, talking with some of the other guys, laughing and joking.

"Now you've got to remember, Simms was an established star by then, had performed so brilliantly in the Super Bowl less than two years earlier. Suddenly, Bill says to me, 'Watch this, I'm gonna get your boy.' With that, he lets out the loudest, angriest, nastiest '*Simmmmms*' you ever heard. It echoed throughout the stadium. '*Simms, it's cold! Why aren't you warming up? You're gonna get hurt! Get your ass moving!*' And Simms runs to put his helmet on, gets the ball, and starts throwing.

"Bill just looks back at me and laughs. Simms didn't know it, but that time he was just screwing around."

No wonder Simms told a story years later, on an HBO special, about coming out of the locker room and getting ready to emerge onto the practice field when he saw Parcells standing there on the field. He stopped.

"Here I am, in the league seven or eight years, an established quarterback, and I'm afraid to walk onto that field," Simms said. "I saw the look on his face and I didn't want to walk past him because I knew he was going to say something."

Despite taking verbal abuse from his coach on a regular basis, a serious Simms would say only good things. "He's very down-to-earth," Simms told a reporter in 1987, "and can communicate with the players so well. No question, this is what separates him from a lot of coaches in the league."

Screwing around or dead serious, Parcells always kept them guessing, always kept them on their toes. As McConkey had said previously, he loved it.

But none of that precluded his ultraserious approach to his football team. Not making the playoffs in 1988 had to have been tough for him to swallow, especially when the team appeared to have righted itself in the second half of the season. If 1988 was a year in which the coaching staff simply fine-tuned the team, the 1989 season would see Parcells and his staff faced with more of an overhaul, and for a variety of reasons.

It was a year in which he lost two of his favorite players. Veterans Harry Carson and George Martin both retired. Joe Morris, after gaining a thousand yards once again in 1988, was injured in the preseason and wouldn't play a down for the Giants ever again. Mark Bavaro would be slowed by a chronic knee problem that would rob him of both speed and power, and reduce him from an all-world tight end to a mere mortal. Defensive tackle and original Gatorade man Jim Burt was also gone. Chronic back problems had slowed him. He would resurface in San Francisco to play some more solid football.

Replacements were also on the way. The 1988 draft had produced two fine young tackles, Eric Moore and John "Jumbo" Elliott. In 1989 the team drafted center/guard Brian Williams, guard Bob Kratch, safety Greg Jackson, running back Lewis Tillman, running back/kick returner Dave Meggett, tight end Howard Cross, and safety Myron Guyton. All would become major contributors over the next two years. Now Parcells had a strong influx of good young players to once again mix with his veterans. In fact, Meggett's talent and versatility meant saying goodbye to another treasured old friend. Once again, the coach was forced to cut Phil McConkey.

In his autobiography, the coach had this to say about one of his favorite players. "Numbers are important. But heart is as important to me. If heart isn't important, then there is no place for the Phil McConkeys in our game. I'm not saying that McConkey doesn't have talent, because he does, a load of talent, and all that toughness, and that spit-in-your-eye attitude of his. But heart got him a Super Bowl ring. There are a hell of a lot more talented people than McConkey who never got a ring."

If you want a definition of a Parcells player, there it is. Talent, toughness, tenacity, heart. But while players like McConkey had what it takes to be Parcells guys, it took the same combination of talent, toughness, tenacity, and heart on the part of their coach to make the players dig deep inside themselves and achieve their ultimate success. Witness Phil McConkey.

"The first time I was cut it was kind of shocking," McConkey said, referring to his four-month hiatus to Green Bay in 1986. "The second time, he prepared me for it, told me about the numbers, and that he hated to do it. Looking back, he made everyone better. Of course, it goes two ways. You can't be a great coach without players. You've got to have the ingredients—the superstars, stars, and role players. But Bill won't take a player unless he sees something he likes or wants. He could have kept someone else instead of me, but maybe he knew he couldn't get out of them what he could get out of me. As far as his personality goes, most of the time he was a prick. But he was also a multifaceted guy.

"Later, I went to Philadelphia and Arizona catching punts. I wasn't the same guy. My focus fell off slightly. It was just an infinitesimal amount, but I wasn't as comfortable because I didn't have Bill Parcells standing there critiquing each catch."

For George Martin, retiring had been a four-year ordeal. He began thinking of leaving after his tenth season, 1984. It was Bill Parcells who kept bringing him back for "one more year."

"He was pretty much adamant the first three years that he wanted me back," Martin said. "Then the fourth year, 1988, he said, 'Listen, George, you know how I feel, that I want you to play as long as you feel you can do it. You'll know when it's time.' To me, I felt it was time to call it quits after 1988. I liked the fact that he respected that."

Martin was a guy Bill wanted back. Others, however, had to go. Yet Martin remembers Parcells the coach turning into Parcells the man when a veteran had to be released.

"He would always do it tactfully." Martin explained, "but he would do it. He always stated that his obligation was to the team. The needs of the many outweigh the needs of the one. He would sit down and tell an individual that his skills had diminished and were no longer beneficial to the Giants. Or perhaps that the individual simply no longer fit into the team's plans. But he would also tell the player that if he wanted to continue his career and try it someplace else, that he would try to make an arrangement for him. In other words, he had discussions where some coaches wouldn't care. Their attitude was that whether you're a rookie or twenty-year veteran, you can't help us, goodbye, have a nice day. Bill always put a sense of humanity into what he did.

"I think Bill's hardnose image is something he does by design. He feels he can use that to an advantage. He doesn't want people to see that beneath that gruff exterior lies a human being."

Martin also remembers Bill Parcells as not only a football coach but also a mentor who taught him a lot more than how to block and tackle.

"Bill Parcells had the greatest impact on George Martin," he said, "not on the field of play, but in the field of life. We always had a great deal in common and I thought of him more as a peer than perhaps many of my teammates did. We had kids in college at the same time, often talked about career transition, life after football, our own mortality later on when he had problems with his health. In other words, we talked about a higher level of athletics and life together, more so than he did with most other players.

"Because of that, he helped me prepare for life after football. I learned about making decisions, tough decisions, and about dedication and commitment. The funny part is we had many of these talks during practice. He was great about pulling a guy aside and have little private conversations with him. That made you feel special, to know he was spending a few minutes with you talking about the things that interest you or will effect you. And we've continued to talk since my retirement. I couldn't have asked for a better mentor than Bill."

There were nine new starters in the lineup for the opening game of the 1989 season. Perhaps the most significant change was the installation of thirty-two-year-old Ottis Anderson at running back in place of the injured Joe Morris. It had been five years since Anderson had been a featured runner. He had just sixty-five carries the season before, and only two in 1987. Could he replace the electrifying Morris and give the Giants the running game they sorely needed?

"Bill knows how to mix younger players with older guys," Anderson said. "In 1989 he began putting some different pieces together. For instance, he knew that both Joe and I were getting older, and he wanted to break in some younger players. So he picked up Meggett and Lewis Tillman. He wanted to put us in a position to make a run. He also made sure he had enough quality veteran players around to educate and make sure the younger players knew what kind of commitment it would take.

"He also knew he needed a big offensive line that would allow us to pound the ball. The only way you could win in the NFC East then was to be a dominant running team that will take time off the clock. His philosophy was that by controlling the ball and the clock, you're keeping the opponents' offense off the field."

The coach also seemed to sense that the veteran Anderson would need some special motivation to keep it going during the long season. Once again, he found a way, a way that would help not one but two of his players.

"He told Lewis Tillman to always follow me, telling him, 'You're the young punk. You just watch this cagey old dog.' That was me. He used to call me Old Red. Then he would tell us a story about Old Red, a dog in his prime who always loved to hunt. He made this analogy with me and Lewis one day. When Red was a young punk, you couldn't keep him on the porch at all. You'd open the door and he was ready to run and hunt. This dog loved to play; you couldn't keep him down. But as he got a little older he didn't feel like getting up and running as much, and he kind of laid around, not doing much of anything. He just started to waste away in middle age. You looked at him and figured he was tired, that he couldn't do it anymore.

"But then when you brought a young pup around, the young pup made the old dog feel young again, made him realize he's not that old and still has a few pelts in his belt and can still do some of the things he did in his prime. The young pup had so much energy that he kept Old Red going. Parcells said that kind of reminded him of me and Lewis.

"That was the motivation for me. Lewis would push me because he wanted to start. He had broken all of Walter Payton's records in college, and he was hungry. But he needed guidance. So Bill put our lockers right together. It was a way to keep me motivated and to teach Lewis what it meant to be a pro, how to prepare and develop a work ethic, things like that."

Those were the lengths to which Bill Parcells would go to motivate his players. This was a well thought-out plan designed to keep the aging Anderson feeling young and frisky, competing with the younger player who wanted his job, while paving the way for that younger player to emerge as a star in the future. That was a helluva lot more than just the yelling and screaming, the insults and intimidation that many feel is the Parcells way. Lurking beneath the surface is a much more complex master plan.

Other new starters included tackle Jumbo Elliott, wide receiver Odessa Turner, Zeke Mowatt at tight end for the injured Bavaro, John Washington at defensive end, Erik Howard at defensive tackle, Gary Reasons at inside linebacker for the retired Carson, and Johnnie Cooks at the other inside linebacker spot for the injured Pepper Johnson. Free safety Myron Guyton was also a first-time starter.

It didn't take long to see that the 1989 Giants were once again a formidable team. What better proof than an 8–1 record after the first nine weeks of the season? The team won its first four, dropped a close one to Philadelphia, then promptly won four more. Simms was still Simms. Anderson, while not nearly as explosive as Morris, was still pounding the ball like an elite back, let by the revamped offensive line.

Simms distributed the ball to a variety of receivers. While none was having an All-Pro year, Turner, Manuel, Ingram, Mowatt, and Bavaro all contributed, as did Dave Meggett, who was proving to be an elusive third-down back and receiver as well as a fine kick returner. The defense still had LT, Banks, and a fine supporting cast. They, too, had stepped up their performance from a year earlier.

"We felt we had all the tools to win it in '89," Ottis Anderson said. "We thought we had everything molded properly to go to the next level."

The second four-game winning streak came to an end with a disturbing 31–10 loss to the L.A. Rams. It was a game in which the Giants did not look like a Super Bowl contender. Perhaps most indicative of the kind of game it had been was that Lawrence Taylor was almost totally ineffective. LT finished the game with just three tackles and no sacks, as he was handled most of the afternoon by Rams tackle Irv Pankey.

Two weeks later, the Giants lost to another Super Bowl contender, the 49ers, 34–24, then were beaten by Philadelphia 24–17. They were still solid at 9–4, but there also seemed to be some chinks in the armor. After that, the ballclub rebounded to win its last three and take the NFC East crown with a 12–4 mark. In a sense, this was a team without superstars. Taylor made his ninth straight Pro Bowl and rookie Meggett was named as a kick returner. Otherwise, 1989 was pretty much a group effort.

Simms threw for only 3,061 yards with fourteen touchdowns and fourteen interceptions. Anderson, at age thirty-two, surprised everyone with 1,023 yards on 325 tough carries. But the leading receiver was Odessa Turner, with just thirty-eight catches for 467 yards. Meggett grabbed thirty-four passes and Manuel thirty-three. Still, the team scored 348 points while giving up just 252. Only the 49ers, at 14–2, had a better record in the entire league. Could the Giants recapture the title? Once the season ended, Parcells admitted that he had taken something of a gamble when he decided to retool the team after 1988.

"When we ended last season, I knew that group had taken us as far as we could go," he said. "That same group would have been 7–9 or 8–8 this year, and we'd just have put off rebuilding for one season."

In the NFC wild-card game that year, the Rams defeated the Philadelphia Eagles 21–7, setting up a rematch with New York at Giants Stadium. Everyone remembered the Rams' easy victory earlier in the season, especially Parcells. The week before the game, he not only worked the team hard on the practice field but also used his special brand of motivation to try to get his guys ready. He kept telling favorite-target Simms, one of the league's hardest workers, that he was "the most pampered quarterback in the league." He dubbed running back Anderson "Encore," wondering often and aloud if the veteran runner could squeeze yet another big game from his aging body.

But he saved the best for Taylor, reminding him all week long about his anemic effort against Irv Pankey when the two teams met in November. More than a week before the game, Taylor walked past while the coach was sitting with Simms at practice.

"I've got a plane ticket for you," Parcells was heard saying to Taylor. "I want you to go to New Orleans and I want you to take your helmet with you." Taylor was totally confused. But it didn't take long for Parcells to straighten him out. "Go find [Saints linebacker] Pat Swilling. You don't need your jersey, because he wears the same number. Give him your plane ticket and your helmet, and let him fly back here. You stay in New Orleans and have a nice time. He'll play [Sunday], because he's the only guy who can handle Pankey. You can't."

It was like the early days, when the coach was always throwing (Tampa Bay linebacker) Hugh Green up in Taylor's face. He wanted an angry Taylor, a determined Taylor, by game time, and felt this was the way to get him there. As so many players had said, Parcells handled everyone individually, the old different-strokes-for-different-folks theory. By this time he had it pretty much down to a science.

The Los Angeles Rams were a pass-oriented, quick-strike team that had put 426 points on the board during the regular season. Only the 49ers had scored more. The sometimes erratic Jim Everett was the quarterback, a strong-armed guy who loved to throw downfield, where he had Henry Ellard and Flipper Anderson to catch it. L.A. would like nothing better than a wide-open, high-scoring game. Parcells knew his team couldn't win that way. No, the Giants would have to control the line of scrimmage, run the ball, use the clock, and let their defense try to overwhelm the Rams on the other side of the ball.

That's just how it went for the first twenty-eight minutes. The Giants' first two drives were methodical and time-consuming, with Ottis Anderson running for sixty yards. Both ended with Raul Allegre field goals, of thirty-five and forty-one yards, respectively. Meanwhile, on the other side of the ball it was Lawrence Taylor playing like his own self and stopping a pair of Rams drives with a couple of major-league sacks of Everett. Then, just before the half ended, the Giants made a mistake.

There was just 1:45 left when the Giants got the ball at their own nine-yard line. Instead of trying to run out the clock, Parcells had his team attack. Five plays into the drive, Simms threw an interception. The pass bounced off Rams cornerback Jerry Gray into the hands of safety Michael Stewart at the 49. He ran it back twenty-nine yards, giving the Rams a first-and-ten at the Giants' 20. An Everett-to-Anderson pass on the next play produced a touchdown and the kick gave the Rams a 7–6 halftime lead.

Another long, methodical, eighty-two-yard drive in the third period led to an Ottis Anderson touchdown and the Giants had the lead back, the point after making it 13–7. But in the fourth period the Rams kept driving into Giants territory, again and again. The result was a pair of field goals that again tied it up at 13–13. Neither team could score in the final minutes and the game went into overtime. L.A. won the toss and chose to receive.

Everett then resumed throwing, passing for a pair of first downs. Then came the turning point. Wide receiver Flipper Anderson ran a deep slant, with cornerback Sheldon White on his tail. Everett let go. The pass was slightly off the mark and Anderson had to dive for it. As he did, White also dove and landed on his back. Flag! The ref called pass interference, giving the Rams a first down at the Giants' 25. White and the Giants protested, saying the pass was uncatchable, which would have negated the penalty, but to no avail. Now all the Rams had to do was push it a little closer and try a game-winning field goal. But after a false start pushed the ball back to the 30, Coach John Robinson sent in a play calling for Anderson and Ellard to both go deep. Ellard had already caught eight passes for 125 yards and was considered the prime target. Instead, Everett whistled the ball to Anderson, who caught the perfect throw over Mark Collins's outstretched hand in the end zone. Anderson just kept sprinting right into the locker room as the crowd sat in stunned silence. The Giants had been beaten 19–13 in sudden-death. Just like that, their season was over.

It was a shocking finished, abetted by a controversial interference call, but it didn't matter. This would be a tough one to swallow. As Ottis Anderson said, "I think we were capable of beating the Rams eight of ten times, but this was just one of those days. Offensively, I think I had over a hundred yards rushing. [He had 120.] We controlled the clock. We controlled everything. We had a few bad plays here and there and they made some plays. But on the whole, I think we pretty much dominated from start to finish, until that overtime. But that's all they needed."

Anderson remembers Parcells speaking calmly to the team afterward. He wanted them to learn a lesson, one he hoped wouldn't have to be taught again. "He told us to remember what we had just seen," Anderson said.

"He said, 'Remember what happened. I want you to always remember it. I want you to know how close you were, how you allowed a team to get back in it, how you should not have given this team a chance.'

"He kind of laid it on our shoulders because we had them and it shouldn't have been even close. Because we made stupid mistakes we kept them in the game. And when you let a team that doesn't expect to win back into the game, you get a dogfight. And when you get in a dogfight, anything can happen. Yep, he really laid it on our shoulders."

In a way, it was similar to what had happened back in 1985, when the Giants were a game away from the NFC title game and lost to the Bears. The coach told them then how tough it was to get to that spot . . . and lose. From that point on he focused everything on not making the same mistakes in 1986. On a January day at Giants Stadium, again he left a similar message. He knew his team was ready and he fully expected them to make one more big push in 1990.

CHAPTER ELEVEN

The Best Super Bowl Ever

THE GIANTS OF 1990 JUST REQUIRED SOME FINE-TUNING. RODNEY Hampton of Georgia was the first draft choice. He would be slotted in behind the veteran Anderson at running back. A trade brought All-Pro cornerback Everson Walls from Dallas and he would step right into the starting lineup. Bob Kratch took over at one of the guard slots, and Steve DeOssie stepped into a starting slot at linebacker. Otherwise, this was essentially the same Giants team that had come close a year earlier.

"We knew we had a good nucleus in 1990," said Ottis Anderson, who was one of a diminishing number of players left over the from 1986 Super Bowl team. "There were players who had matured—like Mark Ingram, Stacy Robinson, Meggett, and others. Bart Oates, our center, really had everyone around him on the offensive line playing up to the level of the '86 team. Then all we did to open the season was win our first ten games in a row. But we always had Parcells there to make sure that we knew we weren't as good as we thought we were. He never stopped telling us that.

"We were a team of opportunity and chance. We knew we weren't as good as the '86 team. Bill would make comparisons to the '86 team and what it took for them to be champions. He just always let us know that we weren't that good. He kept putting that thought in our heads. 'You're not that good.' "

Motivate them up; motivate them down. Parcells always had his hand on the team's pulse. He wasn't telling them they weren't that good to erode their confidence. Rather, he wanted to make sure they didn't become overconfident. Winning ten straight can do that to you. Of the ten victories, only three were by a touchdown or less. The other seven the Giants won comfortably. It was still a team that hadn't truly been tested, pushed hard, forced to see how good they really were.

Ottis Anderson, who had played on the 1986 team, also continued to compare the two, and always coming up with the same conclusion.

"The 1986 team was dominant defensively, which we weren't," he said. "They also were dominant offensively in that they could push people around, which allowed us to run the football. We didn't have that in 1990. We knew we had good leadership in [Phil] Simms and [Jeff] Hostetler, and a good corps of receivers. But we really didn't know how good we were. When we won our first ten we certainly knew we could play with anybody, but when we lost to Philadelphia we had to think again. Maybe we weren't that good. That game was a rude awakening for us."

It came in Week Eleven. The Giants traveled to Veterans' Stadium in Philadelphia and were beaten handily, 31–13. The ten-game winning streak had ended and the self-doubt began creeping in. It intensified the next week when, in a close defensive battle, they lost to the 49ers 7–3, in a game between two teams with 10–1 records. So in successive weeks the Giants had lost to a very good Eagles team and an elite San Francisco squad. The 'club was still 10–2 and in first place, but that wasn't the important thing now. The playoffs loomed and suddenly the team was in a two-game funk.

It must have been good seeing Giants Stadium again the next week. The Minnesota Vikings were the opponent, but on Saturday before the game, the team found itself facing something it hadn't considered—playing without Bill Parcells on the sideline. Saturday evening, the coach was rushed to Morristown Memorial Hospital with an attack of kidney stones. Not one to tolerate malingering players, Parcells left the hospital to coach the game, then returned to deal with his physical problem shortly afterward.

That didn't make it an easy game. The first quarter was more like a baseball game. Early in the first period Simms was sacked in the end zone for a safety. A Minnesota field goal at the ten-minute mark made it 5–0. Matt Bahr then booted a thirty-six-yarder before the first session ended, cutting the deficit to 5–3. The field goal was set up by a Dave Meggett fifty-eight-yard kickoff return. After that, it became a football game.

Minnesota upped the lead to 12–3 on a seventy-six-yard drive midway through the second quarter. The Giants closed it to 12–10 before the half as rookie Rodney Hampton, now splitting the rushing chores with veteran Anderson, kept the drive alive with bursts of thirteen and eleven yards. Anderson finished it with a one-yard TD plunge. In the second half the Giant defense took over, led—as was so often the case—by Lawrence Taylor, who was having a monster game.

The Vikes would manage a third-quarter field goal to up their lead to 15–10. But in the fourth period, the Giants rediscovered the magic that had accompanied them on their ten-game winning streak.

"We all just got together and said, 'There's fifteen minutes left and either we are going to be Eastern Division champs or we're going to be some washouts,'" said linebacker Pepper Johnson. "We didn't want that to happen, and we didn't let it."

Defensive end Leonard Marshall put it another way. "I wouldn't want to come back 0–3 and have to play Buffalo next week. They were the best team in the AFC. I was thinking about that. This game was very much pivotal for us."

This was one time the team didn't need the coach for motivation. They went to work with passion and intensity. A forty-eight-yard Bahr field goal at 1:20 of the final session cut the lead to 15–13. Midway through the period, the Giants began driving again. Once more young Rodney Hampton showed why he was a number-one pick, gaining yards on tough runs. Simms then hit Stephen Baker on a clutch, sixteen-yard throw to keep the drive alive. Anderson finished it with a two-yard TD plunge. Bahr's kick gave the Giants the lead at 20–15.

When the Vikes tried to get back in it, the defense took over. Taylor hit Vikings quarterback Rich Gannon as he tried to pass, altering his throw and allowing fellow linebacker Gary Reasons to intercept. A third Matt Bahr field goal with less than a minute remaining made the final score 23–15, clinching the NFC East title. Hampton had seventy-eight yards on nineteen carries, while LT had twelve tackles and assists, and 2.5 sacks. Despite the painful kidney-stone attack, Parcells returned to the hospital knowing his team was back on track.

The following week the Giants would meet the Buffalo Bills, a team with an identical 11–2 record. In addition, the Bears at 10–3 had already clinched the NFC Central, while the 49ers at 12–1 had racked up another NFC West crown. The playoff pieces were pretty much in place, and the game with Buffalo would set up the drama that was to follow.

The Bills were an up-and-coming AFC power, having won the last two AFC East titles in 1988 and '89, though advancing no further than the second round of the playoffs. Led by quarterback Jim Kelly, running back Thurman Thomas, receiver Andre Reed, defensive end Bruce Smith, and linebacker Cornelius Bennett—All Star–caliber players—the Bills, like the Giants, had built the supporting cast to the point where the team was outstanding on both offense and defense. The two teams met at Giants Stadium on December 15, and the Bills came away with a 17–13 victory.

It was a game that turned into more than a disheartening defeat for one of the league's best teams. The Giants lost the one player they seemed least able to afford. Quarterback Phil Simms went down late in the game with a severely sprained arch. While the injury didn't seem serious at first, it would eventually keep him out of the remaining games and the playoffs. At the time of his injury, Simms was the NFC's leading passer statistically, with a quarterback rating of 92.7, best of his career. He was having a virtually mistake-free season, completing nearly sixty percent of his passes while connecting for fifteen touchdowns with only four interceptions.

It couldn't have happened at a worse time. After a 10–0 start, the Giants had lost three of their last four games, with the losses coming against two division winners and another playoff-bound team. Self-doubt again. Even with Simms in the lineup, the Giants couldn't beat Philadelphia, San Francisco, and Buffalo. Now they would have to rely on a quarterback who, prior to the 1990 season, had thrown just sixty-eight passes in NFL competition, and was already twenty-nine years old.

Jeff Hostetler had been the Giants' third-round draft choice in 1984, coming out of West Virginia where he had thrown for 4,055 yards in two seasons after transferring from Penn State. In his first four seasons with the Giants Hostetler did not throw a single pass in competition. Parcells, who traditionally does not trust young, unproven players, had veteran Jeff Rutledge backing up Simms, while Hostetler stood on the sidelines and learned.

"You prepare yourself," Hostetler said, "and you hope you could get into this situation, but actually, my past experience is such that I've never really believed [it would happen] until now." But Hostetler, who graduated from West Virginia with a 3.85 grade-point average and with a degree in finance, was smart enough not to allow himself to vegetate. "That's one of the things over the years," he said. "You learn not to be complacent, not to say, 'Well, I'm not going to play, so why study?'"

The 6' 3" Hostetler was also a tough cookie. When Buffalo's Bruce Smith was playing at Virginia Tech, he once put a hit on the West Virginia quarterback that he still remembered.

"I got a hit on him that I couldn't believe," Smith said, "full speed, right in the chest. I didn't think he'd get up. He lay there for a few minutes, got up, staggered, and fell down again. Finally he got up and they helped him to the sidelines. Three plays later he came back in and threw a touchdown pass."

Hoss, as Hostetler would come to be called, was also a competitor. He didn't like not playing, to the point where every year he would tell his agent to ask for a trade, but the Giants always refused. So frustrated was he that he volunteered to play on special teams and partially blocked a punt against the Eagles in 1986. He also was an emergency wide receiver and caught a pass in 1988, in addition to having one rushing attempt on a reverse. He saw his first quarterback action in 1988, spelling Simms in a pair of games against the Eagles and starting one against New Orleans late in the year. He completed sixteen of twenty-nine passes for 244 yards and one touchdown. A year later, he got in long enough to complete twenty of thirty-nine passes for 294 yards and three scores. That, however, was the extent of his NFL experience before 1990.

Earlier in the season he had relieved an injured Simms in a game against Phoenix, completing eleven of twenty-one passes for 180 yards in a 20–19 victory. Simms was back the next week and Hostetler returned to the bench. Now, suddenly, in Week Fifteen of the season, Jeff Hostetler was being handed the football and being told, "It's your team. Take us home."

"Just play the game," Parcells told him. "Don't worry about making mistakes. You're not playing for the coaches, you're playing for the team. Just go play and play within the structure, and we'll help you as much as we can. Just don't worry about it."

Words are one things; deeds another. Veteran Ottis Anderson, close to the situation as it unfolded, said that Parcells believed in his backup quarterback all along. It makes sense. The Giants must have seen something if they kept refusing Hoss's requests to be traded.

"Bill seemed to know we weren't gonna miss a beat with Hostetler in there," Anderson said. "Look at it this way. Simms was the kind of quarterback who would stand in the pocket until the last second, then deliver the ball and take a hit. We knew that Hostetler, while he was gonna wait back there, wasn't gonna wait as long as Simms. He was a scrambler and did a lot of things on his own athletically. That made him different. We knew with Hostetler that we had an additional runner in the backfield. With Simms, defenses knew he wasn't gonna run and played him to stay home. With Hostetler, defenses had to change their plan, adjust to Hostetler, because he would run."

Hostetler showed right away that the coach's faith was well-placed. He started the final two games of the regular season and led the Giants to wins over Phoenix (24–21) and New England (13–10). They weren't huge victories but were important ones because they brought the team home at 13–3 and also gave them a winning attitude going into the playoffs. Hostetler wound up completing forty-seven of eighty-seven passes for 614 yards, a fifty-four-percent completion percentage with three touchdowns and just a single interception. He had taken care of the football, the first lesson a quarterback learns.

It was a season of outstanding teams. The 49ers had the league's best record, 14–2; the Giants and AFC Bills were both at 13–3; the AFC Raiders and Dolphins came in at 12–4; and the Bears were at 11–5. The race to the Super Bowl was going to be wide open.

It certainly wasn't difficult to find shortcomings within this Giants team. Their number-one quarterback was finished for the year, and his replacement had the equivalent of less than half a season's experience. Their leading rusher (Anderson) gained just 784 yards and their top wide receiver (Stephen Baker) had just twenty-six catches, while the leading receiver was third-down specialist Meggett with thirty-nine grabs. The offense scored 335 points, ninth-best in the fourteen-team NFC. The defense, however, gave up just 211 points, and that led the entire league. Most experts agreed that the team would need a superlative defensive effort from LT and company if they were to have any chance of winning the championship.

The NFC semifinal game, the Giants' first playoff contest, was played at Giants Stadium on January 13, 1991, a tough test against former nemesis the Chicago Bears. Despite expressions of confidence from coach and teammates, quarterback Hostetler was still something of an unknown quantity in playoff-caliber football, so the Giants planned to turn the defense loose against the Bears. Giants backup safety Dave Duerson had been a Bear for seven years and apparently helped the coaching staff set up the defensive scheme. The plan was to stop the strong Chicago running game, led by Neal Anderson, and force their quarterback, Mike Tomczak, to be faced with third-and-long throwing downs.

To do that, the team made some adjustments in their standard, 3–4 defense. They replaced linebacker Steve DeOssie with the bigger tackle, Mike Fox, making it almost a 4–3 alignment. As Lawrence Taylor put it, the defense was "not really a true 4–3, but more of a wide-tackle, six-man line, because the outside linebackers, me and Carl Banks, were playing so close up."

The plan worked. Chicago's running game was stifled, gaining just twenty-seven yards, its lowest total in twenty-three years. But the Giants' running game also suffered a blow when rookie Hampton broke his left fibula on just his second carry of the game. That put thirty-three-year-old Ottis Anderson back on center stage and the veteran responded, ably aided by fullback Maurice Carthon, Lewis Tillman, and Dave Meggett. When the smoke cleared, Giants runners had gained 198 yards.

That was balanced by the surprisingly effective play of Hostetler. Though he completed just ten of seventeen passes for 112 yards, including a twenty-one-yard touchdown pass to Stephen Baker in the opening quarter, Hostetler also showed the extra dimension that Ottis Anderson spoke about. He converted a pair of fourth-down plays on bootlegs, ran another for a touchdown, and wound up with forty-three yards on six carries, something the Giants rarely got from the more classic pocket-passer Simms. The bottom line to all this was a surprisingly easy 31–3 victory.

The Giants had a 10–0 lead after one, stretched it to 17–3 by halftime, then completely controlled the ball on the ground the entire second half, scoring touchdowns in both the third and fourth periods for the final tally. Now the New Yorkers would have to travel cross-country, to Candlestick Park in San Francisco, and meet the 49ers for the NFC championship. The consensus was that the two best teams in the NFC would be battling it out. This time the Giants didn't have to worry about devising a defense for the running game. Instead, they would have to prepare to face Joe Montana, the best clutch quarterback of his generation. The Niners were coming off two straight Super Bowl triumphs, had a league best 14–2 record in the regular season and had won a close 7–3 decision over the Giants along the way. Everyone knew this game would not be an easy one. Maybe this would be the week the loss of Simms, and subsequent loss of Rodney Hampton, would catch up with the New Yorkers.

Once again, the Giants played a tight, close-to-the-vest, conservative game. You just didn't play wide-open football against Joe Montana, Jerry Rice, Roger Craig, John Taylor, and the rest of the well-oiled Niner offensive machine. With the defense containing Montana and company, while Hostetler relied on his running game and short, dump-off passes, the two teams traded field goals in the first and second quarters, leaving the field at halftime to an unlikely 6–6 score.

In the third period the Niners broke loose for their one big play of the afternoon. Montana dropped from his own thirty-nine-yard line and went long. Wideout John Taylor ran under the perfect throw and completed a sixty-one-yard touchdown play. The Niners had a 13–6 lead and the hearts of Giants fans watching the game 3,000 miles away had to sink just a little. The Niners and Montana rarely lost a lead in the second half. Then before the third quarter ended, Matt Bahr booted his third field goal of the afternoon, a forty-six-yarder to close the gap to 13–9. Small consolation with just fifteen minutes to play.

What followed undoubtedly partially defined the Giants' season, as well as the character of the team. As the fourth quarter began New York had the football. Hostetler dropped back to pass on third down and was creamed low by former Giant Jim Burt, causing his left knee to buckle. Hoss left the field in obvious pain, favoring the knee.

"I figured I was out of the game," he said, later. "It hurt like crazy."

On came the Niners' offense and the Giants' defense. Now it was Montana's turn, dropping back and looking to throw. When he spied LT beating his man and zeroing in from the side he looked to escape, only to be flattened like a pancake by the onrushing Leonard Marshall, who blindsided him from behind. Montana went down and didn't move. He was helped from the field, where it was quickly discovered that he had a broken bone in his right hand and a severely bruised sternum. He was through for the day.

"That's what we call justice around here," Taylor said, afterward. "Jim Burt's hit [on Hostetler] was a cheap shot."

The 49ers had to punt, and on the sideline Parcells grabbed his quarterback by the arm.

"Can you go?" he asked him.

"I think so," Hostetler said.

"You think so?' Parcells repeated. "I'll ask you again. Can you go?"

"I'm going," said Hostetler, as he trotted back onto the field.

Later, the Giants quarterback would say, "At this point in my season and at this point in the game and, really, at this point in my career, I know I wasn't coming out."

On the first play, Hoss tested the knee by scrambling for six yards. It held up, the injury nothing more than a painful bruise. He then led the team downfield until Bahr kicked yet another field goal, this one from thirty-eight yards out. It was now a one-point game, 13–12, with just 5:47 left to play. Only that one point belonged to the 49ers and they would be getting the football. The Niners took the kickoff and began moving, keeping the ball on the ground and trying to take precious time off the clock. They drove into Giants territory and were close to field-goal range when Roger Craig carried up the middle. He was hit, the ball popped loose, and Lawrence Taylor caught it before it hit the ground.

Hostetler and the offense then came in to take over at their own 43. There was 2:36 left in the game and the ball fifty-seven yards away. On the first play, Hostetler sprinted out to the right with the option to pass or run. Just when it appeared as if he would run out of bounds he stopped, pivoted, and threw a strike to tight end Bavaro for a nineteen-yard gain. Two plays later he rolled right again and fired on the run. Stephen Baker caught the ball for a thirteen-yard gain to the Niners' 29. Anderson then carried twice for four yards, putting the pigskin on the 25. It was third-and-six, but there were just four seconds left. Matt Bahr trotted on again, with Hostetler setting up to hold.

"All I said to myself was, 'Please don't bobble the ball,' " Hostetler said later.

Bahr stepped into the kick and booted it through the uprights from forty-two yards out. It was his fifth field goal of the afternoon and perhaps the biggest of his career. It gave the Giants a 15–13 victory, and earned them a second trip to the Super Bowl.

There were plenty of heroes. Hostetler showed everyone that he could, indeed, play the game. He completed fifteen of twenty-seven passes for 176 yards, including two big throws on the final drive. The defense had been magnificent, as usual, holding the Niners early, then knocking Montana out of the game. Old man Ottis Anderson once again handled the brunt of the running chores and got the job done. Afterward, one of the reporters crowding around asked Parcells how his team managed to win.

"I'll tell you how we did it," the coach growled. "We did it by not handing the ball over. We set a record for fewest turnovers (fourteen) in a sixteen-game season. We don't make it easy for people. Yeah, I know, we've been called a conservative team, but you'll notice that this conservative team is still playing."

Now there was one to go, only it wouldn't be easy. In Super Bowl XXV the Giants would be meeting the Buffalo Bills, making the title game an all–New York State affair. The Bills, of course, had beaten the Giants in the regular season en route to becoming the highest-scoring team in the league, with 428 points. To make matters worse, the Bills seemed to be on a playoff roll. First they defeated Miami in a 44–34 shootout. Then, in the AFC title game, they simply steamrolled the tough L.A. Raiders by an incredible 51–3 count. The Giants' defense would have its hands full trying to contain Jim Kelly, Thurman Thomas, and company. Oddsmakers made the Bills immediate favorites.

The Giants had just a week to prepare for their biggest game of the year, which would be held at Tampa Stadium in Florida. But Parcells had been thinking about the Bills for some time and had learned plenty when the two teams had met in December.

"When we played them at home and saw some of the things they were capable of, Parcells was taking notice," said Ottis Anderson. "He knew that a team can benefit by playing a team earlier in the season and even though they lost, be perfectly capable of beating them the next time. I remember him telling us, 'Be careful what you say [about them] because you might face them again. Being a ball-control team, we knew our best chance to win was to keep Buffalo's offense off the field. The way they had buried the Raiders [in the AFC title game], they looked like they could beat anybody.

"So we were total underdogs and knew our only chance was to control the clock and keep those guys off the field. Bill made it an individual challenge to many of us. He challenged Jumbo [Elliott] to stop Bruce Smith. He challenged the entire offensive line to open things up for the running game. He told us that, on paper, Buffalo was the better team by far. Then he said,

"You know what. That's paper. You still have to play the game. If you go by paper, a whole lot of teams are better than us. But who's in the Big Dance? You are. So that tells you that paper means nothing. You can sit there and read it and hear it and believe that they are better than you, that they can do this and do that, and that you just happen to be there for the ride. But if you forget about statistics and what they're printing, you can make a difference. You can make things change.' "

In the week before the game, the Giants practiced intently. Much of the focus was on Jeff Hostetler, who was still going into the Super Bowl as a virtual rookie, despite his twenty-nine years. Hoss was now 6–0 as a starter, but there were still some doubts. Parcells tried to dispel them.

"It's simply a case of the opportunity now availing itself," Parcells said, " and [Hostetler] attempting to make the most of it. He had to make the most of it. That was the only chance we had."

The coach also said that if Hostetler was going to be thrown to the wolves that way, it was good Simms's injury happened when it did and not, for example, in the first round of the playoffs.

"Fortunately," Parcells said, we've had over a month to—and I don't want to use the word 'experiment,' but basically that's really what we were doing. We were just trying to pick and choose, and let him execute some things in the game, and then talking to him about it and finding out what he felt comfortable with."

Game time was quickly approaching. As is usually the case, other stories, underlying dramas, took a bit of the attention away from the game itself. The biggest one was that the United States was engaged in what would become known as the Gulf War, the military action against Iraq in the Middle East. There was some concern about the possibility of a terrorist action to try to disrupt the game, or at least divert attention from it. With more than seventy-two-thousand fans expected at Tampa Stadium, security was high, with more than five hundred security people deployed at the stadium by federal, state, and local authorities. They were augmented by another thousand guards from the league and various corporations.

Handheld metal detectors would be used to scan fans entering the stadium, and security at team hotels was also very tight, especially on game day. Even the lobbies of the hotels were roped off so no one could readily approach the players. Concrete barriers were erected in vulnerable spots around the stadium to prevent possible explosives-filled terrorist vehicles from crashing in. That wasn't all. The entire stadium was surrounded by a six-foot-high chain-link fence. Fortunately, there were no incidents.

Then on game day, another strange and potentially distracting story appeared in the press. A story in the *Orlando Sentinel* said Bill Parcells would be leaving the Giants to coach the Tampa Bay Buccaneers the following season. There were also reports that Parcells was planning to retire after the season. As to the Tampa Bay story, owners Wellington and Tim Mara as well as General Manager George Young issued prompt denials.

"[The Buccaneers] haven't talked to us to get permission to talk to [Parcells]," Wellington Mara stated. "He's under contract to us. As far as I know, he has no intention of not fulfilling his contract."

Tim Mara indicated there was no way the Giants would give anyone permission to talk to their coach, anyway. "If he's going to coach, he will coach for the Giants," Tim said.

General Manager Young's take was that "It's total speculation, an old story they're beating to death. Tampa Bay has said it's not interested in people under contract."

Leave it to Parcells, however, to keep just the slightest aura of mystery to the whole thing. Always private in his thoughts and plans, and especially obstinate when pushed by the press, he refused to address questions about retirement, saying only that he would do what he does after every season. That is to sit down and evaluate his situation, then decide about his future. Retirement must have seemed a wild thought to many. After all, he was just forty-nine years old and was about to lead his team into the Super Bowl for the second time in five years. He was a man seemingly at the top of his profession and already recognized as one of the best coaches in the game. Then there was the fact that coaching the Giants had always been his dream job. To most, Bill Parcells would remain a Giant forever, even if forever was only another ten years.

In his final press conference before the game, Parcells just wanted to talk football. It was no secret what his team planned to do and had to do to win. He didn't care who knew it.

"We have to have some measure of control on offense," he said. "I don't think we can win a shootout game with Buffalo, I really don't. I don't think our team has proved that it can win any kind of shootout game this year. But I think it has proved that it can win a lot of methodical games. If we can play our style and keep them from playing theirs, we'll have a better chance of beating them."

Nothing new and exotic there. Behind the scenes, however, the Giants had planned very carefully just how to make their game-plan happen. Defensive coordinator Bill Belichick had once again made some changes, designing two- and three-man rushing schemes with six defensive backs in the game, and using these formations in certain situations. He also had learned from the two teams' first meeting. Buffalo's no-huddle offense and the Bills' quartet of offensive stars—quarterback Kelly, running back Thomas, and wide receivers Reed and James Lofton—had given the Giants trouble in that first game. If the Giants couldn't stop them, Belichick felt a different defense could at least slow them down. There was no way Buffalo was going to score anywhere near the fifty-one points they had tallied in the AFC title game against the Raiders.

"Great players have moves that are tough to stop," Belichick said, of the Buffalo offense. "When you see them the first time, they get you. The second time, it's a different story."

Finally, the time for talking, planning, and scheming was over. The tone for the game was set in the opening minutes. The Giants took the kickoff and began moving the ball, mixing running plays and short passes, nothing fancy, just the basic stuff they had run successfully all year. They kept the ball for more than seven minutes as they moved fifty-eight yards on eleven plays. Hostetler connected on passes of thirteen yards to tight end Howard Cross and a clutch third-down throw to Mark Ingram that netted 16. Meggett also made a nifty ten-yard run. When the drive finally stalled, Matt Bahr came on and booted a twenty-eight-yard field goal, giving the New Yorkers a 3–0 lead.

Buffalo, however, came right back and did it their way. They moved the football sixty-six yards on six plays, but only one of them did the damage, Kelly's sixty-one-yard completion to Lofton. Then the defense stiffened and Scott Norwood came on to kick a twenty-eight-yard field goal that tied the game at 3–3. After that the defenses took over for a time. Hostetler seemed to lose his early edge and on the Giants' next four possessions he could produce just two first downs.

The quarter ended with the score tied at 3–3, but the Bills were driving once again. This time they started at the twenty and eleven plays later, after the start of the second period, were at the Giants' one. Don Smith ran it in and Norwood's kick gave the Bills a 10–3 lead. Meanwhile, the Giants continued to have trouble getting the offense in gear. At the 6:33 mark, Hostetler was sacked in the end zone by Bruce Smith for a safety. The two points made it 12–3. If the Bills scored again, they might be able to break the game open.

The defense then tightened, stopping the Bills on their next possession. A Buffalo punt gave the Giants the ball at their own 13 with 3:49 left in the half. Hostetler and the offense quickly went to work. It was important that they get a score before intermission, if only a field goal. First, the drive was kept alive by a key third-down pass to Howard Cross. It netted just seven yards, but was good for a first down. Seconds later, Anderson burst through a hole opened by Doug Riesenberg and ran for eighteen yards and another first.

Hostetler then dropped back again and connected with Ingram for twenty-two yards, bringing the ball to the Bills' 41. The Giants were getting close to field-goal range, but wanted more. Dave Meggett took a handoff and weaved his way to the Buffalo 29, a gain of seventeen and yet another first down. Three plays later Hostetler had a third-and-seven from the 21. Once again he came through, hitting Cross, who caught the ball on his knees at the 14. Two plays later, Hostetler lofted a perfect pass to Stephen Baker in the right corner of the end zone for a touchdown. There were just twenty-five seconds left in the half. Bahr's kick made it a 12–10 game.

"That touchdown made us feel like we could move the ball on them," said Giants' offensive coordinator Ron Erhardt. "It gave us a shot of confidence."

At halftime, Parcells's message to his team was a simple one. "I told them," he said, afterward, "that basically I was at a Super Bowl five years ago and some of you guys were with me and we were in the exact same situation we are now. I told them the first drive of the third quarter was the most important of the game. We had to do something with it."

The Giants players also began to feel they could wear the Bills down. Ottis Anderson put it this way. "I think collectively we knew we could put points on the board, that we could control the lock," he said. "We did a lot of things that hurt us at first, but we knew we could keep running the ball, keep pounding heads, and something was going to give."

Tackle John Elliott echoed that thought when he said, "We felt we could establish long drives on them. We just felt we could take the ball and run down the clock. We were executing."

The Giants would prove that at the outset of the second half, at the same time making their coach a prophet. They brought the opening kickoff back to the 25, then embarked on what would be the longest drive in Super Bowl history. It would take them fourteen plays and a record nine minutes, twenty-nine seconds.

The drive was punctuated by a twenty-four-yard run by Anderson, and several key passes by Hostetler. One was a fourteen-yard completion to

Ingram on a third-and-thirteen that brought the ball to the Buffalo 31, Ingram running the last five yards with a determined effort. There was also a clutch nine-yard completion to Cross on a third-and-four play. Finally, Anderson punched it over from the one and Bahr's kick made the score 17–12, Giants. They finally had the lead. At that point, the Buffalo defense was starting to reel from the pounding.

"There was no way our defense could stay in there with the Giants after those eleven- and twelve-play drives they kept coming with back-to-back," said star Bills linebacker Cornelius Bennett. "You have to expect a defense to wear down, and we did. . . . You barely had time to regroup before it was time to go again. I'm not blaming anyone or anything. I'm just saying that the style of the game and the way it was played ended up helping the Giants' chances even more."

Buffalo was too good a team, however, to roll over and quit. At the end of the third quarter the Bills started at their own 37. The difference in the teams was that while the Giants were taking eleven-, ten-, and fourteen-play drives to score, the Bills were doing it quickly. This time they went sixty-three yards in just four plays. The first three were passes to the backs that netted thirty-two yards. The third period ended with the ball at the Giants' 31, and on the first play of the fourth quarter Thurman Thomas took an inside handoff from Kelly, bolted up the middle, then ran away from linebacker Reasons and safety Guyton to score. The kick gave the lead back to the Bills at 19–17. This was turning into a corker of a game.

Before the Bills' scoring drive, they had held the football for just 1:59 of the previous sixteen minutes. Now their offense had struck quickly. While the drive got them the lead back, it happened so quickly that their tiring defense didn't have a chance to regroup. They were back on the field almost immediately, trying to stop the Giants' sledgehammer offense.

Sure enough, Parcells's team began moving again. On this drive, Mark Bavaro came to the fore. The rugged tight end, whose brilliant career was sabotaged by a deteriorating left knee that would cause him to leave the Giants at the end of the season, turned back the clock to grab passes of seventeen and nineteen yards to keep the drive alive. Ingram caught a thirteen-yarder, and Meggett made a clutch six-yard run on a third-and-five play. Finally, the ball was at the three, but on the next play Anderson lost four yards. With another handoff he gained them right back, but when Hostetler tried to throw for the score on third down, Cornelius Bennett batted the pass away.

On came Matt Bahr to boot a twenty-one-yard field goal that gave the Giants a one-point lead, 20–19. Though they had settled for a field goal, the Giants had once again driven seventy-four yards and had taken another 7:24 off the clock. Both teams had the ball once more; neither could mount a serious threat. Finally, the Giants had to punt. The ball wound up on the Buffalo ten-yard line with just 2:16 left. Kelly had to move his team at least fifty-five or sixty yards to give Scott Norwood a chance at a field goal. Against this Giants defense, that seemed like a task of enormous proportions.

Ottis Anderson and the rest of the offensive unit could now only watch. They had done their job; now the defense had to do theirs. "We kind of felt we were helpless now," Anderson said, recalling the moment. "It was out of our hands. We were surprised when the defense started rushing only two guys. We just hoped that if they bent, they wouldn't break. We felt that we had given the team the best chance to win by controlling the ball. Now it was up to [the defense] to hold it."

Kelly and his Bills teammates seemed equal to the task. The quarterback started by running himself for nine yards. Thomas, who would have 135 rushing yards on the day, then rambled for twenty-three, bringing the ball to the 42. Suddenly, Giants fans began sweating, as Parcells and his staff looked on with concern. A four-yard pass to Reed, then another Kelly scramble for nine brought the ball into Giants territory at the 46, with forty-eight seconds left. A five-yard pass to right end Keith McKellers brought it to the 42 with twenty-nine seconds left.

Thomas then showed his greatness once more, taking an inside handoff and running twelve yards to the 29. With no timeouts, Kelly had to spike the ball to stop the clock. There were just eight seconds left. The game came down to one play: placekicker Scott Norwood would try a forty-seven-yard field goal to win the game and the championship. Norwood was just six of ten on field goals beyond forty yards, but only one for six on grass. Tampa Stadium had a grass field.

The Giants held their breaths as the ball was snapped. Norwood stepped into it and snapped his right leg into the kick. It sailed high, and in a flash it became apparent that it had the distance. But would it be straight enough? With time seemingly suspended, every eye followed the flight of the tumbling football as it . . . sailed wide right! The game was over. The Giants had won.

They were Super Bowl champions once more.

CHAPTER TWELVE

Nothing Is Forever

T HE CELEBRATION BEGAN IMMEDIATELY AS BILL PARCELLS ENJOYED his second shouldered ride off a Super Bowl gridiron in five years. The Giants had done exactly what they had to do to beat an outstanding Buffalo team. It was one time a game plan worked nearly to perfection. Ball-control football had kept Buffalo's light-'em-up offense off the field. In fact, the Giants set a Super Bowl record that still stood as the 1900s became the 2000s by holding the ball for more than forty minutes on offense. Their time of possession was officially 40:33, which meant Kelly and company had the pigskin for 19:27. The Giants had run off seventy-three plays compared to just fifty-six for the Bills. Yet it was still a one-point game that could have turned if Norwood's kick had been just a foot or so more to the left.

Hostetler had more than justified the confidence his coach had in him by completing twenty of thirty-two passes for 222 yards. He did not throw a single interception in the entire postseason. However, it was old man Ottis Anderson who was named the game's Most Valuable Player on the strength of his 102 yards on twenty-one carries, spearheading a Giants ground attack that made the time-of-possession difference possible. In fact, he got sixty-three of those yards in the second half when everything was on the line.

Once the Giants hit the locker room there was bedlam all over, as is always the case when a championship is won. But before everyone began spraying the champagne and talking to the hordes of media people scurrying around, Parcells spoke briefly to the team.

"He told us to enjoy the moment," Ottis Anderson recalls. 'You guys were a bunch of overachievers,' was the way he put it. 'Nobody in the world gave you a chance—not the writers, not the oddsmakers. No one thought you could. Mathematically, you had no chance of winning. But the one thing they can't measure is the heart of a man, and his determination. You guys proved that with hard work, dedication, and belief, you could overcome any obstacle. You beat a team that was totally better. And if you look at the numbers, they beat us in every aspect but time on the clock. And the score. So I'm telling you right now, you can take all the statistics and toss 'em out the window.' "

Then it was time for the formalities. Parcells came out to accept the Vince Lombardi Trophy, then was whisked to another podium to face the media. Will McDonough, columnist for the *Boston Globe* and a friend of Parcells's since he coached a year in New England in 1980, remembered the moment.

"I was standing right in front of the podium, the closest person to him," McDonough recalls. "They waited for all the press and media people to run from different angles, looking to get in front of him. It was all taking place in a big tent. While he was waiting to begin he suddenly leaned over to me and said just two words: *'Power football!'*

"If you read my story the next day, that's the way the story starts."

It didn't take a genius to know what won the game for the Giants. Professor Parcells and his staff knew what it would take and fortunately had the horses with which to do it. The coach would willingly elaborate on the two-word statement he had made to McDonough.

"They call us predictable and conservative," he told the press, "but I know one thing, and I've coached this game a long time. Power wins football games. *Power wins football games.*" He said it twice, as if to emphasize his point. "It's not always the fanciest way, but it can win games."

He also knew it was game that could have gone either way. That's how good the Bills were. Maybe he was acknowledging that when he said, "I realized a long time ago that God was playing in some of these games. He was on our side today. We played as well as we could. If we played again tomorrow, they would probably win, 20–19. But I think both teams were valiant. I don't think there's too much to choose between the two teams."

Buffalo Coach Marv Levy, in a perhaps unwitting tribute to Parcells's game plan, said, simply, "We just didn't have enough time to move the ball."

The win was a wonderful wrap for many of the players, as well. Ottis Anderson knew that if young Rodney Hampton hadn't been injured, he probably wouldn't have been in there long enough to win the MVP. Because the game was played in his home state of Florida, his performance had an extra-special significance for him.

"I said a long time ago that if I ever got to play in a Super Bowl, I'd be a most valuable player," he said. "When we lost to the Rams [in the playoffs] the year before I had tears in my eyes because I didn't think I'd get another chance."

Hostetler was another big hero, a kind of Walter Mitty success story, a guy who sat for four years without throwing a pass. Now, at age twenty-nine, he finally had a career.

"I heard so many guys say that I'd never be able to do it, and thank the Lord, it's done and nobody can take it away," Hoss said.

Hostetler would leave the Giants after the 1992 season, then spend several years as the starting quarterback for the Raiders, gaining a reputation as one of the toughest signalcallers in the league, a guy who made the most of his talents.

There were many such individual stories on the Giants that year, but in the days following the victory, more and more attention was being paid to the coach. There were some who said that Parcells and the Giants got lucky that day, something that he would continue to hear about for years. In an interview some ten years after the fact, he almost growled when the game and Giants luck came up.

"They didn't deserve to win," he would say that day. "I'm telling you the truth. We outplayed them big time that day. Forty minutes we had the ball. That's dominating, no matter what you say. No turnovers and forty minutes of possession."

When the question of Norwood's missed field goal arose, he also said that the odds were always in the Giants' favor. "The guy hadn't made that one from that distance on grass his whole life."

Whether the years had changed his opinion slightly or whether he tempered his feelings after the game is hard to say. Sure, the game could have gone either way, but if the Giants hadn't executed their ball-control game plan, it's apparent they wouldn't have won. For building the kind of team he felt he needed to win, and then for motivating them to perform to their utmost potential, Parcells deserved all the credit.

Coach Levy, asked about the game some nine years later, also dismissed the claim that the Giants were lucky. "We had played them earlier in the year and won a close, hard-fought battle," Levy said. "Everybody remembers the missed field goal [in the Super Bowl], but we led late in the game and they had a third and long. Mark Ingram caught a pass and we had two guys bounce off a tackle that would have forced a punt. They didn't make the tackle and the Giants went down and scored the go-ahead touchdown. So it just wasn't the missed field goal. We didn't play well enough to win the game."

In Parcells's postgame press conference, the question of his future arose once again. The rumors that he might jump to the Tampa Bay Buccaneers just wouldn't go away, despite the fact that he had one more year remaining on the four-year, $3.2 million contract that he signed before the 1988 season.

"The last time we won one of these," Parcells said, "there was a little controversy about me and it didn't allow my owners and general manager to enjoy this very much. They're going to enjoy this one, I promise you. There's not going to be any controversy."

That seemed to settle the question of Tampa Bay. If there was ever any contact between the Buccaneers and Parcells's representatives, it never came out. In the days following the Super Bowl, the praise for Parcells's coaching abilities seemed to multiply, the respect for his achievements growing quickly.

"Bill Parcells," said Giants' co-owner Tim Mara, "is the best coach the Giants have ever had."

Others said even more. One newspaper story called him "the National Football League's premier coach as well as one of the best coaches in its history," adding that no team had ever won a Super Bowl with a backup quarterback, and that once Simms went down the Giants' hopes seemed to go down with him. "Other coaches and other teams might have surrendered to such adversity," the story continued. "Not this coach. Not this team."

Typical of Parcells, he would never publicly take one hundred percent of the credit for his team's success. In fact, he showed once again his loyalty and deference to old friends and influences. Not surprisingly, his high-school coach and mentor, Mickey Corcoran, was at Tampa Stadium to watch his former star athlete coach the Giants. Parcells loved having Corcoran around and never missed an opportunity to talk about him.

"Mickey is like my second father," he told an interviewer. "He influenced me toward the profession and he's had a tremendous effect on my life. You're seeing a reflection in me now of what he was as a coach. How things should be done. Things you don't do. Things you do. He's almost seventy years old and all he talks about is winning games. I hope I have something like that to keep me going when I'm seventy."

Everyone who spent any time around Parcells would eventually hear about Mickey. When Brad Benson, the former Giants tackle who retired in 1987, was asked if he knew anyone his coach admired, he said quickly, "Say a prayer to God in the morning, then Mickey."

As Parcells learned the first time, Super Bowl celebrations don't last long. It's soon back to work, watching films, looking at college players, thinking about which veterans are at the end of the line, preparing for the upcoming draft. In fact, Parcells went through the same routine every year, Super Bowl victory or not. The draft was held on April 21, 1991. With Parcells running the show, the Giants chose fullback Jarrod Bunch of Michigan in the first round, also picking up wide receiver Ed McCaffrey of Stanford and linebacker Corey Miller of South Carolina, among others. It seemed like business as usual, except that the rumors hadn't stopped.

Then on Friday, April 26, the *New York Times* ran a story by Dave Anderson titled "Giants Can't Let Parcells Get Away." The story focused on Bob Tisch, who was the team's new co-owner along with the Mara family. Tisch indicated he would be a hands-off owner and leave the football matters to General Manager George Young, as well as Coach Parcells and his staff. The story also said that Tisch and longtime owner Wellington Mara didn't seem to be taking seriously statements made by their coach that he wasn't sure whether he wanted to continue coaching.

"I don't really know what I want to do," Parcells had apparently been saying, on more than one occasion. When he was reminded that he would earn another $750,000 by coaching in 1991, Parcells was heard to reply, "It's not just money."

Again there was speculation that the coach might be looking for a change of venue. He had built the Giants into a Super Bowl team in 1986, regrouped after 1987, and built them back to a second title in 1990. Maybe he was looking for a new challenge, another place to try to work his magic.

In the *Times* story, Bob Tisch was quoted as saying, "I gather that George Young will get into it next week with Bill."

Anderson then concluded his story by saying that if Parcells left, "Wellington Mara and Bob Tisch will deserve to be blamed for losing the best coach in Giants history."

Perhaps people didn't know Parcells as well back then. If they had, they would have realized that his decisions were not predicated by money. No one could be blamed if he left, for the simple reason that once he made up his mind, that was it. His decisions, even unpopular ones, were final. Fini. So the ball was squarely in his court. Any decision he made would be his alone, made with perhaps the consultation of a few—his wife, Judy, and Mickey Corcoran. By the last week in April, there had to be serious concerns about Parcells's future and whether he would return to the Giants. At that time no one knew what was driving him, whether there was a reason that was causing him to even consider leaving what had always been his dream job.

The speculation continued, even when Parcells showed up at the first mini-camp for rookies in early May. Then on May 15, the speculation ended and it ended with a bombshell. Bill Parcells announced he was resigning as head coach of the Giants, in effect walking away from the only coaching job he ever really wanted. His announcement shocked players and fans alike.

"No one knew at the time what Bill was going through," said Ottis Anderson. "I don't think anyone ever knew. He was a very private person about his medical health and his life. So we didn't see it coming. Then we started hearing rumors, like everyone else. By the time it became reality, the decision was made. Supposedly, it was based on his health, but with Parcells you never know.

"In all honesty, I think it was a shock to everyone on the team. If he wanted to leave, there was no better way to do it. He was on top of the world, making it the perfect scenario if he wanted to bow out. He didn't talk to me before he resigned, and as far as I know didn't talk with any of the players."

At the time of his resignation, Parcells the coach became Bill Parcells, private person. He said little and refused to give detailed reasons for resigning when he did. A coach who wants to go out on top usually calls it quits as soon as the season ends, as Dick Vermeil did just two days after the St. Louis Rams won the Super Bowl in January 2000. Parcells didn't do that. He stayed on through the draft and the first mini-camp, then walked in mid-May.

Most of the speculation focused on either his health or his dissatisfaction with GM George Young. Always a man who wanted complete control, Parcells had to defer to Young when it came to personnel decisions. This would become a thorny point in upcoming years. But at the time, he refused to discuss it.

"It's not burnout. It's not my health," were two of the definitive statements he made the day he resigned. He then went on to say that it was time to move on, a rather vague and almost patronizing way to explain to an entire city full of football fans who had grown to love him, respected him, and thought of him only as a New York Giant. He also said that he wanted to go out on top. That was a bit more acceptable. After taking the Giants from 3–12–1 in 1983 to a Super Bowl win in 1986, then building again from a 6–9 season in 1987 to a second Super Bowl triumph in 1990, perhaps he did feel there were no more worlds to conquer as the Giants' coach.

As people would learn in the upcoming years, Parcells came into situations hailed as a savior, but left them under an often acrimonious and ambiguous cloud. In September 1999, he was asked by an interviewer all over again about leaving the Giants some eight and one-half years earlier.

"It was a good time to leave," he said, then. "I'd been there eight years. Ten total, including as an assistant. I just don't think nowadays you can do that anymore. The landscape of this business has changed a lot. After awhile, it's like it is with the players. You've got to move on to something different."

Odd. With the Giants, Parcells certainly was in a position to write his own ticket. He was a strong enough coach that it's nearly impossible to visualize the team—any Parcells team—going through two or three years with big losing records. Unless he reached some kind of personal impasse with management, he probably could have remained with the team as long as he wished. After all, in eight years as head coach he had produced a 77–49–1 record in the regular season and an 8–3 mark in the postseason, with two Super Bowl triumphs.

Time to move on? Maybe. A new challenge? Not exactly on the horizon. Conflict with management, e.g., George Young? Sure, he always liked control, but the success ratio and team full of "Parcells guys" pretty much negated that. No, the major reason was apparently the one he denied at the time of his resignation. "It's not my health," he said, then. In truth, however, it was. Ottis Anderson's recollections of his coach's departure were made nearly nine years later, when the whole story was known. That's why he referred to no one knowing "what Bill was going through," and mentioned his "medical health."

Once Parcells left, the Giants moved quickly to maintain continuity, as they had when Ray Perkins left and Parcells was hired. This time the job went to offensive coordinator Ray Handley, who undoubtedly had the approval of the former coach as well as General Manager Young. Parcells kept a low profile for a few months, then resurfaced in the fall as an NBC studio host for NFL pre- and postgame shows. He worked with Bob Costas, O. J. Simpson, and Will McDonough, and was a genial, often smiling presence, a far cry from his acerbic coaching persona. Then, after just a couple of months on the job, the true nature of his resignation became apparent.

On December 16, Parcells entered Valley Hospital in Ridgewood, New Jersey, where Dr. Michael Kresselbrenner performed an angioplasty to correct a mild cardiac blockage. He was quickly back at work, but it was the first indication that a heart problem was the real reason he left the Giants. Over the next year or so, he would have two more minor "procedures," culminating with single-bypass heart surgery on June 2, 1992, that would finally correct the problem. It wasn't until years later that he would fully discuss what had happened during that great 1990 season.

"I didn't want to leave football, but I knew I had to do something," he told the press in 1997. "I knew I couldn't keep going like I was or I wasn't going to make it. For a long time, I didn't know what was wrong. Quite frankly, it took six months to find out. I knew something was wrong because I could feel it, even though it wasn't showing up on the tests."

Symptoms included an irregular heartbeat that would trouble him from time to time. His condition wasn't diagnosed until just before the angioplasty in December 1991. By that time he was so frustrated and perhaps a bit frightened that he said to his doctor, "I tell you what I'm going to do, doc. I'm going to get on this treadmill right now, and I'm either going to drop dead or I'm going to find out what's wrong, because I can't take this anymore."

He also admitted that by the time Super Bowl XXV rolled around, he felt he was ready to collapse. "I was very, very tired, physically, almost exhausted. I just wasn't doing as well physically as I am now. All of those things [back then] added up."

At that time, Parcells wasn't taking the best of care of himself in a demanding, high-stress profession. He was a heavy cigarette smoker, drank potfuls of coffee, and one of his favorite foods was peanut butter, which he often ate to excess. Always a big man, he had become somewhat overweight, his more-than-ample midsection often visible through the sweaters he sometimes wore on the sidelines. Upon learning the nature of his problem, he quit smoking cold-turkey, improved his diet, and began working out more regularly. Returning to NBC for the 1992 season as a game analyst, providing color commentary alongside top play-by-play man Marv Albert, he seemed comfortable in his new surroundings—but the question was: for how long? Once a coach, etc., etc., etc.

A rumor in December 1992 held that George Young was going to step down as the Giants' GM and that Parcells would take his place. Again, it was a rumor, which Young quickly dispelled.

"I am very satisfied with my health the way it is right now," said Young, who also had some physical problems, "and I will be general manager of this team next year. There is nothing wrong with me and I have no intention of leaving."

Young would remain the Giants' GM through the 1997 season, when he finally left to take a job in the NFL home office. So there was no merit to the rumors. What of the Giants, however? Did they miss Bill Parcells? That quickly became apparent. With basically the same cast of characters returning for the 1991 season, the team began to struggle, losing their final three games to finish at 8–8. A year later, they had an even more difficult time, coming in at 6–10, and Handley was gone, replaced by Dan Reeves.

What happened? Did losing Parcells really affect the team that much? Veteran Ottis Anderson, who had been with losing teams in St. Louis before joining the Giants in 1986, stayed on through the 1992 season and thus saw the difference.

"One thing I can say about Parcells is that he made every position competitive. Even if you were a starter, it didn't matter. If you didn't perform well in practice there was a chance you would be demoted. Bill knew that certain players and certain individuals couldn't be given the freedom to make their own decisions, because they weren't mentally prepared for it.

"Ray had the American attitude. A man prepares for his job, gets paid good money for it, and thus shouldn't have to be motivated. Motivations should come from the fact that you play on national television, get paid well, and therefore should do your job to the best of your ability. You shouldn't need someone to yell at you, challenge you, challenge your manhood, challenge your character. You should be responsible for yourself. But I think we needed that. I don't think we were ready to have the reins pulled from our backs.

"As a football team, we were always well prepared. No team could throw a blitz at us that we weren't ready for. But I think [Coach Handley] gave a lot of people the opportunity to be men who weren't prepared to be men. And it backfired."

If Ray Handley didn't think his players needed to be challenged, Bill Parcells had to be the ultimate challenger. Challenging his players was something he did from the first day of training camp to the final quarter of the final game. It was constant, and it worked. Phil McConkey, who had left the Giants after the 1988 season, continued to follow the team closely through Parcells's resignation and Handley's two unsuccessful years. He, too, felt that the Parcells approach was the right one, and its absence was a prime reason the team faltered.

"Any time you hear a player say, 'He's a player's coach, he understands us, he's one of us, he treats us like men, he treats us with respect,' I'll tell you they will lose," McConkey said. "In this league you need discipline. A lot of players are like twelve-year-old boys. I'd much rather play for a hard-nosed guy who's a prick a good percentage of the time and win, then play for a compassionate, respectful guy who treats us like men, and lose.

"When Bill left the Giants a couple of guys still on the team said to me, 'Ray Handley treats us like men, takes our input, listens to what we have to say.' These are the kinds of guys Bill likes to weed out."

Maybe the team slipped back because the players were used to a challenge, used to having a coach who refused to let them get away with anything, refused to allow them to play to even the smallest notch below their ability. Whatever the reason, the Giants did not respond as well to Ray Handley as they had to Bill Parcells. Ironically, the veteran players who knew Parcells best seemed to have the most respect for him, especially those who became *his guys.*

Phil Simms, who achieved his greatest success with Parcells and yet was one of his favorite whipping boys, remembers an incident in 1988 that he related for an HBO special on Parcells in 1999.

"We've already had a lot of success together and we're out on the practice field one day during training camp. He comes up to me and says, 'Hey, boy, you're having a good camp, but I'm gonna tear you up out there today.' Then he adds, 'If it's okay to get on you, then it's okay to get on the rest of them. You'll put up with it because you know it's gonna make you win.'

"I'll never tell him this," said the smiling Simms, speaking from pure respect, "but that fat s.o.b. was right."

Ottis Anderson took a more direct approach. "He was a giant among Giants," Anderson said. "He stood taller than everybody else and he knew what we had and how he could get what he had to get out of each and every one of us. That gives a man a special quality. He believed in me and gave me a chance, but he told me it was on my shoulders. 'You're a veteran and you know what you have to do. It's your job, but if you can't hold it, somebody else will.' I think when they made the movie *A Man Among Men* they were talking about Parcells."

The younger players from his Giants years, guys who didn't know him as well, had an entirely different perception. Tight end Howard Cross, who joined the Giants in 1989, remembers a tough coach, but little more.

"He beat the heck out of us all the time," Cross said, in 1996. "I have a black belt in karate because Bill was on me all the time. I went to karate every day after practice [to alleviate frustrations]. Did he make me a better player? I have no idea. It think Mark [Bavaro] and Zeke [Mowatt] and Coach [Mike] Pope had more to do with my development as a player. Bill wasn't very encouraging when he was here."

Brian Williams, a center/guard, who was a first round pick in 1989, held out before reporting to camp late. That didn't put him in good stead with the coach. His memory of his first day in training camp is still negative.

"There was nothing good," Williams said. "It was just a hard day, that's all. They put me in at center, immediately called for a blitz, and a wave of defenders ran over me. Bill's philosophy is you have to prove yourself before he's willing to give you any respect. I respect that of him, but that was the toughest part."

Then there was linebacker Corey Miller, a sixth-round pick in 1991, who joined the team a month before Parcells resigned. Miller remembers being excited about getting a phone call from his first pro coach. The phone call he got deflated him within seconds.

"He said, 'Corey, this is Bill Parcells. Congratulations. But don't get too excited about playing linebacker. You're probably going to play tight end.' "

Miller also remembers the mini-camp just before Parcells left. He recalls the first meeting of the camp, held the afternoon before the first workout, which was scheduled for the following morning. He said that Parcells just barked out the schedule, the time the bus would leave the hotel, and the time practice would start.

"Then he said, 'We just won the Super Bowl. I've got all the players I need. I don't care if you get on the bus or not.' He just seemed angry," Miller continued. "He didn't smile a lot. He just hated rookies."

So the coach took some getting used to. Those who didn't really know him and would never play for him again would be missing a unique football experience. If they were able to handle him and perform, they undoubtedly would have been playing for a winning team. Those who stayed around long enough to become Parcells guys (and not every player can do that), would probably ended up feeling the same as Anderson, McConkey, and Simms.

Those seeing him on television and not knowing about his coaching personality saw a pleasant, smiling presence, a man knowledgeable in football, joking with the likes of Bob Costas and Marv Albert, and analyzing games dispassionately. But there was one football player-turned-broadcaster who felt he saw something beneath Parcells's broadcasting facade. Bob Trumpy had been an All-Pro tight end with the Cincinnati Bengals before becoming an NBC analyst. Trumpy remembered covering a game in New York when Parcells was still coaching the Giants. Afterward, there was going to be a small press conference.

"He came into [the conference room]," Trumpy recalled, "and immediately said to me, 'Trumpy, get on the other side of the table.' I said okay, but I asked why. He said, 'I'm the coach and that's just the way it is. That's the wrong side of the table to sit on.' It's insane, but those are the things that set some coaches apart from others. He's probably the most superstitious person I know."

Maybe it was because Parcells paid such close attention to every detail of his coaching life, and seemed to revel in it, that Trumpy reached another conclusion.

"It was never going to work out for him in television. Parcells was a lot more involved in football than thirty-five-second clips."

While Parcells continued to work the television booth during the 1992 season, those on the inside who knew about his heart problems also knew that his surgery had been successful. His health restored, his doctors gave him some news that gave him an option he thought he might never have. In late 1992, they told Parcells that he had medical clearance to coach again. If he wanted to do it.

CHAPTER THIRTEEN

The NFL Wars, Round Two

W HEN THE DOCTORS TOLD PARCELLS IT WAS MEDICALLY SAFE FOR him to coach again he was fifty-one years old. He had been away from his chosen profession for two years, which wasn't long, and would undoubtedly be able to step back in without missing a beat. Yet he seemed to have a solid niche at NBC, projected himself well as a broadcaster, and probably could settle in for a long run, especially with the proliferation of television coverage of both college and professional football. Not only was it a comfortable niche, it paid well, wasn't especially stressful, and seemed to be something he enjoyed.

Why, then, would he want to re-enter the NFL wars, where being a head coach was an increasingly complex, pressure-packed, stressful job. Nine-to-five it wasn't, with many NFL coaches arriving at the office before sunrise and staying long into the night. It wasn't unusual for a coach to simply pass out on a couch at the stadium, catch a few hours' sleep there, and begin working once again before the roosters crowed.

Preparing weekly game plans had become an ordeal of meetings, videotape analysis, poring over scouting reports and statistics, discussing an opponent's offensive and defensive tendencies, debating the best way to attack and defend against them, and finally agreeing upon a way of hopefully winning the game, with the head coach usually making the final decisions. Computer-generated game plans for an offense can run upwards of 125 pages or more, while the defensive counterpart takes up another hundred or so pages. This has to be done sixteen times in a season and, if a team is good enough to make the playoffs, maybe another three or four times, depending on how far the team goes.

In between are the practice sessions, personnel decisions, checking on injured players, deciding who can and can't go that week, and contemplating last-minute changes. Coaching the actual game is often the easiest, and in some ways the most relaxing, part of the week. The coach can go out there and be competitive along with his players. A number of coaches have stayed the course for more than twenty years. George Halas remained on the Chicago Bears sidelines for forty years, while Curly Lambeau piloted the Green Bay Packers for thirty-three. Both of them, however, coached in earlier times, when the game was more basic. They had another advantage, as well: they also owned their respective teams. No one could fire them.

Seven other coaches went over the twenty-year mark—Don Shula, Tom Landry, Chuck Noll, Chuck Knox, Steve Owen, Paul Brown, and Weeb Eubank. Brown started with the Cleveland Browns in the rival All-America Conference, while Eubank bounced from the NFL to the upstart AFL and stayed through the merger of the two leagues. All were successful. Still, the twenty-year coaching club doesn't have many members considering the long history of the league.

"The game is definitely more complex now in that you have more diverse offensive schemes, sometimes four wide receivers, nobody in the backfield, shotgun formations," said Chuck Knox, who coached twenty-two years with the L.A. Rams, Buffalo Bills, and Seattle Seahawks. "You've got all these things that at one time you didn't have. You used to have two backs in the backfield, a tight end, and two wide receivers. That's all you saw. To react to the new formations, you've got to have complex defensive schemes that might involve five or six defensive backs. So the game has changed tremendously, plus it's much faster and so much tougher physically."

Knox also said there was a time when head coaches had some time off between seasons. That's no longer the case.

"We used to have the college draft in late January," he said. "That meant you relied more on your scouting department to get information on the available players. Now, with the draft in late April, there is more time and everyone has to know all the available information on each player out there. You not only send your assistants out on the road, but you also become involved. You go to all-star games, the combine meeting for four or five days, where you might look at four hundred college players. It's all very time-consuming.

"Then there is free agency, something else we didn't have years ago. Now you have to spend a lot of time looking at films of players and getting a rundown on the pro personnel who will be available through free agency. You go out and court them, bring them in, show them your facility, talk to them about the team and your coaching philosophy. Then you must pay attention to money management. That has become even more important because of the salary cap, something else we didn't have to contend with years ago.

"Finally there are the mini-camps. You're permitted to have a few legally, but there's nothing to prevent some of your players from staying around during the month of June, for instance. Say your wide receivers, defensive backs, and quarterbacks stay. Now, you've got a passing mini-camp. The next thing you know, you're going to training camp about the middle of July. So while both you and your assistants used to get some time off during the off-season, you can't do that anymore."

Chuck Noll, who coached the Pittsburgh Steelers to four Super Bowl triumphs in the 1970s, then stayed on during some difficult, losing years, described the job he held for more than twenty years as very tiring.

"It takes a toll on you the longer the season goes on," Noll said. "My wife used to talk about how drawn all the coaches looked. While you're out there, you don't realize it, but now that I'm out and I go back and see some of the guys, I understand what she was talking about. You're working fifteen-to-eighteen-hour days, but you try to be efficient; not let it drag too long because you want to keep your staff fresh. When they're on the field and teaching, you don't want them falling asleep."

Both Chucks, Noll and Knox, agreed that the biggest stress is the kind a coach brings on himself.

"The goal of the organization is to win," Knox said. "So the head coach has to create a climate in which the coaches and players can be successful. You try to keep the pressures away from them. Yet you can't get completely away from the pressures. You've got to win. If you don't win, you're gone."

According to Chuck Noll, "The fruits of all your preparation comes on Sunday. The game, in a sense, is enjoyable, especially if you're doing well. If your team is not doing well, it becomes very depressing. Either way, when the game is over, there is an immediate letdown. You have to be thinking about next week, so you can't even enjoy a victory for long."

One coach who seemed to handle stress extremely well was Marv Levy, the losing coach in Super Bowl XXV. The oldest coach in the league, Levy stayed at the helm of the Bills into his early seventies, and took his team to the Super Bowl four times. Even though they lost each time, he and his staff, as well as the players, never quit. Levy said it was the love of the game that kept him going.

"Coaching, to me, was sheer enjoyment," he said. "I would feel an adrenaline rush, but I never felt stress. I only felt exhilaration. I might feel moments of despair when we lost a game, particularly a momentous game, but you go through a little period of mourning and then you get right back at it again.

"Even with the ups and downs, I never said, 'How am I gonna handle this? Can I hold up? What am I doing to my family?' Those kinds of things."

For the families of head coaches, the life can also be difficult. Chuck Knox says the family must have a very strong bond. "It helps if you have a very, very understanding wife," he explained. "Your wife and kids are always going to wonder, are we going to be here next year? Are we going to be in the same school? Are we going to be moving someplace else?"

Noll agreed. "The sacrifice you make is all the time you're away from your family. You start early in June and you're gone seven days a week. You're gone so much that your input with your kids is minimal. Your wife does that most of the time, to the point where the image they have of you is what she gives them. We used to try to take one month, usually June, to do things as a family. I would always try to do the things that interested them. Hopefully, you have a partner who does a great job, something I was blessed with.

"There are some guys who keep their families completely separate. They choose to do that. But if your family is important, then [being away so much] is a problem."

Some coaches handle the stresses better than others. Marv Levy said coaching wasn't stressful. Yet Dennis Erickson, who moved from the college ranks, where he was very successful, to the Seattle Seahawks, where his teams struggled, said the job really took a toll.

"It's about as stressful a situation as you can get," Erickson said. "Your nerves are shot. Your stomach is shot. You tie yourself up in knots. You don't sleep with any kind of regularity. The surprising thing is that more coaches don't have really serious problems with their health."

But there certainly have been health problems among coaches, with maybe more lurking beneath the surface than made public. Perhaps the first highly publicized incident that showed the tremendous stress some coaches were under came after the 1982 season when Philadelphia's Dick Vermeil resigned, citing physical and emotional "burnout." Vermeil was a workaholic who drove his team and drove himself. He had the Eagles in the Super Bowl following the 1980 season and ultimately had a fairly successful seven-year run. That was enough. Vermeil, of course, would resurface sixteen years later with the St. Louis Rams, taking them to a Super Bowl triumph in 1999, then retiring once more at age sixty-three.

Some coaches have continued after health problems. The highly emotional, often explosive Mike Ditka suffered an "inferior wall heart attack" in November 1988 while he was coaching the Chicago Bears. It was a relatively minor episode and Ditka was back on the sidelines in two weeks. He said the most difficult thing for him was watching the Bears play from his hospital bed, where he had no control over the outcome.

"My [heart] rate and blood pressure went off the charts," Ditka said. "They all thought that I would have another heart attack."

Coaching has always remained in Ditka's blood. After leaving the Bears, he later resurfaced in New Orleans, where he coached several more years through the 1999 season. Still emotional, still explosive, Ditka has seemingly avoided recurrence of his heart problems.

The most recent episode was that of Atlanta Coach Dan Reeves, who underwent quadruple bypass surgery in December 1998 while his Falcons marched toward the Super Bowl. Like Parcells, Reeves had undergone angioplasties in 1990 and 1991. He somehow managed to return in time to coach the Falcons at the Super Bowl in late January, and indicated that he would return to coach again in the 2000 season.

A number of other coaches and assistants have battled health problems in recent years. Whether they simply represent a segment of the overall population or whether their professions tend to increase the likelihood of problems isn't known. But perhaps former Kansas City coach Marty Schottenheimer put it best when he said:

"You're in a business where sometimes you get caught up in the same syndrome as the players. You feel you're bulletproof and that 'It can't happen to me' mentality takes over. But it does happen."

Of course, not everything about the profession is negative. Coaches love what they do, the stress and strain notwithstanding. There is tremendous satisfaction that comes from building a team, taking them to the playoffs, and maybe winning it all. Then there is the power that comes from being the leader, the commander. It's like a war out there on Sundays and the head coach is the general. He and his aides have prepared a battle plan; now he leads his troops to see if they can prevail. Writer Will McDonough touched on this, as well as on another aspect of being the boss.

"A head coach today is like a star," McDonough said. "He's the big guy when he walks into the office every day. 'Hi, Coach. How ya doing?' He's like the king. He controls all their lives. He's the one who has gotten most of these people their jobs. He's the first guy on the bus, the first guy on the plane. He's out front. He's the celebrity, the one doing the commercials and everything that goes with it. A coach has to have a real sense of power, and that's a rush. In [Parcells's] case, however, I think the competition overrides everything else."

To coach or not to coach. This was the situation Parcells faced in the fall of 1992. He had recovered from bypass surgery and his doctors said the recovery was so complete that he could now coach again, if he chose to. By December there were the rumors that he might take over from George Young as Giants GM. But it's doubtful he would have taken that job, even if it had been offered. He was first and foremost a coach. If he returned to football, it would surely be in that capacity.

The only analogy that could be drawn was his one-year sabbatical in 1979, when he decided to sit out in deference to his wife and girls. Though he enjoyed some aspects of real estate, the lure of the gridiron was still there, eating away at him and driving him batty. Finally, Judy Parcells told her husband to get back into football, and fast. Same thing in 1991 and 1992. While he enjoyed broadcasting, it had to be difficult covering games every week and watching other coaches work the sidelines. He must have been thinking about things he would have done differently, about players who could become *Parcells guys* and about the challenge of turning another team around.

In fact, just before he had his bypass surgery he told a *New York Times* reporter, "If I feel right, I want to do it again."

The "it" was coaching, but once he recovered from the surgery and resumed his broadcasting career nothing concrete was said, only the rumors that surfaced from time to time. What no one knew then was that by the end of 1992, Parcells was in serious negotiations with the New England Patriots. The rumors really started on January 8, 1993, when the New England team fired its coach of two years, Dick MacPherson. The team had a new owner, James B. Orthwein, who had purchased controlling interest in the franchise from Victor Kiam, II, in May 1992. Orthwein then watched the team go through a miserable 2–14 season that fall. When he removed MacPherson, it appeared that he was looking to build a winner. That's why he went after a man who had already shown the ability to do that—Parcells.

On January 21, 1993, Bill Parcells became the 12th head coach in the history of the Patriots franchise. The *Boston* Patriots had been one of eight teams comprising the brand-new American Football League in 1960, a league created to rival the older, more established National Football League. Ten years later the two leagues finally merged, with the Patriots becoming part of the newly formed American Football Conference. A year later, in 1971, the team changed its named to the *New England* Patriots.

The team had some winning seasons and made the playoffs a couple of times, but all told wasn't an exceptionally successful franchise. Finally, in 1985, the Pats surprised everyone by taking a wild-card playoff berth all the way to the Super Bowl. But once there, they were soundly beaten by a very powerful Chicago Bears team 46–10. The next year, when the Giants and Parcells were 14–2 and headed for the Super Bowl, the Patriots won the AFC East title with an 11–5 mark but lost to Denver in the second round.

Four years later, in 1990, when Parcells had the Giants heading for a second Super Bowl triumph, the Patriots had crashed to a league-worst 1–15 record. A year later, they rebounded slightly to finish at 6–10, then in 1992 regressed once more and finished last at 2–14. So Bill Parcells would be inheriting a team that had a combined 9–39 record over the previous three seasons. This wouldn't be an easy ship to right, but the Patriots hoped they had the right man to do it.

"I want to improve the Patriots to the point where we can compete for a championship," the new coach said when he was introduced. "I pledge to the fans and the players that I won't rest until we approach that goal."

Parcells had signed a five-year contract worth about $6 million. He was being well paid for his talents, but he had come back for reasons other than money. "I feel good about it," he told the press. "I missed football.

I missed the competition. I just look forward to it and try to build a new team. And I missed the camaraderie with the players."

Some wondered if coaching the Patriots was the job that Parcells really wanted. If he had left the Giants purely for health reasons, wouldn't it be reasonable to think that, given a choice, he would have preferred to return to his former dream job? After all, the Giants had dismissed Ray Handley after the 1992 season and immediately begun searching for a new coach. They were turned down by Tom Coughlin (who decided to coach the expansion Jacksonville Jaguars), explored some other possibilities, then finally settled on Dan Reeves. Whether Parcells was considered or contacted isn't known. George Young was still the general manager and there were always lingering stories that the two didn't get along. But writer Will McDonough, who has known Bill since he was an assistant with the Patriots in 1980, felt that his Giants days were done, that he didn't want to go back.

"I think Bill felt it was time to move on from the Giants," McDonough said, "even though he has his roots there. He had lived in New England in 1980 and liked it there. His wife liked it, too. So I think it become of matter of if he had the opportunity to come here, he would come. That message was passed along to James Orthwein, who owned the team at the time. [Bill] even knew exactly where he wanted to live. Obviously, it wasn't that far from New Jersey or New York, if he had to go there to visit or on business. So, no, I don't think he wanted to go back to the Giants. That was behind him. He felt it was time to move on.

"He also liked the situation with Orthwein. He was a hands-off owner who planned to live in St. Louis and wouldn't even be around the team. He told Bill, 'This is it, carry the ball. You're the boss.' "

That was definitely the kind of situation Parcells wanted. Though he coexisted with George Young when he was coaching the Giants, and the result of their collaboration speaks for itself, Parcells still wanted total control over the entire football operation, including the acquisition and movement of all personnel. Orthwein gave him that. Parcells took it, and was back in business.

The task he was given, however, seemed nearly impossible. A team that was 9–39 over three seasons, including years of 1–15 and 2–14 can't have too many positive things going for it. Shortly after he arrived, Parcells described the entire New England setup as "the most down-and-out, despondent, negative atmosphere you could imagine." It was difficult to find a starting point.

Of the three major sports—football, baseball, basketball—turning around a bad football team is the most difficult. A coach has to deal with a forty-five-man roster and taxi squad, with twenty-two starters on offense and defense. Baseball has nine starting players and a twenty-five-man roster, while basketball can play just five at a time. Add a couple of twenty-game winners and maybe a forty-five-home run, 120-RBI slugger, and a baseball team is well on its way. A basketball team can go a long way just with the addition of a seven-foot center who can play offense and defense, a point guard who takes care of the basketball, and a coach to put it all together.

It's different with a football team. Add a great quarterback and you still need some wide receivers to get open and catch the ball. Then you need a strong running game so that the quarterback can direct a balanced offense. That's still not enough. From there, you need a good offensive line or the quarterback, no matter how good he is, will spend most of the afternoon running for his life or getting up from a sack. Build your offense so it can score thirty points a game, and it won't do any good if the defense gives up forty. With a football team, all the pieces must be in place. Once that happens, then your outstanding players at the so-called skill positions can help make you a champion.

It was apparent what Parcells had to do as soon as he joined the Patriots: Make a quick study on personnel. Get rid of the deadwood and do it quickly. (A 2–14 team always has a lot of deadwood.) Before the 1993 season opened, Parcells went about completing this first step. The turnover was enormous. By the time the season opened, there were some thirty new players donning Patriots uniforms.

He also took a huge step through the draft when he made quarterback Drew Bledsoe the number-one pick of the entire league. Bledsoe was a six-foot-five, 220-pounder with an exceptionally strong throwing arm and quick release. He had started just twenty-eight games at Washington State from 1990 to 1992, but in that time established himself as one of the finest collegiate passers in the land. He capped his career by completing thirty of forty-six passes for 476 yards as Washington State topped Utah in the Copper Bowl. Bledsoe entered the NFL draft after his junior year and gave Bill Parcells a quarterback that the coach felt would be a cornerstone to a winning franchise.

Parcells also picked up linebacker Chris Slade and wide receiver Vincent Brisby as two of his three second-round choices. In addition, there were a number of trades, free-agent signings, and other non-roster players added. When the team reported to training camp at Bryant College in Smithfield, Rhode Island, the players found a very different kind of coach awaiting them. His former Giants players could have told them what to expect. Had they seen him in action, they would have thought he had never been away.

When he saw several players high-fiving each other during practice, he bellowed out, "You guys high-five every fucking thing. Wait until you beat somebody!"

Minutes later, he began getting on rookie Bledsoe, reminiscent of the way he always rode Phil Simms. "Let's go, Drew," he shouted. "This isn't homecoming against Oregon State!"

Bledsoe, apparently, got the message and knew what he was dealing with from the first. Or at least he thought he did.

"He's very easy to play for from the standpoint that you know exactly what he expects," the rookie quarterback said. "He's very up-front about it and then you can either do it or you don't do it. If you do it, he's happy with you and you can play. If you don't do it, then you're out of here."

One player who was already familiar with the coach was Reyna Thompson, who joined the Patriots as a cornerback and special-teams player. Thompson had been part of the Giants in 1989 and helped win a Super Bowl in 1990. Thompson saw a little bit of a change in the Parcells demeanor.

"I would say that the key thing is that now when he blows up, it's more direct," Thompson said, "where it used to be like a hand grenade going off or something. Now it's real pinpointed. It's like a direct hit on the target. But he has been a little bit—I don't want to say calmer—but a little bit more smooth than I recall. It's not a situation where he'll go up and whisper in a guy's ear. I think part of the reason he's so boisterous and to the point is so that the other guys can also benefit from the experience."

Looking to create the same atmosphere, the same formula, he used with the Giants, Parcells hired Johnny Parker to be the Pats' strength and conditioning coach, the same Johnny Parker he had brought to the Giants. He felt that the program Parker installed with the Giants had not only had a hand in limiting injuries, but helped foster team unity as well. The weight room was always off-limits to everyone but players and coaches; no press or any other visitors allowed. In addition, his coaching staff included longtime Parcells disciples Romeo Crennel, Al Groh, and Charlie Wise. His offensive coordinator was old friend Ray Perkins, who was Parcells's first boss with the Giants. Perkins had left the Giants to become head coach at the University of Alabama and, true to Parcells's prediction, he was back in the pros. The first one to offer him a job: Bill Parcells. Again, there was always the loyalty to old friends. The coach also acknowledged that he was prepared to work his team extremely hard.

"This is a murderous schedule," he acknowledged. "Two-a-days for six straight days is a tough schedule for any football player. I would say a lot of teams in the league are on a more moderate schedule now than we are, but I think we need more work than some of the teams. That's why we elected to push."

After one practice, the coach showed his tendency to be unpredictable and to surprise. It had been a rough practice, as usual, and the players thought they were about to be dismissed. Instead he held them there and had them run two hard, 220-yard wind sprints.

"Here's the deal," Parcells said. "I'm looking for players that have some staying power. That's part of being in pro football. If they can't take the whole deal—the physical part of practice, the mental part of practice, the hot weather, the coaches harassing them, those kinds of things—if they can't get through that and do it, then they don't have enough staying power. It happens every year. You see what happens to some guys, they can't do it."

The coach knew that staying power was what won games in the fourth quarter. Those who understood what he was doing, what he was trying to achieve, were only too happy to work through his arduous program. Marv Cook, who was the Patriots' backup tight end, summed up the feelings of many during that first training camp.

"[Coach Parcells] is very organized and very discipline-oriented," Cook said.

"He's a great leader. . . . He's been [to the Super Bowl] twice and he's won it twice. As a player, that's what your goal is. That's what we're excited about. . . . It's Bill Parcells. The players love to play for him."

The Patriots of 1993 were still not a good team. Bledsoe made rookie mistakes and was inconsistent, but showed great promise. He completed just under fifty percent of his passes—not good by today's standards—throwing for 2,494 yards, fifteen touchdowns, and also fifteen interceptions, and missing three games with a strained knee. That, however, was just part of the story. With thirty new players the Patriots were almost like a group of strangers, and it took a while for them to know each other. The team lost its first four, beat the Phoenix (formerly St. Louis) Cardinals, then lost their next seven. At 1–11, it looked like another total disaster.

Then in the final four weeks, the team started to jell. They won each of their remaining games, with their biggest victory of the season in the finale, a 33–27 overtime win against Miami, a game in which Bledsoe completed twenty-seven of forty-three passes for 329 yards and four touchdowns. There was little doubt that he had the talent to be a big-time quarterback. For the season, Leonard Russell ran for 1,088 yards, tight end Ben Coates caught fifty-three passes for 659 yards and eight scores, and rookie Vincent Brisby grabbed forty-five for 626 yards. The team was 5–11, a bit better than the 3–12–1 disaster in Parcells's first year coaching the Giants. The New Yorkers had quickly become winners in his second year. Because Parcells hated losing, couldn't tolerate it, he fully expected the Patriots to do the same thing in 1994.

CHAPTER FOURTEEN

Winning, Then Losing, Equals Problems

S HORTLY AFTER THE 1993 SEASON ENDED, THERE WAS A CHANGE IN the Patriots hierarchy that would eventually have a profound effect on the future of Bill Parcells and the entire New England franchise. James Orthwein was seriously considering moving the team out of Massachusetts, with Hartford, Connecticut, targeted as a potential landing site. The Patriots had been part of the Boston area since the team's inception in 1960. Once it became apparent that Orthwein was serious, Robert Kraft stepped into the breach.

Kraft was a highly successful Boston businessman who owned, among other things, Foxboro Stadium. He had been a Patriots' fan since *Boston* Patriots days of the American Football League, and a season-ticket holder since 1971. Not wanting to see his favorite team leave the area, Kraft did the pragmatic thing. He decided to buy the ball club, making Orthwein an offer he couldn't refuse. The NFL approved the transaction on February 25, 1994. Orthwein was out, albeit some $200 million richer, and Kraft was in. Unlike the previous owner, Kraft showed immediately that he wanted to play a major role in the everyday running of the team. If he was going to write the checks, he wanted to know about the people receiving them. The first year he took it slow, watching how his coach and team performed.

That performance turned out to be one of the big surprises of the 1994 season. The Pats didn't have a strong running game; Leonard Russell left via free agency and the team's top rusher turned out to be journeyman Marion Butts, acquired in a trade with San Diego. Parcells also signed, via free agency, three former Giants: linebacker Steve DeOssie, safety Myron Guyton, and guard Bob Kratch. He always felt comfortable having familiar faces around, especially players he knew could perform, and those he considered Parcells guys. Because they knew him and reflected his values, they could only be a good influence on the others. None of that, however, was surprising. The surprise was that the team won and, being a Parcells team, the way they did it.

"Bill was strictly a power-football guy when he coached the Giants," said writer Will McDonough. "He designed the team that way specifically so he could beat the Washington Redskins, who were bigger and stronger at the line of scrimmage in his first few years. He simply went out and got bigger and stronger players than they had. When he came to New England he didn't have those kinds of guys. He knew he couldn't play power football, even if he wanted to.

"So he turned Drew Bledsoe loose and began throwing the ball all over the field. With no running game whatsoever, he got the team on a terrific run the second half of the year. Throwing the football and playing finesse defense did the trick. And he showed for the first time that he was capable of changing his coaching style to adapt to whatever he had, doing whatever it took to win.

"I know he still preferred playing power football, to hold the ball and keep the defense off the field. That's always been his whole philosophy, but if he can't do it, he's not going to sit there and watch his team not score points."

Perhaps Parcells himself described his own ability to adapt and change when he talked about wanting players who have the desire to reach their own potential.

"The ability I have as a coach is to see the end picture," he said. "I've been around long enough to know what it takes to get a team to reach its potential, and I want players who want to reach their potential. Because I feel I can see the end picture, I'm less tolerant than I used to be, less tolerant of mistakes and players who aren't giving everything. I'll tell you when I knew that was the way I had to be: right after I almost got fired."

Once again he was referring to his first year with the Giants, the now infamous 3–12–1. It was almost as if that single season continued to haunt him the rest of his career, haunt and motivate him at the same time. At any rate, he unleashed Bledsoe right from the opening bell and didn't rein him in for the entire year. Wide-open football was not his thing, but if his vision of the end picture were to end positively, it was the only way to get there.

The Patriots scored thirty-five points in each of the first two games . . . and lost both: to Miami 39–35, then to Buffalo 38–35. But the tone was set. Against the Dolphins in the opener, Bledsoe threw the ball fifty-one times, completing thirty-two for 421 yards and four touchdowns. He also had a pair picked off. A week later, he aired it out forty-two times against the Bills, hitting on twenty-six for 380 yards and three scores. But again, two of them were intercepted. The team then won its next three, with the quarterback throwing fifty or more passes in two of them.

The streakiness continued in the form of four more losses that dropped their record to 3–6. It was beginning to look like the same old Patriots. Then in Game Ten, against the Minnesota Vikings, the Pats won a 26–20 overtime thriller in Foxboro. In that game, Bledsoe threw the football seventy times, completing forty-five for 426 yards and three scores. It was a game the Pats trailed 20–0 with fifty-eight seconds left in the half. Bledsoe completed four straight passes for forty-eight yards, enough for Matt Bahr (another former Giant) to kick a thirty-eight-yard field goal, putting the Patriots on the board. In the second half they tied it, and Bledsoe won it in OT by completing five passes in a row and hitting Michael Timpson with a fourteen-yard game-winner in the corner of the end zone.

The come-from-behind victory seemed to put the Patriots on the right track. With Bledsoe continuing to throw and the defense coming together, the team ran off six straight wins, not only getting over the .500 mark but also suddenly moving into playoff contention. The sixth victory was a 41–17 triumph over Buffalo, bringing the Patriots record to 9–6. It wasn't the victory that was so impressive, but the way they won it. Buffalo scored on its first three possessions, taking an early 17–3 lead. The old Patriots would surely have mailed it in the rest of the way. However, these were the Parcells Patriots of 1994. Bledsoe and company tied it by halftime, then forced five Bills turnovers after intermission and completed their run of thirty-eight unanswered points to the final gun.

"This was our best game of the year," the coach said, afterward. But he continued to tell anyone who would listen that his was an "upstart" team that didn't have great talent. Another Parcells ploy, trying to lull the opposition to sleep and maybe motivate his team at the same time. He tweaked them even more by saying that teams without great talent can win.

"There are a lot of teams that have won that don't have those things," he said. "It's [a question of] can you just, for the day that you're playing the important games, can you be at the top of your performance level. Can you muster up enough energy and will and fortitude and whatever else it takes—toughness, preparation. Can you do it at the right time?"

The coach also felt his team was beginning to understand how to handle adversity and come back from early deficits. "This team can still be night and day," he said. "It wasn't going very well [early in the game], in case you didn't notice. On the sidelines there was no sense of chaos. There was no sense of panic. There was nothing but determination. At halftime I told them, 'We've taken their best shot and we're even. Now, let's see if they can take ours.' "

The overachieving Patriots obviously believed in their coach and were almost playing to him, to his challenges, to his daring them to rise and beat teams with more talent. They finished running the table the following week, beating Chicago with a fine 13–3 defensive effort to finish at 10–6. Miami also won, so the Patriots were the wild-card team, but in the playoffs nevertheless.

The one stat worth mentioning, besides the surprising final record, was that Drew Bledsoe threw the football more than any other quarterback in NFL history: 691 times. He completed four hundred of his passes, four short of Warren Moon's record, for 4,555 yards and twenty-five touchdowns. There were still lapses—he was picked off twenty-seven times—but there was little doubt as to how the Patriots were winning.

Tight end Ben Coates also had a great season, with ninety-six catches for 1,174 yards and seven touchdowns. Michael Timpson had seventy-four catches for 941 yards, and three other receivers caught fifty or more passes. The team scored 351 points, while the defense gave up 312. The Patriots were the surprise team of the 1994 season and Bill Parcells's reputation as a coach with an innate ability to produce winners continued to grow.

Despite the Pats' unexpected regular-season success, the playoffs proved another story. It was a really a matter of "he who lives by the pass, dies by the pass." New England traveled to Cleveland to meet the AFC Central Browns in the wild-card game and came up on the short end of a 20–13 score. Once again Bledsoe put the ball in the air fifty times, completing just twenty-one for 235 yards. He had a TD pass, but also threw three pickoffs. Since the Pats had no running game, the Browns were simply laying back to stop Bledsoe's aerial attack.

By contrast, Cleveland quarterback Vinny Testaverde threw just thirty times but completed twenty of them for 268 yards and a score. Testaverde had the benefit of a running game that provided him with 125 yards of support, while the Patriots runners combined for just fifty-seven yards. As disappointing as it was, the season gave Pats fans hope for the future, but the coach knew that there was still a lot of retooling necessary before his team could seriously contend for a championship.

It was at this point that owner Kraft decided that Parcells needed some help. On February 6, 1995, the owner appointed Bobby Grier Director of Player Personnel. Grier had been an assistant coach and since 1993 had been the club's Director of Pro Scouting. Parcells, of course, felt he didn't need help with personnel. Because of his penchant for surrounding himself with his type of player, Parcells guys, he always preferred to have the final say on all personnel decisions. Now he would have help, help he didn't appreciate. It was the beginning of a deteriorating relationship between coach and owner, one that would soon put them on a collision course.

In a way, it seemed a strange time for Kraft to make that kind of move. All Parcells had done was take the 1–14 team he inherited to 10–6 in two years. Yet Will McDonough, who was friends with both men, already sensed the relationship beginning to go sour.

"I had become aware through conversations with Kraft and Parcells of a growing mutual dislike between them," he said. "Parcells considered Kraft a meddler and double-talker. Kraft regarded Parcells as an ingrate and someone who had no respect for him. At the same time, Kraft thought Parcells had done a poor job of selecting talent."

That was difficult to fathom, especially with the team having completed such a surprising season. Because Grier was new to the position, the draft calls were made mostly by the coach in 1995. It would prove an extremely beneficial draft. The top pick was cornerback Ty Law of Michigan; the second, linebacker Ted Johnson of Colorado; and the third, running back Curtis Martin of Pittsburgh. All three would become starters as rookies and play a large role in the team's future fortunes. In addition, another Parcells guy joined the team when he signed former Giant Dave Meggett as a free agent. Meggett would become the team's kick-returner and a situational running back, a valuable contributor.

With Curtis Martin looking like the real deal, Meggett providing a valuable backup, and Bledsoe a year older and more experienced, it seemed the offense should flourish. Defensively, there was still work to be done, but the D had held its own for much of the previous season. When the team opened with a 17–14 victory over the Cleveland Browns, the team that had knocked them out of the playoffs the previous season, everything seemed back on track. New England had won the game with a clutch fourth-quarter drive, and many of the writers and observers were saying that the 1995 Patriots should challenge the Miami Dolphins for AFC East supremacy.

Parcells, of course, wasn't getting excited. "I told the players in the locker room after the game to be happy and enjoy it," he said. "But this is a marathon we're in, not a sprint. It was only one game. We've got a long way to go yet. I'm still not sure if maturity was the overriding factor today. Every year is different. Every team is different. The question is, how's this team going to respond when it's down 17–0? How's it going to respond when it's ahead? Those are the things that need to be answered every year."

The coach admitted he was happy with his team's eighty-five-yard winning drive, with rookie Martin taking the ball over with just nineteen seconds left on the clock. But he cautioned everyone about getting too pumped, citing his displeasure with the Pats' special teams and the "too casual" way the defense played in the last nineteen seconds, when only a dropped pass prevented the Browns from getting a chance to kick a field goal for the tie.

"We didn't finish the right way," said the ever-cautious coach. "If that guy had caught the ball and gone out of bounds, we would have been in overtime."

Martin had gained 102 yards on nineteen carries in his first pro game and had the look of a guy who could singlehandedly give the Pats a running attack. At first glance, then, the team looked more rounded and balanced than the ball club of a year earlier. That makes what happened next a bit difficult to explain. In a nutshell, the roof suddenly fell in on the Patriots and on Bill Parcells, something that almost never happened to a Parcells-coached team that had seemingly found its legs and its winning ways.

First it was an early season showdown against Miami in which the Pats came up on the short end of a 20–3 score. Next came the always-tough

San Francisco 49ers. Parcells tried to confuse the air-minded Niners, opening up with a 3–2–6 defense, a nickel defense, instead of the expected 3–4. It threw the Niners off stride to the point where they didn't score until thirty-five seconds before the half. The problem was that the Pats hadn't scored at all. In the second half Steve Young and his receivers adjusted and cruised home with a 28–3 victory.

Parcells was already getting testy. After the Miami game he banned the press from practices and drove the team mercilessly, having them dress in full pads all day. It didn't help.

"I'm just going to have to think about it right now," he said, after the San Francisco game. "This is not a good time for me to comment on what I'm going to do. It was pretty much the same story [as it was against Miami], with the exception that we added some turnovers today. San Francisco has a good team, and I congratulate them. But like I said, I've got problems of my own. I can't worry about congratulating them too much."

The next week was open, then the club lost to Atlanta 30–17, with Bledsoe out with a slight shoulder separation. He came back only to quarterback a 37–3 debacle against the Denver Broncos. Suddenly, the team was at 1–4, the euphoria of the 1994 season long gone. If there was any chance of the team turning this season around, it would have to happen almost immediately. It didn't look good, however. While Curtis Martin had given the Pats a running game, Bledsoe was still throwing fifty passes a game. In the first four in which he played, he threw the ball 205 times without a single touchdown pass. The offense was out of sync and the defense wasn't playing as well as it had in '94. In five games, the team had been outscored 129–43—despite the addition of some strong personnel. None of it reflected well on anyone.

"I'm running out of patience," Parcells growled after the Denver game. "There's lots of players I'm mad at . . . for what's going on down here. But I take responsibility for that because I'm the one that's allowed this to happen somehow. When you feel like . . . your team has better ability than what they're showing, then you feel like you're failing as a coach."

It had to be a trying time for a coach who not only hated to lose but also thought he was on the brink of putting together a very solid team. In truth, while there were more front-line players, many of them were still very young. Behind them, however, there wasn't a great deal of depth. Remember, the most difficult sport in which to turn a team around is football, with a forty-five-man roster. A contending team has to have the backups as well as the stars. Parcells said as much by stating, "I think maybe I assumed that there was a little more maturity here than there really is."

There was also a question of the coach's staying power. He was now fifty-four years old. Maybe the two-year layoff also took the edge off his ability to drive and motivate a team. Someone asked if he felt he was still capable of leading a team to a title. It was the kind of question he might have ignored, or chafed at, in better times. Now, he answered it.

"I would hope so," he said, quietly. "Right now, it doesn't appear that I'm doing that."

In a nutshell, everything was going wrong. The stress of losing that other head coaches had spoken about now appeared to be getting to Parcells. A week later the Patriots lost again, 31–26 to Kansas City. After the game, the coach complained of not feeling well. Doctors determined that he was suffering from dehydration. It wasn't serious, but just another indication of the kind of season it had been. Murphy's Law: Whatever could go wrong was going wrong.

Despite his hatred for losing, Parcells never stopped coaching. A 1–5 record doesn't mean you throw in the towel. You keep working with the young players, trying to teach and motivate, trying to assess which players will help you next year and which ones must go. And you try to win. You always try to win. A 27–14 victory over Buffalo took the team out of its dive. Beginning with that game, the Patriots won five of their next eight, making their record 6–8 after fourteen games. Two more victories and the team would finish at .500. At that point, as well, there was a still a mathematical chance to grab a wild-card spot in the playoffs.

Then came a Saturday game at Three Rivers Stadium in Pittsburgh. It was an old-fashioned barn-burner that was tied at 27–27 late in the fourth period. With just 1:28 left in the game, the Steelers' Neil O'Donnell hit Ernie Mills with a sixty-two-yard bomb for the go-ahead score. The kick made it 34–27. As Parcells gathered his team on the sidelines, he told them, "We've got time."

After the kickoff Bledsoe went right to the air, connecting with tight end Coates, who tried to struggle for a few extra yards, was gang-tackled and fumbled the ball. Pittsburgh's Chris Oldham grabbed the loose pigskin, took off, and ran it all the way in for another score. Two touchdowns on two plays gave the Steelers a 41–27 lead and the game. It also finished the Patriots for the year. At the press conference afterward, the losing coach was asked the inevitable question: Would he be back again next season?

"I hope so," Parcells answered, adding the old caveat that as always he had to check his gut feelings once the season was over. "You really need to step back from it and get away from it and think it over. This game involves a stronger commitment than anyone in here really knows."

He also said that one bad season was not enough reason to make him quit. "Let me tell you about football and me," he continued. "There is no possible chance that I will leave this game being bitter. There are a lot of people who . . . leave their profession bitter. There is no chance that will happen to me. Zero. This game has been great to me. It's been a good livelihood. . . . So there is no chance that I'm ever leaving this game with anything but good feelings."

As to 1995, he acknowledged that he hadn't expected this kind of outcome. "Am I disappointed that we've got six wins? Yeah, I'm disappointed. I really am disappointed. [But] this year isn't over yet and I've got a lot of things to talk over with Mr. Kraft. But by and large I [still] enjoy the game very much."

He didn't sound like a coach ready to pack it in. Yet at the same time there was always that postseason gut-check, an analytical look deep inside oneself to see if the fire was still burning. Every coach has to have it. If you just go through the motions, you don't do justice to the team, the fans, or yourself. Parcells knew this. If he couldn't be Parcells, he couldn't coach.

The following week the Patriots ended the season with a 10–7 loss at Indianapolis. The reversal was complete. The team had gone from a surprisingly good 10–6 in 1994 to a surprisingly bad 6–10 in '95. The offense had scored fifty-seven fewer points (351 vs. 294) than a year earlier, while the defense gave up sixty-five more (312 vs. 377). Not a good ratio.

Offensively, Curtis Martin had been an instant star, gaining 1,487 on 368 carries while scoring 14 touchdowns. He had all the earmarks of a big-time running back. Despite the strong running game, Bledsoe still put the ball in the air 636 times, an average of nearly forty passes a game. Yet this plethora of passes resulted in just thirteen touchdowns via the air lanes, while sixteen of his throws were caught by players wearing the opposing uniform. Once again he was inconsistent. The big P for potential still hadn't been lifted from his resume. He needed to improve. As with many young teams, the Patriots also had trouble finishing, on both offense and defense. The team continued to lack both depth and confidence. The depth would come from acquiring more of the right players. The confidence had to come from within, by way of Bill Parcells.

Three days after the season ended, the suspense about the coach's future was put to rest. The Patriots announced that Parcells would indeed return for the 1996 season. However, the public pronouncements made to the press on the day after Christmas belied an undercurrent that would grow in intensity during the coming months, a time when Parcells would encounter the worse possible scenario—a battle of wills with his boss, team owner Bob Kraft—which clouded his future at the very time he was trying to coach his team. But on this day, at least, everything seemed to be coming up roses.

"I'm looking forward to next year with a lot of anticipation," Parcells said. "In fact, I'm looking forward to it as much as I have for any season. I know I have the support [of Bob Kraft] to get the team back into the playoffs, where I believe it should be."

Just two weeks earlier he had told the press he had to be away from the game before he could assess his own feelings. It must have been a quick assessment, undoubtedly based on the fact that Parcells did not want to go out on a losing note. He still believed in the team and must have felt they were close, that the 6–10 of 1995 was an anomaly, not truly indicative of the talent level but rather the by-product of young players who simply lacked experience.

"I feel fine now," he continued, answering the usual questions about the state of his health, adding that he would undergo a complete physical the following month, "I do this every year at this time, and I expect everything will continue to be as it has been, which is good."

Parcells also talked about improving Bledsoe's performance at quarterback, saying that the strong-armed signal-caller had failed to fulfill the potential he had shown in his first two seasons. Though no one knew it at the time, what the coach discussed next would serve as a foreshadowing of events to come, creating a rift in the hierarchy that couldn't be repaired. He was asked about stories that he and Kraft were already in disagreement over the team's priorities at the upcoming draft. There were reports that the owner wanted to go after one or two wide receivers, while the coach favored getting a top defensive lineman.

"I've said he's a little bit of an offensive owner," Parcells said, smiling at his perhaps intentional play on words. "I tease him about that."

The coach then confirmed that personnel decisions would no longer be his alone, that they would be discussed and decided upon by a four-man committee—Kraft, personnel director Bobby Grier, vice president of business operations Andrew Wasynczuk, and himself.

"I don't think I'm stubborn, I don't think I'm narrow-minded," Parcells said. "Some of the things I've done haven't worked too well, and I'd be the first to admit it. But if you're batting .500 in this business you're doing pretty well, and a lot of people aren't. When I came here, it was with the intent to fix this franchise to the best of my ability and to make it competitive. It wasn't when I got here. I was hopeful we were moving in the right direction, and we were . . . and we're not as far removed from it now as it might appear."

By mid-February, everything seemed on course. It was announced that the Patriots had hired Bill Belichick as assistant head coach and to work with the defense. Belichick had been Parcells's defensive coordinator with the Giants, and had recently been the head coach of the Cleveland Browns before his dismissal following the 1995 season, the year the Browns moved the franchise to Baltimore.

"Bill Belichick is one of the most respected defensive coaches in the game today," Parcells said. "He was an instrumental part of my staff for eight seasons in New York and helped build one of the premier defenses in the league at that time. He is familiar with everyone on my staff and will be a tremendous asset to the team."

The hiring of Belichick completed the picture. Not only was Parcells's right-hand man back in the fold, but Belichick would also play a major role in the drama that was to come. In fact, Belichick would figure prominently in both Act One and Act Two, which was still several years down the road. Suffice to say, his hiring in 1996 was strictly business, Parcells bringing in the best man for the job.

At this time no one outside the confines of the inner circle surrounding the Patriots knew what had transpired in the months leading up to Parcells's proclamation that he would return in 1996 and the hiring of Bill Belichick. The college draft was coming up at the end of April and, outwardly, that would be the next thing on the agenda. To fully explain what happened next, however, it necessary to backtrack a bit.

Parcells's original five-year contract with the Patriots was signed with former owner James Orthwein in January 1993. It contained a clause that stated if the coach decided to leave at any time before the contract was completed he would have to pay the owner his salary for that season. The contract would pay Parcells $1.2 million for 1996 and $1.3 million for the final year of 1997. But there was something else, something the coach would come to see as a loophole.

When he joined the Patriots, Parcells made a separate marketing deal with a clothing company called Apex One. It gave him the rights to the clothing worn on the sidelines by Patriots personnel. In 1995 Kraft bought the rights for $800,000, to be paid out over three years. In other words, Kraft would pay Parcells $400,000 in September 1995, which he did. The next payment was to be $300,000 on September 16, 1996, and if Parcells was still coaching the Patriots on that date, he would be paid the final $100,000 in September 1997.

What no one knew at the time was that Parcells gathered his coaches together the night before the final game of the 1995 season and told them his tentative plan. It was related to Will McDonough by Al Groh, who was the Pats' defensive coordinator that year.

"[He] told us he had a plan, and we should know what it was," Groh said, "because it concerned all of us. He said that he was going to meet with [Kraft] and offer him $300,000 to get out of the final year of his contract. He said that if Kraft did not want to do it, then he probably would not be coaching here in 1996. The next meeting we had, he said that Kraft agreed to it, so he was going to coach for one more year, and that was it."

Why did Parcells think that a $300,000 payment would get him out of his contract, when the document stated he would have to return the final year of his salary—over a million dollars—in order to leave early? It turned out that on January 12, 1996, Parcells had signed an amendment to his original contract that deleted the final year, 1997, as well as his $1.3 million salary for that year. There was, however, a paragraph in the amendment that stated that if he didn't coach New England in 1997, he could not coach anywhere else. Parcells said later that he signed it without consulting his attorney or his agent, Robert Fraley.

"It was my fault," he told Will McDonough. "I was stupid. I should have been smarter than that."

Apparently, Parcells had also signed a separate agreement giving up the $300,000 he was due for the clothing deal. This one said nothing about his coaching arrangement, yet he mistakenly thought it would let him out gracefully after 1996, allowing him to coach elsewhere, if he chose, in '97. He told Kraft to use that money to help bring Belichick in as assistant head coach. This had all transpired by the end of February and when it was done it looked as if things would go along smoothly, at least through the 1996 season. The problems, however, weren't over yet.

The next crisis came the first day of the 1996 draft, April 20. Parcells still wanted a defensive lineman. Will McDonough, whose beat is the NFL, asked Kraft about the Patriots first choice and was told it would, indeed, be a defensive lineman. The owner mentioned three names: Cedric Jones, Duane Clemons, and Tony Brackens. When McDonough relayed to Parcells what his owner had said, the coach agreed, "That's right," he said. "One of those defensive linemen. That's where we need the help. We stink on defense."

But there were also rumors that Kraft really wanted to draft Terry Glenn, a top-flight wide receiver out of Ohio State. When that was mentioned to Parcells, he said no.

"We're not taking a receiver there," he said, sounding definite. "We're going to get the defensive lineman and then get the receiver at the top of the second round. There still will be some good ones left around."

The Patriots had the seventh pick in the first round that year. When it came time for the choice, Parcells announced that the team was picking Terry Glenn. Later, the coach would say that Kraft called him and Bobby Grier into a private office just before it was time to pick.

"I didn't know what was happening," he would relate. "Then they said that Glenn was going to be the pick. I said we had agreed it was going to be a defensive player and that was it. I was mad as hell. I said, 'OK, if that's the way you want it, you got it.' "

After that, Kraft and Grier took over the rest of the draft. Parcells felt they had made a fool of him. "When the draft was all over," said Al Groh, "Bill called us all together and told us that this was done to publicly humiliate him and that he would never forget it."

As it turned out, the team didn't pick a defensive lineman until the fourth round, using their fifth pick. Their second choice, defensive back Lawyer Milloy of Washington, would turn out to be an outstanding player, but it was still apparent that the draft had not gone the way the coach wanted and that the actions of Bob Kraft had produced a chasm between the two that couldn't be repaired. Then, in early May, Parcells went to play golf in a threesome that included Will McDonough. He told the *Boston Globe* writer that he had almost resigned about a week and a half after the draft.

"For about twenty-four hours, I made up my mind I was finished here," he said. "I didn't want any more to do with this guy [Kraft]. But now here's what I'm going to do. I'm going to get in the greatest shape of my life. I already started to lose weight. I'm not leaving here 6–10. I'm going to come back here and prove I'm better than that.

"I did a lousy job. I know that. But next year we've got a chance to be pretty good. I'm just going to have as little to do with this guy as I can and just focus on coaching the team. Then when it's over, I'm out of here. I'm going to retire. This will be my last year coaching."

It wasn't the first time, and wouldn't be the last, that Bill Parcells reserved the right to change his mind. Obviously disgusted by the events of the past few months, he probably felt if he could put the Patriots back on a winning course it would then be a good time to pack it in. Yet by early June there was a story that Parcells and Kraft had met to discuss the situation and it both parties felt it was workable and beneficial to the Patriots, that Parcells might indeed coach again in 1997. Parcells would later tell McDonough the story was true.

"That's right," he said. "If I want to come back, I come back. If I don't, I'm out of here free and clear. That's the deal."

Yet just a week or so later, with training camp getting close, Parcells again met with McDonough. He had lost twenty-five pounds and according to McDonough looked great and seemed happy. Once again, however, he talked about working his tail off coaching in the upcoming season, then stepping down.

"I don't need the money," he said. "I got a house here. I got a house in Florida. I'm going to sell my house in Foxboro, spend the winters in Florida and the summers in New Jersey."

As for Bob Kraft, he claimed his biggest issue with Parcells was the lack of respect. He told McDonough, "I almost fired him right after the draft. I had it up to here with that guy. It just isn't any fun to go down there. [What happens with Parcells] is my decision. I own the team. He works for me. With me, it's a matter of respect. We give him everything he wants, and still he shows no respect for me."

In a sense it was like two kids playing in the sandbox and fighting over who gets to fill up the pail with sand. That's usually when the owner of the pail threatens to take it and go home, and neither will have any fun. Here, the stakes were higher. The acrimonious feeling between the two men, as well as their ambiguous—I'm out, I'm in; you're out, you're in—

protestations could only hurt the team. As with any business, it's only as good as its product and, in the long run, the man capable of best putting that product on the field in 1996 was Bill Parcells. Deep down, both men knew it . . . at least for one more year. If they couldn't resolve their differences, business or not, there would probably have to be a split after 1996. But for the moment, Bill Parcells was still the coach and his objective was the same as always: to get his team into the playoffs and beyond.

CHAPTER FIFTEEN

Super For A Third Time

S O MUCH OF WHAT HAPPENED WAS BEHIND THE SCENES THAT MOST of the Patriots' fans didn't know how deep the rift between the two men had become. Sure, there were stories in the local press, especially when the draft disagreement arose. It was also made public that the coach had agreed with the owner about leaving the team following the 1996 season. But the public pronouncements almost made it seem like a mutual admiration society.

At the beginning of May, Kraft issued a statement saying that he had agreed to a request from Parcells to shorten his five-year deal to four. "At the same time," Kraft said, in his statement, "we agreed that at the end of this season, if there were a mutual feeling that he should coach the Patriots beyond the 1996 season, he would have that opportunity. I believe we have one of the best coaches in the NFL. Bill continues to have my full support, professionally and personally."

Parcells, for his part, didn't comment at the time of the statement. But he had made public comments that indicated he had no problem distancing himself from personnel moves and leaving them to others.

"I am not the general manager," he said at his year-end press conference after the 1995 season ended. "I don't care about control, I never wanted that. . . . I am not one of those guys who wants to call all the shots."

A strange statement coming from a guy who was always involved with every aspect of his football team. When he was with the Giants, Phil

McConkey said, "his fingerprint was on everything, from the captain of the team to the assistant ballboy. It was a dictatorship, but that's really the only way it can be. A total dictatorship."

Dictators demand control. When Parcells was asked during an HBO profile in 1999 about his battle with Kraft in New England, he answered this way. "I would have liked to coach another year with the Patriots, but I didn't feel I was in control of my situation."

So the public statements from both coach and owner were seemingly a matter of making nice for the press, sugarcoating what was slowly churning in the cauldron and might explode at any time. The only thing that quieted matters down for awhile was football. When the new season rolled around, Bill Parcells didn't have time for extracurricular battles. He had a football team to prepare. If 1996 was, indeed, going to be his last year in New England, and perhaps his final year as a coach, he wanted it to be a memorable one.

He worked the team hard and rode the players hard during training camp, a typical Camp Parcells. Terry Glenn, the wide receiver and first draft choice, as well as the man the coach didn't want, took his share of the Parcells wrath. Parcells even dubbed the wide receiver "she" at one point, causing some flap within the team.

"Coach Parcells stayed on me the whole training camp," Glenn would say. "Little gestures, know what I mean? I knew he was serious. He wanted to see if I was tough."

An old Parcells ploy, especially with a rookie. *"You're shit, kid. Prove to me you aren't."* But Glenn wasn't the only one. Parcells chided and challenged Bledsoe to prove his number-one selection three years earlier wasn't a fluke, made sure Curtis Martin didn't become complacent after his outstanding rookie year, and kept telling the entire defense that they would have to play better than they had a year earlier. He rode herd on everyone, including his assistant coaches.

Parcells probably had more loyal assistants than anyone, coaches who followed him from college days. Some, like Belichick, left when there was opportunity elsewhere, then returned when they once again needed a job. Knowing the man and his ability, Parcells would take him back. Brad Benson, the outstanding Giants tackle who was also one of Parcells's guys, remembers the way the head coach was with his assistants, even back in Giants days.

"I had a chance to coach with him one year in training camp," Benson said. "It was after I retired and he was trying to talk me into coaching. Anyway, I had a chance to see him in action when he met with coaching staff. He was relentless with these guys. I remember him ripping Romeo Crennel, just ripping him. But Crennel was with him for years, and all [the assistants] were intensely loyal to him."

It's sometimes difficult to explain the loyalty to the coach. He isn't easy on anyone. He doesn't even allow his assistant coaches to talk to the press, a rather autocratic dictum in an age of free speech and a probing, sometimes swarming, omnipresent press. Yet his loyal assistants remain mum, letting the big man do the talking. As usual, Parcells has his reasons, even though they sound as if they strain the bounds of logic a bit. He explained the what-for of his long-standing practice during a 1999 interview.

"I don't want anybody's agenda to come out but mine," he said. "The coaches don't have the big picture. They're going to get talking about subjects that aren't in their domain, and they're going to have an opinion, and someone's going to entice them to say something, and it may be in direct conflict with what someone else says.

"I've seen assistant coaches talking in the press. I know coaches that were going behind the head coach's back, calling members of the media, telling them things right in this town (New York). . . . If they're doing it with me, they'd better do it in a closet."

He obviously wanted his coaches to coach. That was the extent of their job. Teach and coach. Keep everything inside the team. When he explained why he didn't want them speaking to the press he made it sound as if he didn't trust them completely, or at least trust their judgement. Yet these coaches were as loyal a group as you could find in the NFL. There are two things that can be gleaned from this. First, don't believe that Parcells doesn't want complete control of his football team. If a coach puts a permanent clamp on his assistants, he is making sure all control stays with him. The buck not only stops here; it belongs here. At the same time, there was a kind of magnetism in his personality that somehow made his assistants overlook the very rough edges—the abrasiveness, the churlishness, the stated and unstated reminders that *I am the boss!*

Parcells ran as tough a camp in 1996 as he had ever run. He wanted his team out of the gate fast. It's more difficult to right a sinking ship than it is to keep one operating at full speed, especially in a sixteen-game season. Yet with all the preparation, the Patriots opened the season exactly the same way they debuted in 1994—losing to division rivals Miami and Buffalo. The Dolphins beat them 24–10, and the Bills triumphed by a 17–10 count. Someone was quick to point out that when this happened in '94, the team rebounded to finish 10–6. The question was which Patriots team would this one more closely resemble, that 1994 team that did bounce back, or the '95 version that had a disastrous 1–5 start and wound up 6–10?

More disconcerting was that Bledsoe once again looked liked a mediocre, mistake-prone quarterback. He failed to complete fifty percent of his passes in the first two losses, including a twenty-one of forty-six effort for 210 yards against Buffalo. Then in Week Three, everything suddenly changed. It was as if this team, one that certainly had enough talented players, had realized that it was time to grow up. That, and the persistent prodding of their coach, finally began showing results.

It started with a 31–0 whitewashing of Arizona. The Cards weren't a great team, but the Pats won decisively and received a fine performance from Bledsoe, who completed twenty-one of thirty-five passes for 221 yards and three touchdowns. More importantly, he didn't have to put the ball in the air sixty times and he didn't throw an interception. In addition, Terry Glenn, the receiver Parcells didn't want, was beginning to look like the real deal as well. After missing the first game with an injury, Glenn caught six passes against Buffalo and came back to grab six more in the win over Arizona. Teamed with tight end Coates, newcomer wide receiver Shawn Jefferson, Martin, and Meggett, the Pats had more than enough players to catch the ball. In addition, Martin was proving that his rookie year wasn't a fluke. He continued to look like a big-time runner, dependable and durable, as strong in the fourth quarter as he was in the first.

That was the beginning of a surprising turnaround. After Arizona, the Pats beat a good Jacksonville team 28–25, then topped Baltimore in a shootout, 46–38. After losing to Washington by five, they beat Indianapolis, Buffalo, and Miami, avenging both opening season losses. They beat the Bills 28–25, then shocked the Dolphins 42–23. Against Buffalo and Miami, Bledsoe completed more than seventy percent of his passes, hitting sixty-two of eighty-six in both games combined for 792 yards. Finally, he was playing at an All-Pro level. In the closing seconds of the Miami game, the usually surly coach walked over and embraced his improving quarterback.

"That was something that doesn't happen all the time," said Bledsoe, afterward.

How true. Bledsoe had been hearing the opposite for more than three years, getting the full treatment from his coach. Parcells was always smart enough not to push too hard, especially with players he knew could help him.

"I'm a jerk three-quarters of the time," he said, laughing. "So they have to see another side once in a while."

It was a time for some laughter. The team had won six of seven to bring its record to 6–3 and a share of the AFC East lead with the Bills. Nothing heals better than winning. Will McDonough saw the difference in Parcells. "During the season, [he] was as happy as I've ever seen him," McDonough said. "He liked his team. They had some players he had drafted at the beginning who were coming of age. Drew, Curtis Martin, and some of the others were giving them big years. In his mind, he was keeping Kraft at arms length and getting his job done."

It was at this point in the season that the speculation began anew as to whether he might return to the Pats in '97. As usual, there were rumors. There was even one report in the New York press that Parcells would turn up as the coach of the New York Jets the following year. He made it a point to call that a "very distasteful" rumor. He said, outwardly, that his immediate goal was to simply coach his team.

"I'm coaching this year the best I can, trying to get my team as far down the road as we can get it," he said. "Anything else is separate and distinct from that."

He also told the press that the 6–10 finish the year before had really affected him adversely because he felt the team was much better than that. "When you're 6–10, you have to rethink what you're doing," he said. "I don't feel like I got everything out of the team last year. Very seldom have I ever felt that way. So I said to myself, 'Parcells, you better get your butt in gear and get going.' I made a promise to myself that I was going to enjoy this season and the players, regardless of the outcome."

Then there were the stories about Parcells changing his mind and now wanting to come back to the Patriots, even though he had gone to great lengths the year before to get the final year lopped off his contract. Will McDonough reported that Bob Kraft called him on October 30 and said, "Your boy wants to coach again. Asked me about it today."

The "your boy" was a reference to Parcells. McDonough admitted being surprised, because Parcells had told him he was through after 1996, that he would retire from coaching. Kraft couldn't resist getting in a dig, adding, "See how this guy changes? He does it all the time. Now he wants to coach again."

McDonough immediately put in a call to Parcells, who confirmed what Kraft had said. The coach explained it to McDonough this way.

"[Kraft] was talking to me about all the stuff in the media about us not getting along and how it was hurting the franchise," Parcells said. "I told him, 'OK, let's do something about it right now. We can end all of that stuff with a new contract. Let's talk right now.' He told me that I really didn't know what I wanted to do, and he didn't want to talk about it until the year is over."

Kraft's reluctance to re-sign Parcells, even to negotiate with him, was understandable—the acrimony between the two had been so great just a short time earlier, with the coach adamant about not coming back, almost quitting before the current season began, and Kraft angered to the point of nearly firing him. Kraft may not have been an angel in the fray, but he was right about Parcells's now-you-see-me-now-you-don't act. For one of the few times in his life, the coach seemed to be reacting to his emotional swings. When things were bad and seemingly getting worse, he wanted out. Now that the team was winning and again looked like a ball club with a future, he suddenly thought about staying. Kraft was basically calling for a time out. This part of the drama would have to continue later.

A week after the big win over Miami, the Pats almost suffered a letdown. They traveled to the Meadowlands to meet the Jets, a downtrodden team that had won only a single game all year. Lo and behold, the Jets suddenly looked like world-beaters and raced off to a 21–0 lead by the second quarter. The Patriots got one TD back before the half, but still faced an uphill climb in the final thirty minutes. If the team was going to become part of the NFL's elite, it simply couldn't lose a game like this. At halftime, Parcells knew he had to challenge his team.

"If you carve out a championship," he told them, "it will be with you the rest of your life. A prime example was the guy last night. There's still time to win the game. You need to decide if you want to be champions."

The "guy last night" was Evander Holyfield, who had just KO'd Mike Tyson in one of boxing's monumental upsets. Parcells would use any means at his disposal to motivate his team. Whether the challenge ignited a spark or whether the talent level simply evened out, the Patriots began dominating as soon as the third period began. Bledsoe caught fire, throwing to Glenn, Coates, and Jefferson as well as his running backs. At one point at the end of the second and into the third quarter, he completed eleven straight passes. The Pats were closing the gap. Finally, with 6:45 left in the game, the Jets were clinging to a 27–24 lead and the Patriots had the ball. They moved it to their own 49, where the drive stalled and the team was faced with a crucial fourth-and-two. On the sidelines Parcells signaled for them to go for it.

Bledsoe fired a quick-out to Coates, who was tackled almost immediately. The Jets thought they had stopped the big tight end, but the line judge spotted it just far enough upfield for a first down. To most observers it looked like a bad spot in the Patriots' favor. But good teams need some luck, as well. Several plays later Bledsoe handed the ball to Martin, who took a couple of steps toward the line, then turned and flipped it back to his quarterback—the old flea-flicker. Bledsoe then hit Terry Glenn for a 28-yard gain to the two. A quick pass to veteran Keith Byars gave New England what would be the winning score in a 31–24 victory.

"I'm trying to win the game," Parcells said, when asked about his fourth-down gamble. "I just had a feeling we could do it. We made it. Just by inches, but we made it. We've been showing some maturity. But the comeback today wasn't about maturity. It was about getting your butt kicked and having enough guts to get back up. We've been talking about [being a champion]. I've been trying to point out to them what it takes to be one of those."

Bledsoe had been white-hot in the second half, completing seventeen of twenty-two after intermission with a pair of touchdowns. For the game he completed 70.6 percent of his throws, the third straight time he was over the seventy-percent mark. After ten games he had eighteen touchdown passes as opposed to just eight interceptions. It was apparent that this was finally a breakthrough season for him. In winning seven of their last eight games, the Patriots were averaging thirty-two points per contest, leading their coach to say that he now had as much confidence in the Patriots' offense as he had in the Giants' defense years back.

"Some guys are club fighters," the coach told his players. "Other guys have the heart of champions."

The game with the Jets was interesting for another reason. The New York press had been on the Jets' situation for years, a team that never seemed able to rebuild or get to the elite level. The latest Jets coach was Rich Kotite, who had previous coaching experience with the Eagles. Now in his second season with the Jets, Kotite's record going into the game with the Patriots was a dismal 4–21. There was already speculation whether the Jets' owner, eighty-two-year-old Leon Hess, would admit his mistake and dismiss Kotite at the end of the year. So it was natural when the Patriots came to town that comparisons would be made with Bill Parcells, still so much a hero in New York because of his successful tenure with the Giants. Oh, how Jets fans would love to see Parcells coaching Gang Green and hopefully giving them a shot at the Super Bowl, a place they hadn't been since the 1968 season.

When asked about the Jets' situation, Parcells was diplomatic. "I think Rich has done an excellent job of holding the team together," he said. "They've improved as the season has gone on. That's what I go by."

Most other people went by the bottom line: wins and losses. One writer even put it this way: "Imagine going from Kotite to Parcells." He also found a common denominator, cornerback Otis Smith, who was cut by the Jets in late September and had signed with the Patriots. Smith was asked to compare the styles of the two coaches.

"Richie [Kotite] is more of a laid-back coach; Bill is really aggressive, more hands-on," Smith said. "Richie lets the position coaches do the coaching [in practice]. If Bill sees a mistake, he jumps on it right away and doesn't let it happen again."

Smith also said that the two coaches treated injured players differently. "Richie gives you a rest when you need it. Bill doesn't do that. He expects you to get over little nicks immediately. Richie will give you a day or two to rest up. . . . You're talking about two totally different coaches."

And, apparently, with two different kinds of results. The Jets would continue to plummet, failing to win another game all year. The Patriots, however, kept it going, bouncing back whenever they hit a bump in the road. They encountered a bump the following week, losing to the Denver Broncos 34–8. It would be their worse loss of the year. But the team showed its mettle, coming back for big wins over Indianapolis (27–13) and San Diego (45–7), before beating the Jets for the second time, this one much easier at 24–20. The only disturbing thing about the big loss to Denver was that the Broncos were considered the class of the AFC and heading toward a 13–3 season. The Patriots and Parcells must have wondered if they were yet an elite team, having been handled so easily.

After beating the Jets the team sustained another tough loss, this one a 12–6 decision to the Dallas Cowboys, another top team. During the week approaching the game with the Cowboys there was yet another distraction.

A story in the *New York Post* on December 12 indicated the New York Giants might have an interest in bringing Parcells back as their coach. The Giants were still coached by Dan Reeves then, but in the midst of a losing season. Losing, it seems, always breeds speculation.

In the *Post* story, Giants' co-owner Robert Tisch reportedly said, "If anything happens with Dan [Reeves], and if anything happens with Bill, Bill's name will be part of the equation, I guess." Co-owner Wellington Mara, also asked to comment, said he didn't see why Parcells and Giants' General Manager George Young couldn't work together again, and that he didn't hold a grudge against Parcells for leaving after the 1990 season.

It was thought that Tisch's comments, in particular, might result in tampering charges against the Giants. No team is allowed to publicly covet or court a coach who is under contract with another team. The Giants, doing some instant damage control, quickly issued another statement to the press, making sure they also threw the Jets into the mix.

"Neither Dan Reeves, Bill Parcells, and Rich Kotite, nor George Young, Bob Kraft, and Leon Hess deserve to be subjected to any further tabloid trash talk," the statement read. "It is apparent that any statement whatsoever can be used to start a fire where none exists. Accordingly, the status of Dan Reeves or any other coach is a closed subject, and we will not answer any further questions on the matter."

Tampering or not, the can of worms had once again been opened, as least to the point where someone had pried the lid. Every Sherlock Holmes–style reporter began scratching around for comments and, hope-fully, answers. It wasn't surprising that someone approached Bob Kraft about the story.

"I can just answer that for the seven-thousand-six-hundred-and-thirty-seventh time," the Patriots owner explained, sardonically. "We said once the season's over, we'll sit down and talk and see what's in our mutual best interest."

Another reason for the speculation was a story in a Boston paper report-ing that Parcells could be leaving the Patriots after the season. That story stated that Parcells had talked with alleged "friends" about the Jets' situa-tion. Then Parcells himself, appearing on a Boston radio station, was asked about a comment he once made that the Patriots job would be his last.

"I think I can reserve the right to change my mind, okay?" he said.

Others wondered why Parcells would even consider walking away from a team that had rebounded (at the time of the story) to 10–4 and might have a chance to go to the Super Bowl, if not this year, then definitely next. Along the same lines, why would he leave a team that it took him four years to build, to start all over again with another down-and-out club? Finally, the irascible Parcells emerged as he was asked about the Patriots, Jets, Giants, and who knows what else for the umpteenth time.

"Here's what I'm saying: I'm saying I'm not answering any more questions about that," he snapped. "So it's going to be dead silence when that comes up. So write dead silence."

More and more, however, it was beginning to look as if Parcells wanted to continue coaching. There was a quote from his agent, Robert Fraley, saying that he did, indeed, want to coach next year, but only in the right situation. That was taken by some to mean a situation where he had total control. Kraft didn't seem inclined to give it to him, and he never had it with the Giants because of George Young's presence, and Young was still there.

Will McDonough confirmed that he had spoken to Parcells in mid-December and, at that time, Parcells stated that he did want to coach again, that he was having fun once more, and no longer had the health concerns that had plagued him for a number of years. Apparently, agent Fraley called Kraft on December 16, several days after all the speculation arose in the New York papers, and asked to talk about a new contract for Parcells. Once again, Kraft said he didn't want to talk about a new contract until the season was over.

"That was twice he had the chance to sign Bill and decided not to do it," Fraley told McDonough. "We got the message. He didn't want Bill to coach the Patriots again, no matter what happened."

That bit of information was not made public at the time. The Patriots still had one game left in the regular season, a December 21 meeting with the Giants, once again at Parcells's old haunt, Giants Stadium in the Meadowlands. It would mark the first time the Patriots and Giants had met in the regular season since Parcells took over the New England club, adding to the game some special significance for him. But for one half he probably wanted to bury his head somewhere in the end zone, or maybe even switch sides. It was the 6–9 Giants who were acting like a playoff team as they raced to a 22–0 halftime lead. Their defense had completely stopped the Pats' running game, while the offense capitalized on every mistake the Pats made. Bledsoe was called for intentional grounding in the end zone, which is a safety. A TD drive and field goal made it 12–0. A second Brad Deluiso three-pointer gave the Giants a 15–0 lead, then just before the two-minute warning, Jason Seahorn stepped in front of Terry Glenn, picking off Bledsoe's pass and returning it twenty-three yards for yet another TD. So much for that half.

Like the first game against the Jets, the Patriots made the second half theirs. Martin still couldn't get untracked on the ground, so Bledsoe's right arm had to take over. A field goal started the comeback in the third. Then early in the fourth quarter Bledsoe led a ten-play, eighty-eight-yard scoring drive by completing six of eight passes and finally hitting Glenn in the corner of the end zone from twenty-six yards out. The kick made it 22–10. Minutes later, Dave Meggett helped make it 22–17 by returning a Giants punt sixty yards for a score.

The winning score came with just 1:23 remaining in the game. The Pats had a fourth-and-seven from the Giants' 13. A field goal wouldn't help, so Bledsoe dropped back once more. He spotted Coates open and rifled a pass to his tight end at the Giants' two. Coates refused to go down when a pair of tacklers hit him and fell into the end zone with the winning touchdown.

"Everybody knows how I feel," Parcells said afterward. "I grew up just up the street here so this is a home away from home. This will always be my home."

Once a Jersey guy . . . "I was a little emotional because I wasn't sure how I was going to react," the coach continued, "but it's just very gratifying and not because it's the Giants. That doesn't make it any sweeter. I just mean it's gratifying to see these kids rally back and do what they did today."

What they did was finish the season at 11–5 and clinch the AFC Eastern Division title. That meant a bye in the first week of the playoffs and at least one game at Foxboro Stadium. The team had come all the way back from the 6–10 of a year earlier. The offense, led by Bledsoe, Martin, Glenn, and Coates, scored 418 points, while the defense gave up 313.

The old power-football coach now had a quarterback who had thrown more than six hundred passes for the third straight season, only in 1996 it was a much more balanced offense than ever before. Bledsoe was 373 for 623 for 4,086 yards and twenty-seven touchdowns with just fifteen interceptions. More importantly, his completion percentage was 59.9— the best of his career. Martin, in his second season, gained 1,152 yards on 316 carries, while Terry Glenn set a rookie record with ninety catches for 1,132 yards. Coates, still a clutch receiver at tight end, had sixty-two grabs for 682 yards and nine touchdowns.

In the final regular-season game, against the Giants, Glenn had eight catches for 124 yards and a touchdown. He was happy because, as with so many players who were doubted, then challenged, by Parcells, he felt he had finally proved himself.

"I got hurt with a hip pointer," Glenn said, "but I showed him I was mentally tough. I could see it in his eyes. Beating the Giants was something he really wanted for himself. And it was something we wanted."

It was almost as if the entire team was doing it for Bill Parcells. They felt they had let themselves and their coach down the season before. Now, he had challenged them to show the heart of a champion and they had learned their lessons, winning several games after being what appeared to be hopelessly behind. That was all the coach ever asked: play hard, don't make mistakes, don't quit. If they could carry that into the playoffs, there was no limit as to how far the team could go.

The Pats' first playoff game was against the 10–6 Pittsburgh Steelers, the AFC Central Division champions. The Steelers were known for their hard-hitting defense and were expected to give New England problems. The day before the January 5 game, Parcells was discussing strategy when he said, "[Rod] Woodson will come up on first down and try to intimidate my quarterback. We'll see if we can get him to bite on the up-and-go."

Sure enough, on the Patriots' first play from scrimmage cornerback Woodson came creeping up on Terry Glenn. Glenn faked, then sprinted past Woodson. Bledsoe hit him on the fly for the fifty-three-yard gain. The doors were open. Martin scored the first touchdown on a two-yard run in the first. Byars caught a thirty-four-yard scoring pass from Bledsoe later in the period. In the second, Martin burst right up the middle past the startled Steeler defenders and went seventy-eight yards for the third score. It was 21–0 at the half and all but over. The 28–3 final was a foregone conclusion. The Patriots had not just won, they had won impressively.

Martin and the offense controlled the football in a manner reminiscent of Parcells's Giants days. The second-year running back gained 166 yards on nineteen carries. Because the ground game was working so well, Bledsoe had to throw just twenty-four times, completing fourteen for 164 yards. At the same time, the improving New England defense held Pittsburgh's star running back, Jerome Bettis, to just forty-three yards on thirteen carries, while their quarterbacks were a combined sixteen of thirty-nine for just 110 yards.

The victory put the Patriots into the AFC title game, only they wouldn't be playing the team they expected, a team they might have feared. The day before they had beaten the Steelers so easily, the Jacksonville Jaguars had upset the favored Denver Broncos 30–27. The Broncos were the one team that had really blasted the Patriots in the regular season, winning 34–8. The Jags were just a second-year expansion team that surprised everyone by getting in the playoffs as a wild card. Now they had upset the Broncos. Will McDonough, for one, feels that the sudden change in matchups gave the Patriots a huge psychological boost.

"They got a tremendous break when Jacksonville had the stunning upset over Denver," McDonough said. "All of a sudden they began to think, if we beat Pittsburgh on Sunday, we've got the home field for the AFC championship against Jacksonville, and we already beat Jacksonville this year. I think there were two keys that opened the door—beating the Giants in that come-from-behind game to end the season, which got them at least one home playoff game, then having Jacksonville knock off Denver. All of a sudden they realized they had a great shot at getting to the Super Bowl.

"In other words, their talent was every bit as good as Pittsburgh's or Jacksonville's. Their talent was not as good as Denver's. Denver had absolutely kicked their butts two years in a row. So it wasn't likely that the Patriots were going to go out and win at Denver that year, but Jacksonville got it done for them."

The Jaguars were coached by Parcells disciple Tom Coughlin, who not only served as one of Parcells's assistants with the Giants, but was also a good friend. Coughlin had brought his expansion team in at 9–7 in just its second season. Then came an upset of Buffalo in the wild-card game, then the great victory over Denver that put Jacksonville on the brink of a possible Super Bowl appearance. Only Parcells and the Patriots stood in their way. Though it was business as well as a crucial game to each franchise, Parcells really didn't like coaching against such a close friend.

"I don't enjoy it," he said. "It's not pleasant for either of us. But that's the way the business is. He is one of my favorite guys I ever coached with. It's simple, really: I like him. Of all the things that are very important in a coach, he is all of those things. And he is not afraid. That's the main thing. He's got conviction."

Ironically, Coughlin was already known as one of the most demanding coaches in the game, a no-nonsense dictator who controlled virtually every aspect of the Jacksonville franchise. Sounds familiar. There were players who couldn't handle his tough style and complained about him in the Jags' first season. Now, however, the team was winning and the complaints stopped.

"I am proud of Tom and what he has done," Parcells said. "He's a terrific coach."

The game was tough from start to finish, with the outcome still in doubt right up to the final minutes. New England scored first, Martin finishing a first-quarter drive with a one-yard plunge. The kick made it a 7–0 game. In the second period, the Patriots kicked a pair of field goals while the Jags got one, making the score 13–3 at the half.

In the third quarter, both defenses gave up very little, the only scoring a twenty-eight-yard Jacksonville field goal. So moving into the final fifteen minutes of play, the Pats held a slim 13–6 lead. It was still anyone's game. Once again the defenses refused to yield, but in the last five minutes Jacksonville got the ball and began driving. With 3:43 left, the Jags had the ball at the New England five-yard line. It was second and goal as quarterback Mark Brunnell dropped back to pass. The southpaw signal-caller spotted tight end Derek Brown in the end zone and zipped the ball in his direction. At the last second, free safety Willie Clay darted in front of Brown and made what could have been a game-saving interception. Parcells and the Pats had dodged a bullet.

But it wasn't over yet. New England couldn't move the ball and had to punt it back to the Jags. Jacksonville now had it at their own 42 with 2:36 left, still plenty of time for Brunnell to engineer another drive. On the first play the Jags tried a draw, with Brunnell handing off to running back James Stewart, who ran straight ahead into the line. Patriots' linebacker Chris Slade went after the ball and got it to pop loose. Cornerback Otis Smith, playing Johnny-on-the-spot, grabbed the loose pigskin in midair and ran it back forty-seven yards for the game-clinching touchdown. The kick made it 20–6, and that's the way it ended. The Patriots were AFC champions and in two weeks would be playing in the Super Bowl!

The victory immediately put Bill Parcells in select company. He was about to become just the second coach in NFL history to take two different teams to the Super Bowl, joining Don Shula, who had done it with Baltimore and Miami. That, however, meant nothing at the moment. The coach knew there was still very little to celebrate. For the moment one game is over, you begin preparing for the next. Now the "next" was the big one, the Super Bowl. The Patriots would be underdogs to the powerful Green Bay Packers, led by the league's Most Valuable Player, quarterback Brett

Favre. Knowing what his team would be facing, Parcells didn't want them to get too full of themselves. He gave his players the AFC championship trophy, then walked away, his face still red from the cold, no smile, just a look of determination, a readiness to deal with what was to come.

Wanting to keep his players grounded, he made sure he tempered his remarks carefully, even when he spoke with the press the next day. "We played very well Sunday," he said. "Here's the difference. We played so hard, the mental errors we made did not show up. Even when we would do things wrong, we'd tackle the guy for a loss three of four times.

"We have to be careful not to overload this team; they were a little bit overloaded Sunday. On the line, we aren't using a couple guys for just three or four plays and others for seventy-two plays. Now, we're playing six to seven guys thirty or forty plays each."

Once again, however, he was proud of his defense. In the seven games since the team's blowout by Denver, 34–8, the defense had allowed just seventy-three points. After holding Pittsburgh's star running back Jerome Bettis to just forty-three yards in the first playoff game, the New England D held Jacksonville's Natrone Means to the exact same amount.

"On defense we're making plays, not just keeping it status quo, and we're giving our offense chances to score," said linebacker Ted Johnson. "We took a lot of heat, living in the shadow of our offense—and rightfully so. But things have changed."

As one writer said, they had won it Parcells's way, "a simple way. They ground out the game on a frozen Foxboro Stadium field." He went on to say that the stars were not the big-name quarterbacks or the outstanding running backs. Rather, the stars were the Patriots' defense, unheralded guys like Willie Clay and Otis Smith, who made the big plays when they had to. "They were the players who mattered yesterday," the scribe went on. "They made this a Bill Parcells kind of victory."

Now, it was down to one game. With two weeks between the conference championships and the Super Bowl, there was more than enough time for hype. Only much of the hype this time would involve a coach. As the game approached something very unique began happening, a kind of skewed perception on the part of the upcoming media bonanza preceding one of the major sporting events of the year. This was the first Super Bowl where there was more focus on a coach than on the two teams and the game itself.

Not surprisingly, that coach was Bill Parcells.

CHAPTER SIXTEEN

Bad Endings All Around

THERE WERE ALWAYS CRITICS OF THE TWO-WEEK GAP BETWEEN THE conference title games and the Super Bowl. Teams lose momentum and become stale, some felt. Others might overwork, drill too much, and leave their game in the locker room, coming up flat at the opening whistle. Maybe that explained why so many previous Super Bowls had resulted in blowouts. The fourteen days also gave the media time to work itself into a frenzy, reporters, writers, and TV and radio people from all over the world searching for stories in every nook and cranny, under every rock.

For Bill Parcells, the primary job was to figure out a way for his Patriots to defeat the Green Bay Packers, then—and maybe this was the toughest part—make the players believe they could do it. Unfortunately, that wasn't the only thing on his mind. There was always the overriding question of his future. Would he sign a new contract and return to the Patriots? Would he quit? Would Bob Kraft fire him? If he left, where would he go? Would he retire? Would he return to the Giants? Would the Jets rope him in? Would some other team suddenly enter the picture and land the Tuna?

The Tuna? That was a nickname Parcells had picked up way back in 1980, his first year in the NFL, when he was an assistant with the Patriots. The prevailing story was that one day a player tried to put something over on him. Wily even then, Parcells quickly spotted the transgression and quipped, "Who do you think I am, Charlie the Tuna?" Charlie the Tuna was a popular cartoon-like figure featured in commercials for a certain brand of tuna fish. Charlie was always trying to fool someone but getting caught, passed over for a better quality of tuna. Though none of Parcells's close friends used the nickname, the press loved it, especially in New York, where it was easy to coin quick headlines with word plays using a simple, four-letter word—Tuna—as a synonym for Coach Bill Parcells.

In retrospect, it is one of the more ill-fitting nicknames in sport.

At any rate, the speculation about Parcells's future, both immediate and long-term, was running rampant during the two-week wait. Add to that his reputation as a coach, motivator, and winner, and it led to even more stories. Some portrayed him as a modern-day Pied Piper, with his players believing so strongly in him that he could almost will them to win the game. At any rate, it seemed that the fourteen days before the game were filled by a steady dose of Parcells, Parcells, Parcells.

"Rarely has a coach been the focus of a Super Bowl week like Parcells has been during this one," one story said. "Not only is he by far the most recognizable Patriot, but Sunday's game against Green Bay is likely to be his last in New England, a subject he's unsuccessfully tried to dodge this week."

Another pregame story from the *Detroit News* included the following paragraph:

"The Tuna reportedly brought a team here [to New Orleans] which goes by the name of 'Patriots,' but no one really notices or cares. The Green Bay Packers are battling Parcells and his remarkable record, his savvy, his toughness, his ability to convince an undermanned team that it has a chance."

A third story, this one in the *Washington Post*, read, "If I had to win one football game to save my life, I'd pick Bill Parcells to be the coach. . . . Parcells has proven beyond a doubt that he's one of the great leaders of men not just in the NFL, but in all of professional sports. The Patriots believe so profoundly in their coach that there's no way the Packers are going to win the Super Bowl by fourteen points, if at all. Parcells is that good."

Parcells, Parcells, Parcells. Even his players couldn't stop talking about it. Safety Willie Clay, who made the key interception against Jacksonville, spoke for many when he said, "Guys believe in Coach Parcells like you would never believe. He's been here. He knows what he talking about."

So the team got ready, the reporters had their tongues wagging, and the writers kept pounding on their keyboards. Meanwhile, Will McDonough was right in the middle of the Parcells–Kraft situation, which wasn't getting any better despite some cursory efforts to work things out. McDonough apparently began hearing from Kraft shortly after the playoffs began. The Patriots owner was concerned that once the season was over and Parcells was gone, he (Kraft) would take a beating in the media. Because of the year the team was having, Kraft was wise enough to know that the Patriots' fans would not be pleased to see the coach leave. He said he didn't think he and Parcells should be critical of each other.

At that point it was a foregone conclusion that the owner–coach marriage was over. It was just a matter of how the split would be handled. As with most divorces, both parties wanted to come out with the advantage— both in the public's perception and the financial settlement. At that point, McDonough apparently relayed Kraft's fears to Parcells and the coach said he would not be critical when he left.

The day of the AFC title game, January 12, 1996, what was left of the relationship between the two men had taken the proverbial turn for the worse. That morning, Parcells had seen a story by Kevin Mannix in the *Boston Herald* which said there was a signed agreement between Parcells and Kraft that gave the Patriots the right to deny the coach permission to sign with another team unless New England was compensated satisfactorily. Parcells went nuts.

He told McDonough, "Imagine, we're here today playing [to go to] the Super Bowl, and Kraft is planting this garbage in the paper. This is unbelievable. This never stops."

McDonough then arranged a meeting between Parcells and Kraft. According to McDonough's story that followed the meeting, Parcells extended his hand across the desk to Kraft and said, "Bob, this is what I'm going to do. When the season is over, I say that it is time for me to move on. That I've enjoyed my time here. The fans were great. You treated me well. I wish you the best, and I even give you a plug for a new stadium. And the next day, you notify [NFL Commissioner Paul] Tagliabue that I am free and clear with no further obligations to the New England Patriots."

When he made the final statement, the one about no further obligations, McDonough said Kraft "withdrew his hand like a piston."

Finally, the battle lines were drawn. The next day the two antagonists met again and, according to McDonough, Kraft told Parcells flat-out that he would stop him from going to another team. By that night, Parcells had hired a Boston attorney to represent him. Without going into the legal details, it soon became apparent that a decision on the circumstances of

Bill Parcells's future employment would be made by Commissioner Tagliabue, and that the decision would have to wait until the season was
officially over. As for the Parcells–Kraft relationship, that ended the minute Kraft withdraw his hand at the January 12 meeting. It just hadn't been
made public yet.

But, as they always say in sports, there was still a game to play. In the
Green Bay Packers, the Patriots would be facing a formidable foe. The
Packers were 13–3 in the regular season, strong on both sides of the ball.
Quarterback Brett Favre was not only the league's Most Valuable Player,
but the team's on-field leader—a tough and resourceful quarterback who
would run through a brick wall if he thought it would help win a ball game.
He had also thrown a league-high thirty-nine touchdown passes that season, with just thirteen interceptions. He was the guy the Patriots knew
they had to stop.

"He's like a linebacker playing quarterback," said Patriots linebacker
Chris Slade. "The more you hit him, the better he seems to play. The guy
is dangerous."

The Packers' defense was no slouch, either, led by veteran defensive
end Reggie White, the NFL's all-time sack leader and a pro since 1984,
but a player who had never tasted a championship. He wanted one and
wanted it badly. White and his fellow defenders had given up just 210
points during the regular season, more than one hundred fewer than the
Patriot defense. In the playoffs, the Pack had won both its games easily,
beating San Francisco 35–14, and then the Carolina Panthers 30–13.
Those with the courage to pick the Patriots to win the Super Bowl were
few and far between. The consensus was that the Patriots' best chance to
win was Bill Parcells. There were actually some who felt that Parcells
would figure out a way for his team to win. That's the kind of reputation
he had. Many people though of him as something of a miracle man, especially when it came to winning big games.

At one of the final press conferences before the game, Parcells and
Kraft stood at the podium, side by side, and once again tried to give the
appearance of a mutual admiration society, a couple of old buddies working things out.

"I know there's been a little bit kinda swirlin' around here, so my final
statement on this to everyone is the same as it has been," Parcells said.
"Bob and I agreed a long time ago that we would go through this year and
we would discuss the situation about the future when the season's over

and we're gonna do that as expeditiously as possible, and I also can assure you that it's gonna be done in a very civil and a very friendly manner. That was our agreement and that's what we're gonna do as soon as this season's over. Okay?"

Kraft made a couple of jokes that didn't go over. Then, he added, "Also, I thank [Coach Parcells] for one thing: with everything that has been stirred up over the last week, three years ago and one day, to the day, we bought the team . . . and here we are in a Super Bowl. There's a pretty special karma going on, and we're excited about it, and I thank you for the opportunity."

Smiles abounded at the press conference as the lawyers continued to work feverishly behind the scenes. Cynics called it the Bill and Bob Show. By that time almost everyone knew that Parcells would be leaving, and probably not on a very pleasant note. In fact, there were even some New York writers who said that Parcells was basking in the sunlight, manipulating the media with the deft hand of a practiced politician and setting himself up in a no-lose situation. If the Patriots beat the Packers, his coaching reputation would be elevated beyond the top floor. However, if they were to lose, he had still brought a second team from the depths to the Super Bowl in a relatively short time, and his reward most likely would be a new contract in excess of $10 million, probably from the Jets.

Super Bowl XXXI was played at the New Orleans Superdome on January 27, 1997. Before Parcells took his team onto the field he reflected briefly on what it meant to be in this game for a third time.

"I probably appreciate this one more than the others in terms of gratification after all these years," he said. "I have a greater appreciation for how hard it is and how much it takes."

Whatever the game plan might have been, all bets were called off on Green Bay's second play from scrimmage. The ball was at the Packers 46-yard line and Favre dropped back, looking downfield. Then he fired . . . deep. Veteran receiver Andre Rison, streaking between a pair of Patriot defenders, grabbed the football and ran it into the end zone for a touchdown. The extra point made it 7–0 with just 3:32 gone. Already, the Patriots had to play from behind, and that's not a position any team wants to find itself in after less than four minutes of play. Then it got worse.

The Packers scored again on a thirty-seven-yard Chris Jacke field goal midway through the period. Worse yet, it was set up by an interception of a Bledsoe pass. That made the score 10–0 and, to many viewers it began to look like another one-sided Super Bowl romp, not a competitive game. On the sidelines Parcells told his offense not to panic, to stick with the game plan and they would move the ball.

On their next possession, that's just what happened. Bledsoe began moving the team, mixing running plays to Martin with several passes, including a thirty-two-yarder to Keith Byars. They drove downfield, and from the one the QB tossed a short pass to Byars in the end zone. Adam Vinatieri's kick made it 10–7. The next time the Pats had the ball, they did it again. This time the big play was a forty-four-yard pass to Terry Glenn. From the Packers' four, Bledsoe flipped a short pass to Coates for the go-ahead score. The kick made it 14–10 Pats with 2:33 still left in the first quarter. The momentum had definitely changed and it began to look as if Parcells might be walking off the field with yet another Super Bowl ring. Even some of the Packers were worried.

"We were completely baffled," said veteran Green Bay safety Leroy Butler. "We were missing tackles, they were flying right past us, and they were pushing us around. No one had pushed us around all year, and they were killing us, doing stuff we hadn't seen before. It was a great game plan."

It was Brett Favre who had the answer, however, Less than a minute into the second period he went to the bomb again, hitting wide receiver Antonio Freeman on what would be an eighty-one-yard touchdown. The kick made it 17–14 Packers and signaled another change in momentum. Before the period ended, the Pack would score twice more, on a thirty-one-yard Jacke field goal and a two-yard run by Favre. The game had turned into an offensive explosion, with the Packers taking a 27–14 lead into the locker room. It didn't look good for the Pats.

Parcells knew the third quarter would be key. For most of the period, however, the wide-open game of the first half turned into a defensive struggle, neither team yielding much. Then, toward the end of the period, the Patriots began driving. They brought the ball to the Packers' 18, where Bledsoe handed it to Curtis Martin. The star running back burst through a hole, turned on the speed, and ran it into the end zone for yet another touchdown. Vinatieri's kick made it 27–21, giving the Patriots and their fans hope. Unfortunately, that hope lasted for less than a minute.

On the ensuing kickoff, the Packers' Desmond Howard took the ball at the one, burst straight up the middle, made one cut to his left . . . and was gone: a ninety-nine-yard runback for a touchdown. It all but drove a stake through the Patriots' hearts. After the TD, the Packers went for a two-point conversion and made it, Favre passing to tight end Mark Chmura. The score came at the 11:50 mark of the third quarter, making it a 35–21 game. It would be the final score of the afternoon. Both teams were scoreless in the fourth period, giving Green Bay its first Super Bowl triumph since the 1960s heyday of Vince Lombardi. The Patriots had lost, a defeat that also somewhat shattered the myth of big-game invincibility around Bill Parcells. Still, the coach was gracious and analytical in defeat.

"I thought the game, obviously, turned on special teams," Parcells said afterward. "We were worried about [Howard], but I mean, you can't cancel the game. You gotta play it. But I credit him. He made some guys miss on his own. That's the first time this year we've been outplayed on special teams."

Outplayed, they were. Howard not only turned the game with his ninety-nine-yard kickoff burst, but was a terror all afternoon, garnering a Super Bowl-record 244 yards on kickoff and punt returns and being named the game's Most Valuable Player for his efforts.

"It is frustrating to get to this point and not take advantage of it," the losing coach continued. "I've been fortunate, you know, in the past to do that. I know how hard it is to get here. It is very disappointing to [lose], particularly in a game that I thought was fairly well played by both teams. I thought we kept it exciting for a long time."

Parcells had told his team their best chance for victory was to force the Packers to turn the ball over. Unfortunately, the Packers took care of the ball, while two interceptions of early Bledsoe passes led to ten Packers points. All told, Bledsoe was intercepted four times, the last two coming later in the game when the Pats were forced to play catch-up. Yet even Parcells admitted the Howard kickoff return had been key.

"In big games, when you fail to concentrate on just one play, that's when it could make the difference," he said.

What next? That question didn't escape too many people at the post-game press conference. Once more, however, Parcells deflected it with the same public pronouncement he had made during the two weeks leading up to the game.

"As I've said all week, I'm not going to do anything until I sit down and talk to Bob Kraft," was the way Parcells put it. "So you might as well try a different question."

When Parcells doesn't answer, he doesn't answer. Yet the next day

FOX-TV commentator John Madden reported that Parcells was not even going to fly home with his team. Madden suggested that the coach was already beginning talks with the New York Jets, the team most observers felt was most likely to hire him. Asked if the report about separate transportation was true, Parcells again made light of the report.

"Whether or not I'm going home with them doesn't make any difference," he said.

Even the players were aware of the impending changes. Drew Bledsoe, the first player Parcells picked when he was made the Patriots coach in 1993, certainly didn't sound like someone who wanted a new coach, not now.

"I told Bill before the game, 'Hey, it's been a great experience playing for you,'" Bledsoe said. "'I'm glad I've had the opportunity to play for you.' I don't know what's going to happen this off-season, but if Bill comes back, he gives us a great chance to be back here next year and possibly win the thing. Bill's proven time and again that he is a great football coach and we feel as a team that we believe in him. Especially after the way he was able to keep us focused these last few weeks. We believe if Bill comes back he gives us a great opportunity to be back here next year."

Bledsoe's comments were interesting. For one thing, it showed that the players did not know the full extent of the Parcells–Kraft rift, and thought there was still a chance that their coach would return. It also showed the respect that quarterback had for the coach, at least from a working standpoint. There had been stories from time to time over the previous four years that Bledsoe found it difficult coping with Parcells's pointed barbs, his sarcasm, his criticism—the usual stuff you get if you're a Parcells quarterback—and had often said the two were not exactly buddies off the field. Yet, in a way, he was making a kind of plea for his coach to return.

But Bledsoe wasn't the only one reacting to the rumors and stories. Veteran Keith Byars was another who felt a departing Parcells would be missed. "This team has all the pieces in place, and the centerpiece is Bill Parcells," Byars said. "We need to do everything in our power to make sure he stays. Hopefully, the organization can get it right.

"We need a guy like Bill Parcells. The way I feel about Bill Parcells is the way Bart Starr felt about Vince Lombardi. He's a great coach."

Guard William Roberts, who had played for Parcells with the Giants, thought the coach's loss would especially tough on the young players.

"If the coach leaves, it's going to have a devastating effect on the young players," Roberts explained. "In many cases, he's the only pro coach they've ever had. They've listened to him and they believe in him. Now they're going to get somebody else."

The team returned home on Monday, January 27. Parcells flew back separately. Three days later, NFL Commissioner Paul Tagliabue ruled that Parcells's contract with the Patriots was valid through 1997. For Parcells to jump to another team, that team would first have to ask Kraft for permission to talk with him, then arrange some kind of compensation, probably in the form of draft choices. The ruling fueled some speculation that Parcells might bite the bullet, coach the Patriots for one more year, collect his $1.3 million, then move on when he would be free and clear to make his own deal.

In fact, his attorney, Joel Kozol, made that very suggestion. Parcells nixed it in a second. He wanted no more of Bob Kraft. "Bill never wanted to go to court with this," said attorney Kozol. "He said only as the last resort. He wanted this to be settled by the NFL. We even told him to consider the option of going back to Kraft and calling his bluff on coaching the Patriots in 1997. But he didn't want any part of that. And believe me, I've got plenty of clients who would have done just that."

On Friday, January 31, 1997, Bill Parcells officially stepped down as coach of the New England Patriots. Three days later, on February 3, the Patriots named Pete Carroll as their new head man. Carroll had spent one season coaching the Jets in 1994, and for the next two years was defensive coordinator of the San Francisco 49ers. Now he was getting a second shot at being a head coach, and his first at replacing a legend.

At the same time, the speculation swirling around Parcells continued. Mike Lupica, writing in the *New York Daily News*, said what many people were thinking. "Parcells can do everything except make an exit," Lupica wrote. "He seems to be a terrific head coach and a terrible businessman."

Parcells had left the Giants after winning a Super Bowl. Now he was leaving the Patriots after getting them to a Super Bowl. The average football fan didn't want to hear about the infighting between coach and general manager, coach and owner. They didn't want to hear about multimillion-dollar contracts, long-term deals, a more comfortable situation, total control. All the average fan sees is a coach defecting, leaving a situation where he has been successful. They tend to resent him, especially when his replacement doesn't live up to the same level of success.

When Parcells left the Giants, he wasn't completely open about his health problems which, considering the private person he is, shouldn't be surprising. However, that left his reasons for departing open for speculation, and the transition wasn't as smooth as it could have been. Now, with the Patriots, things were even worse. The depth and finality of the split between Parcells and Kraft wasn't fully known by the public. To some, Parcells simply seemed like a mercenary, parlaying his success at bringing the Patriots to the brink of a championship in four years into a high-dollar contract with another downtrodden team in need of a savior.

Now, it turns out, he didn't even realize what kind of documents he was signing. One NFL executive was quoted as saying, "You have to wonder if Parcells understood the ramifications of his own contract."

In the eyes of some, Kraft was completely in the driver's seat. Parcells gave up $300,000 (part of the clothing-deal payment) for nothing. He would not be paid the $1.3 million for the final year of his contract. Sure, he might make that up elsewhere, but at what price? Now, if a team signed him, they would undoubtedly have to relinquish a number of top draft choices, mortgaging part of their future for a coach. The other side of that argument was simple. Getting Bill Parcells to coach your team is worth more than almost any draft choices. Draft choices are never sure things. As a coach who can forge championship teams, Parcells was.

The day after Parcells resigned from the Patriots, Kraft made it clear that the ball was in his own court, taking Tagliabue's ruling and using it like a trump card.

"I'm making my position clear," he said. "I'm not playing chicken. I'm not bluffing. I'm not even threatening. I'm just saying, 'Guys, if you want Bill as your coach in '97, make sure your first-round draft choice is there in its current position.' " Then he added a kind of veiled threat. "The longer it goes on, the more expensive a solution will be," he said, adding that he still planned to be "reasonable."

It became increasingly obvious that the team courting Parcells and the one he wanted was the New York Jets. This was a franchise starving for a winner. A New York team in any professional league is supposed to be a flagship franchise, but the Jets were doing little better than stumbling and bumbling. From 1994 to 1996, the team was in a downward spiral, going from 6–10 to 3–13 and finally to an abominable 1–15 in 1996. Team owner Leon Hess was known as one of the finest gentleman in sports. He was now eighty-two years old and wanted, more than anything else, to see his team win a championship. To be honest about it, he didn't know how much time he had left. He couldn't wait much longer.

All that made Parcells the logical choice. Not only did he still have a huge following in New York from his Giants days, his success with the Patriots proved he hadn't lost his touch. Now it was up to owner Hess and team president Steve Gutman to somehow get a deal done with Bob Kraft. There were ongoing talks, but nothing concrete was yet settled. That's when the Jets decided to make something of an end run, setting up a scenario that would continue to play out over the next three years.

On February 4, the Jets called a press conference for a major announcement. It took everyone—including Bob Kraft—by surprise. The Jets had made a twin-Bill hiring. Former Patriots defensive coordinator Bill Belichick had been hired as the Jets' new head coach. Surprised? Not yet. Bill Parcells had also been hired by the Jets. He would serve as a "consultant" in 1997, then on February 1, 1998, become the head coach and chief of football operations, while Belichick would become the assistant head coach, defensive coordinator, and heir apparent when Parcells decided to step down.

Kraft cried foul. "It's like rules don't matter for the Jets and Bill Parcells," he carped. But the Jets claimed that by making Parcells a consultant, they were not violating NFL rules or the dictate set down by Commissioner Tagliabue.

"Consultants consult," Jets President Steve Gutman said. "He does not make decisions. He does not run the football team. He does not coach the football team. This [double hiring] is designed to create an element of stability and create an opportunity to put a football program together, and have it last for a very, very, very long time."

As for Belichick, he also seemed happy with the situation. "I wanted to be with Bill," he said, "and I wanted to be in a good program. To be with Bill in a good program, that's the ultimate situation."

Apparently, negotiations with the Patriots broke down when Kraft insisted on the Jets' number-one draft choice. The Patriots quickly released a statement denouncing the Jets' signings.

"This so-called consulting agreement is a transparent farce," the statement read, "and the latest in a series of actions by the New York Jets and Bill Parcells which further demonstrates it has been their intention all along to have Bill become head coach of the Jets for the '97 season."

At this point everyone was jockeying for position, looking to secure the best deal for themselves and their teams. No one following the chain of events that had transpired since the end of the Super Bowl doubted for a minute that Parcells would be on the sidelines when the Jets opened the 1997 season. The posturing, the complaining, the statements, the threats, the Commissioner's rulings—all of it was just preliminary posing for the Jets and Patriots to finally agree on a deal that would free Parcells to coach. It was just a matter of time.

Ironically, the day after the Jets' announcement Commissioner Tagliabue put a freeze on the hirings, claiming he wanted to study the contracts of Parcells and Belichick before approving the deal. The next day, Parcells signed a $14.2 million, six-year contract that called for him to take over as coach following the 1997 season. According to terms of the contract, he would coach the Jets for at least four years. It was obvious that the whole messy business would soon be resolved. Three days later, it was.

With Commissioner Tagliabue acting as intermediary, the Jets and Patriots agreed on a compensation deal. The Patriots would get a third- and fourth-round draft pick from the Jets in 1997, a second-round pick in 1998, and a first-rounder in 1999. In return, Bob Kraft would release Parcells from his contract. As soon as that was completed, the Jets announced that Bill Parcells would indeed assume the head coaching position immediately. Bill Belichick would be assistant head coach and defensive coordinator. It was also written into Belichick's contract that he would be elevated to head coach whenever Parcells decided to step down.

Who said you can't go home again? After six years, Bill Parcells was doing it. But then again, Bill Parcells had been doing the unexpected for a long time. Would this, then, be the final chapter?

CHAPTER SEVENTEEN

Master Rebuilder

"I JUST WANTED TO MAKE SURE EVERYBODY KNEW I WAS IN THIS for the long haul," Parcells said, upon signing his six-year deal. "I'm going to coach a minimum of four years and hopefully more. We'll see."

Parcells also said the Jets were willing to write just two years of active coaching into his contract, but he was the one who asked them to up it to four years so the players wouldn't look at him as a short-term coach.

"In my mind I wanted to make sure the players here know that and that the fans know it," he said. "As long as I'm physically able to do it, I'm doing it. That's not a change in thinking. This deal was negotiated in a very short period of time."

Once again, Parcells was locking himself into a long-term deal. He had resigned from his "dream" job with the Giants after the 1990 season, and didn't finish the term of his contract in New England. Now he was saying he wanted his players to have "coach security," so he was pledging to coach at least four years, maybe more. As always, when Bill Parcells arrived on the scene, everyone was happy.

It was also at his introductory press conference that he uttered his now well-known line, which probably defined the real reason things had fallen apart in New England: "If they want you to cook the dinner, they at least ought to let you buy the groceries."

Control over personnel, the thing that had been taken from him in New

England, had now been returned to him with the Jets. After all the guessing, that was the biggest single cause of the rift. It was when Kraft pulled rank on his coach at the 1996 draft and picked Terry Glenn first instead of the defensive lineman the coach wanted that it all came apart. Parcells's buy-the-groceries-cook-the-meal analogy pretty well summed it up.

Now he was joining a franchise that had peaked nearly 30 years earlier, following the 1968 season. That was the year of Super Bowl III, when the Jets were in the process of being integrated into the NFL along with a number of other teams from the upstart American Football League, which had begun play in 1960. The NFL teams still had a patronizing attitude toward the old AFL teams, exacerbated by the Green Bay Packers' annihilation of the Kansas City Chiefs and Oakland Raiders in Super Bowls I and II. The next year, the Baltimore Colts, with a 13–1 regular-season record, won the NFL championship easily and headed into the Super Bowl to meet the Jets, a team that was 11–3 on the regular season but considered no match for the powerful Colts.

His team a huge underdog, brash Jets quarterback Joe Namath seemed to put his white football cleats squarely in his mouth when he "guaranteed" a Jets victory. NFL people laughed. Only they weren't laughing after the game, not after Namath and an opportunistic defense engineered a 16–7 victory, still considered the greatest single upset in league annals. The game not only helped make Namath a legend but also put the Jets and the old AFL teams on the map. They weren't inferior; they were equal.

However, the franchise couldn't stay on top. Two years later, the Jets had fallen back to a 4–10 record. It was 1970, the first year of the complete AFL–NFL merger and new league alignment. The Jets wouldn't have another winning season until 1981, the year Bill Parcells joined the crosstown Giants as an assistant. In 1982, the year of the strike, the Jets made the playoffs in a shortened, nine-game season. Then in the special Super Bowl tournament, a revised playoff schedule, they made it all the way to the AFC title game only to be turned back by the Miami Dolphins. It was their best chance to return to the top. Though the team had several more winning seasons in the 1980s, it never again reached the AFC championship game, let alone the Super Bowl.

Then came the mid-'90s crash. For some reason, fans latched on to the 1995 and 1996 seasons under Rich Kotite, and the aggregate 4–28 record, as a symbol of Jets futility. They complained that owner Hess didn't know how to run a football team and couldn't even find a coach who could rebuild the team. They saw the octogenarian as little more than a doddering old man, an anachronism hanging onto his toy of a football team, a man without a clue.

In his many travels, however, Hess, of Hess Oil fame, had a taste of a world that most mortals never see. He once even negotiated an oil deal with Libyan strongman Moammar Gaddafi.

"I had a meeting many years ago in Libya," Hess said, "and a revolver was put on the table. Well, I'm still here."

In other words, Hess could be tough when he had to. As an owner of a major sports franchise, he knew he had made mistakes. Most owners do. This time, however, he knew what he wanted. Parcells was the only candidate he considered for the Jets' head coaching job. Hess did not conduct a single interview once the Jets' season ended. He simply waited for the New England season to end, then went after his man.

"We were contacted by twenty-four highly qualified coaches," said Jets President Steve Gutman. "Leon's sights were set on the superstar we ended up with."

Bill dug in quickly and went to work. He surrounded himself with familiar assistants, many of them the usual cast of characters—Belichick, Al Groh, Charlie Weis, Romeo Crennel, Maurice Carthon, the loyal crew that seemed to follow him from job to job. The first order of business was to evaluate talent, both the players who were there from a year earlier as well as available free agents and college stars eligible for the April draft. Parcells was now a New York Jet. As always, he didn't like to talk about the past. Mention his tenure in New England, and you would find he had already relegated it to the realm of ancient history. That was often his answer when asked about the past, even the immediate past. *Ancient history*. What was important was the here and now, and that meant making sure the Jets were nowhere near the team that had been 1–15 in 1996.

Ironically, things were not so quiet in New England. Parcells had been gone just a little more than a month when Drew Bledsoe was quoted as saying some negative things about his former coach. At new coach Pete Carroll's first team meeting, the quarterback took Parcells to task for not addressing the team after the season.

"He didn't say anything to any of the players," Bledsoe told the Boston media. "You'd like to think that, when you go through some of the things we all went through with the guy, he'd at least say goodbye. But from the get-go, Bill has been about Bill. That's the way it is; that's the way he is."

How quickly people forget. Funny how if Bill was just about Bill, he seemed to take the rest of the team along for the ride, all the way to the Super Bowl. But Bledsoe wasn't finished yet.

"It's exciting to come in here to a positive atmosphere, where the coaches are excited about working with you and where you're excited about being here," he said. "It's not like before, when you came in every day wondering if you were going to get beat down. You always wondered what [Parcells] was going to say. Now you don't feel like somebody is waiting to cut you down when you come to work."

Bledsoe concluded by saying that he "wasn't dissatisfied with Bill. He has his style of coaching, Pete has his. Both can work. It just so happens that Pete's way suits me a lot better."

The quarterback wasn't the only one ready to take a shot. Linebacker Chris Slade was quoted as saying, "If I was getting $10 million and he was coming back, I wouldn't want to be there."

Maybe Bledsoe and Slade should have spoken with Phil McConkey and listened to the ex-Giant's theories about "the popular player's coach," something he always equated with losing. Or more pointedly, they should have heard what McConkey said when he was traded back to the Giants after a month in Green Bay.

"The grass is greener, my ass," McConkey told Parcells then. It would take Bledsoe, Slade, and some of the other Patriots a little longer to learn the same lesson McConkey had learned very quickly.

Will McDonough, who still covers the Patriots as well as the rest of the NFL for the *Boston Globe*, explained that it took Drew Bledsoe a couple of years to fully realize the impact Bill Parcells had on him.

"Drew came in as a twenty-year-old," McDonough said, "a kid who played for his father in high school and had an upbeat relationship with his college coach. He was a number-one draft pick and Bill always dumps on his number-one pick, to show the rest of the team that we're not gonna kiss this kid's butt, whether it's Drew or somebody else. For example, in training camp he always used to have his number-one choice go get the Gatorade.

"So for awhile they went head to head. But I think after Bill left Drew realized—and it took a couple of years—that this guy, even though he didn't like the way he did it, this guy was doing everything in his best interest to make him the best possible quarterback and football player he could be. I remember after the Jets beat New England the second time they played in 1998, Drew came across the field and congratulated Bill. That was the first time they had spoken since Bill left New England.

"A few days later Bill called Drew on a Wednesday and told him he wanted him to know that he was pulling for him, that he liked him, and that he tried to do all he could to make him a better quarterback. They have gotten along fine ever since."

McDonough also said there was reason for Chris Slade's remark. "Bill had benched Chris on and off during his final season in New England because he thought of Chris as strictly a pass rusher and didn't have confidence in him on rushing downs. When Bill left, the first guy they signed to a long term contract was Chris. He was still upset and said what he had to say. But I think after awhile, when the teams played each other, Chris also went up to Bill and talked to him."

It almost seems that Parcells has a delayed effect on players. Sometimes it takes a few years for them to realize there was a method in his madness. It can also take time for a player to know how much respect the coach really had for him. While they are with him, players are sometimes too busy dealing with his barbs and his challenges to forge a real relationship. Jeff Hostetler is a perfect example.

Hostetler was the long-suffering backup quarterback with the Giants, a guy who sat for nearly four years as Parcells deflected his trade requests and pleas to play. Hoss finally got his chance and wound up a hero in 1990, helping the Giants get to and win Super Bowl XXV. Asked to comment a few years later on his coach, Hoss made the previously mentioned statement: "I have nothing but great things to say about the man as a coach, but I didn't enjoy one minute of my time with him. I know that sounds strange, but that's how it is when you're around Bill Parcells."

Funny, Hostetler didn't enjoy one minute of his time around Parcells. Yet when he was called upon to play in the Super Bowl with limited experience he was ready, both mentally and physically. Then, when Parcells joined the Jets in 1997, Hostetler received a surprise phone call.

"He offered me the job of quarterbacks coach with the Jets," Hostetler said. "It was one of the most flattering calls I ever got when he asked me to join his staff, because he had never given the slightest indication I had earned his respect when I was with the Giants. But I honestly don't know if I could work with him. He makes a lot of demands, and I don't know whether I could make that commitment."

Hostetler decided to remain active as a backup in Washington that year, but the phone call that surprised and flattered him so much once again speaks volumes about a coach that many players don't understand and continue to have a difficult time tolerating. It takes time. As a coach, Parcells has said he can always see the end picture. Maybe it's that way with his players, as well. Maybe he knew it would take five or six years with Bledsoe, as it had with Simms. Who knows? Bledsoe didn't quite get it while Parcells was there. Neither did Hostetler. Both do now. That doesn't mean they love their former coach, but they do have a more complete understanding of some of the reasons for his success.

Could Parcells, however, do it one more time with the Jets? The 1997 version of the franchise had more talent than the 1–15 record of '96 indicated. Offensively, the team seemed quite capable of scoring points. Veteran Neil O'Donnell was the quarterback. He had been signed away from the Pittsburgh Steelers following the 1995 season. The Jets felt their huge, $25 million investment was worth it, since O'Donnell had led Pittsburgh all the way to the Super Bowl that year. Behind him was a feisty battler from Boston College, Glenn Foley.

Adrian Murrell was the team's top runner, a guy capable of getting 1,000 yards. The wide receivers could compete with anyone. Keyshawn Johnson had been the team's, and the league's, number-one draft choice in '96. A big-play, big-game guy, Johnson quickly showed he had talent, snaring sixty-three passes as a rookie and scoring eight touchdowns. That was during the 1–15 season, and Johnson was a player who hated losing. So he often sulked and complained, and showed a penchant for ripping teammates as well as the organization. Some thought he was lobbying for a trade to a west-coast team, since he had played his All-America college ball at USC. But at the outset of '97 he was still there.

On the other side was veteran Jeff Graham, a fine receiver for whom the Jets had also shelled out pretty big bucks. Young Wayne Chrebet, a sleeper out of Hofstra, had proved a gutsy, clutch pass-catcher who was especially valuable on third downs. He was a guy not expected to make it, but whenever cut time came around, the coaches couldn't seem to cross his name off. Add a couple of massive tackles, Jumbo Elliott from Giants days and David Williams, and Parcells had the makings of an offensive line. This was not a 1–15 offense.

The defense had given up more than four hundred points in 1996, yet had some fine individual performers, such as linebackers Mo Lewis, Marvin Jones, and Hugh Douglas; cornerbacks Otis Smith and Aaron Glenn;

and safety Lonnie Young. It was a defense that had no business being so porous. They needed direction and a few more talented bodies.

The holdover players seemed to sense a big change as soon as the new coach signed on. They knew things would no longer be the same.

"They finally got it right," said veteran defensive end Marvin Washington. "We went from laughingstocks the last two years to a legitimate football organization. I'm happy for the Jets. They finally got someone who can turn it around."

Safety Lonnie Young said the team had reached a point where they couldn't sink any lower. "It got to a point where we couldn't back up anymore," he said. "We had to go for the big fish. Thank God luck was on our side. We were finally able to land the big one."

Once training camp began it was the old Parcells again, working every angle at practice, ripping guys, questioning them, challenging them, his tongue as acerbic as ever, maybe more so. He knew that these guys were used to losing and he wanted to make sure that mentality changed fast. His former coach and friend Mickey Corcoran saw him in action at the Jets' training camp at Hofstra University and knew immediately that his protégé was beginning to work his magic.

"I was out there with a friend of mine and I said, 'Watch him, he'll interact with every one of these guys that he possibly can," Corcoran said. "When they're stretching, he's kibitzing with this guy, he's kibitzing with that guy. He interacts with all the players every chance he gets. I told you this before and I'll say it again: the player–coach relationship is the secret to coaching. He's a master at it and these guys [already] believe in him, and well they should. He's honest with all of them. He doesn't try to bulldoze anyone, just tells them what they have to do to win."

It wasn't long before the players sensed the difference. They already knew what kind of coach they had.

"He doesn't take losing lightly," said linebacker Hugh Douglas, "and he wants a smart team, no dumb mistakes. It's kind of to the point if you do something [wrong], you know you have to come to the sideline. You'd rather just leave. When I glanced over there, he just gave me this look. I don't even want to hear what he has to say. You know it's all bad. It's the kind of look you get from your father sometimes when he's about to whip your butt."

Keyshawn Johnson, who had been critical of just about everything in the Jets organization since he arrived on the scene the year before, did an about-face as soon as he met Parcells. "The thing about Bill Parcells is that he's not one of these over-the-hill coaches who keeps getting recycled," Johnson said. "He still seems like he's, you know, right there."

Parcells would soon learn that Johnson was a lot like Lawrence Taylor, his star linebacker with the Giants, in one respect. He didn't really have to be motivated. Johnson was one of the super-competitors who just wanted to win and would do anything on the field to accomplish that end. Johnson, in his west-coast way, was a Parcells guy, even though you might want to describe him as second-generation.

The definition of a Parcells guy hadn't really changed over the years, not since the days of guys like Carson, Taylor, McConkey, Benson, Simms, and Ottis Anderson. Keith Byars, the veteran who played for Parcells in New England, and would eventually join him with the Jets, said that the coach had certain requirements of players at each position.

"The wide receivers have to be guys who don't wear gloves and mittens on cold days," Byars said. "The running backs are the old down-and-dirty warhorses who could have played in any era."

Parcells himself defined what he wanted a quarterback to be. "They are battlers," he said, "players who pick themselves up and get back in the action. If there's one thing I can't stand, it's a quarterback who thinks playing quarterback is just about passing."

Once the preseason began it was apparent that this was not the same Jets team that had won just a single game a year earlier. Though the roster wasn't a whole lot different from '96, these Jets responded to Parcells from the start. They won their first three preseason games, and while those games didn't count in the standings, they meant something in that they helped forge a winning mentality. Now there was a single preseason game left, the Tampa Bay Buccaneers in Orlando—and the coach seemed to think he had his team headed in the right direction.

"[Playing in Orlando] gives us a chance to do some different things," Parcells said. "We haven't really played on the road and the hot weather will get us better prepared for various conditions. We need to get to the point where the guys can predict what I'm going to do. If they know what I'm going to do, then they can help me get there. I don't know how far we are from that. We need to get in sync with each other. We can't just be reacting.

"Winning is not doing dumb things and we still do too many dumb things. You have to learn how to take calculated and upside risks."

The coach also seemed pleased with his new quarterback, Neil O'Donnell, who was a Jersey guy like himself. Parcells had old friend Ron Erhardt as his offensive coordinator and he was just trying to get everyone on the same wavelength.

"Neil is in tune with what Ron Erhardt is doing," the coach said. "He just has to get a feel for me. There was so much pressure on Drew we had to start from scratch, and it's a completely different situation here. Neil has won before and thinks he has something to prove."

Did Bill Parcells have something to prove, as well? He said no. This job, with his third pro team, continued to be something of a labor of love. It wasn't any different from the year he took his hiatus from coaching in 1979 and tried selling real estate. He found he could do it, but also learned that he was a football coach, that football was where he really wanted to be, what he loved to do. Despite all the water under the bridge, nearly 18 years later the feeling was still there.

"I'm just trying to do this because I want to do it," Parcells explained. "That's the only reason I'm doing it. I don't feel like I have anything to prove to myself or anyone else. I just still like doing it. It's hard for people to understand that."

As the regular season approached, the Jets players could see that a fire still burned inside their new coach.

"It's hard to put into words the vibes that the players are feeling around here," said veteran running back Adrian Murrell. "It's definitely become a unit, as one. The guys actually want to play for him. He's definitely a teacher that you would like to please. I can see it in my teammates' eyes. I see the drive that I hadn't seen here [before]."

Cornerback Otis Smith had observed both sides of the coin. He started the 1996 season with the Jets, playing for Rich Kotite. Then he was acquired by Parcells and the Patriots for the stretch run. Now he was back and could sense something special immediately.

"When I first was employed by Bill Parcells and the Patriots, when I first heard him speak, I was like, "Whoa. There's something different here with this guy," explained Smith. "It's winning. Winning makes him tick. All he cares about his winning. Being a big-time coach and the aura of 'Mr. Bill Parcells,' I truly don't believe he cares about that. . . . He just cares about . . . not just winning football games, [but] winning championships, playing like champions, and walking around like a champion should walk around."

So the pre-season makeover seemed complete. Players knew what they were expected to do, what the coach wanted, what would and wouldn't be tolerated. Now it was the fans' turn to wonder. Would they be seeing the same old Jets, a team that not only failed to live up to expectations most of the time but also always seemed to find new and innovative ways to self-destruct and tumble out of contention? Of course, those Jets teams never had Bill Parcells standing on the sidelines, refusing to let that happen.

The Jets opened the 1997 season at the Kingdome in Seattle, playing a Seahawks team that wasn't upper echelon, but wasn't that bad, either. A good first test. There was a great deal of anticipation. Steve Serby, writing in the *New York Post*, felt a large segment of the pro football world would be watching the coach as much as his team.

"This is the day all eyes are on Parcells," Serby wrote. "This is the day every Jet fan, every Giant fan, every Patriot fan, every fan of football everywhere, really, wants to know how Parcells did at the start of his ultimate challenge only seven months after taking his third team to a Super Bowl in ten years."

There was so much emotion that day, so much adrenaline—it was as if this *was* the Super Bowl, so badly did the players want to come through for their new coach. They did. The Jets not only didn't resemble their 1996 counterparts, they looked like a combination of Lombardi's Packers, Noll's Steelers, and Parcells's Giants rolled into one. They just buried the Seahawks, 41–3, a debut so stunning that nobody could have predicted it. Neil O'Donnell looked like the second coming of Joe Montana when he threw five touchdown passes and made the Seahawks' pass defense resemble a block of Swiss cheese. It couldn't have started any better. Everything went right.

The next week, however, it didn't go so right. The Jets came home to an enthusiastic, packed Giants Stadium in the Meadowlands and were beaten by the Buffalo Bills 28–22. It was a competitive game, one the coach felt his team should have won.

"Overall, I was disappointed and pretty upset that we played the way we did," Parcells said. "But we've got to go forward now, take a look at this and see if we can improve upon it. If we can't, it's going to be a long year."

To make matters even more pressing, the next game on the agenda was at New England. It didn't take long for Parcells to tire of the questions regarding his return to Patriot-land.

"I'm going to say this one time and I'll end it for the week," he told the press. "There's no use to revisit history. I'm coaching *this* team. [The Giants] have a new coach. Their team is playing well, and we're hopefully going to play better than we did last week. That's going to be about it for me. I'm not getting into this revisiting history. It's not worth it."

That was Parcells. He never liked looking back. He would look ahead to playing the Patriots, but not back to when he was coaching them. Unfortunately, a number of his former players continued to take shots, talking as if they had been freed from coaching bondage. Patriots safety Willie Clay was the latest.

"Pete Carroll has turned the team over to the players," Clay said. "It's different this year. This is the New England Patriots, coached by Pete Carroll. It's our team. Last year, we were just players on Bill's team."

Interesting. As players on Bill's team, the Patriots went to the Super Bowl. Suddenly, a number of them were sounding as if they were unhappy. Would they be happier at 8–8, with a coach who gave them free rein to do as they please? Maybe with today's modern athlete, some of them would. But guys like that would never play for Bill Parcells. That wasn't what he was all about. His former players understood. Whether those playing for him in the late 1990s would ever understand might be a different story. Athletes were changing. Their values were changing. The money was changing. Not all of them, mind you, but enough. More than before. A coach like Parcells had to be even stronger. He had to continue to impose his will on young, wealthy players. He had to make them want to commit, to sacrifice, to do whatever it takes to win.

A week later the Jets went to New England and were beaten by the Patriots 27–24. Every loss hurts, but the Jets were certainly competitive and gave the Pats a scare, because the game went into overtime before being decided on a field goal. They were learning, though. In the next three weeks Oakland, Cincinnati, and Indianapolis all fell before Parcells's rejuvenated troops. Suddenly the club was 4–2 and had an upcoming date with tough Miami. What was more interesting, however, was that after just six weeks of the 1997 season the team had won as many games as it had in the last two years put together, through a total of thirty-two games. Better than that, the team was beginning to look like a playoff contender.

Miami, however, was still too tough. The Dolphins won the game 31–20 and it didn't make the coach happy. One Jet, who didn't want to be named, said he hadn't seen the coach that angry since his arrival.

"He was fired up. Just mad. Rage and anger," the player said. "I guess he feels some people didn't compete for sixty minutes. He didn't mention any names or anything."

At this point in the season, Parcells was still evaluating his players. He had basically the same team that had been 1–15 the year before. No superstars or impact players had been added. Yet he had the team at 4–3 almost halfway through the season and he had to be thinking that the team was good enough to sneak into the playoffs. The schedule, however, wouldn't get any easier. Coming up next was a rematch with New England. This was a game that would have a major effect on the future of the Jets franchise, because it marked the beginning of some eventual hard decisions that the coach would soon have to make.

In the first half, neither team could move the ball as the defenses dominated. The Jets' John Hall kicked a thirty-five-yard field goal in the opening period to give the Jets a 3–0 lead. In the second quarter, the Pats got two points for a safety, then three more on a field goal to take a 5–3 lead at the half. During the intermission, Parcells looked at the stats and decided that it was time for a change. He wasn't really happy with the way Neil O'Donnell had been playing in recent weeks. In the first half O'Donnell was just six-of-fifteen for fifty-nine yards, as the offense looked stagnant. When the team came out for the third period, the coach ordered young Glenn Foley in at quarterback.

After the Patriots scored on the first drive of the second half to take a 12–3 lead, there was even more pressure on Foley. But the youngster responded. Playing with the verve of a gunslinger who had ice water in his veins, Foley promptly directed a ten-play, seventy-four-yard scoring drive. On one play he hit Wayne Chrebet for a twenty-yard gain. Then he was the lead blocker on a reverse by rookie receiver Dedric Ward that gained twenty-one yards. After that he connected with tight end Kyle Brady for eighteen more, bringing the ball to the New England 11. A pass interference penalty put the ball on the one. Rookie Leon Johnson ran it in and Hall's kick made it 12–10 with 9:24 left in the third quarter.

"I was just going out there, going with the flow," Foley would say. "We have so many weapons on offense, you want to go out there and let them work."

But it wasn't over yet. Bledsoe came back to take the Patriots seventy-five yards in just five plays for yet another score. The kick made it 19–10 Pats. Foley, however, wasn't intimidated. He completed all four of his passes on an eight-play, fifty-nine-yard scoring drive, with Adrian Murrell taking it the final five yards. The Jets had pulled to 19–17 with 1:51 left in the third quarter.

In the fourth period, the Jets' defense shut down Bledsoe while Foley wasn't yet ready to call it a night. The young quarterback led his team on another eight-play drive, this one covering seventy-six yards. The longest play was a twenty-three-yard pass to Keyshawn Johnson, but Foley's five-yard toss to fullback Lorenzo Neal gave the Jets the go-ahead touchdown and ultimately a 24–19 victory, the team's biggest win of the season.

Foley had come on to complete seventeen of twenty-three passes for 200 yards and a score. He also completed fourteen in a row at one point. He was that hot.

"All I know is we needed a spark today," the coach said, afterward. "I think what's important today is we were able to win a big division game. That was a big win for us and will help our players' confidence genuinely."

Would it mean a playoff spot? Not yet. The following week, against the Ravens, the coach once again yanked O'Donnell, this time in the fourth quarter. The Jets won 19–16. After a 24–17 loss to the Dolphins, Parcells named Foley the starter against the Bears. Though the Jets won 23–15, Foley went down with a knee injury and O'Donnell had to finish up. A win at Minnesota the next week brought the team to 8–4 and first place in the AFC East. It looked as if coach and team were about to pull off a real miracle. Then the Bills beat the Jets 20–10, dropping the team to 8–5. Parcells was now increasingly certain that O'Donnell wasn't his kind of quarterback. Playing for the ultracritical Parcells, O'Donnell seemed to be increasingly fearful of making mistakes, and his conservative approach was hurting his game. Foley, on the other hand, had the kind of brass balls the coach liked. But he was injured and it was questionable whether he would be able to return.

The low point of the season came the following week when the Jets were beaten 22–14 by the 1–12 Indianapolis Colts. It was the game that would eventually cost them a playoff shot and one that left the coach searching for answers.

"This is the first day I've been a little discouraged since I've been working here," Parcells said. "Even though we've lost some games, I was never discouraged. But when you perform like we did [Sunday], you can't help but be a little discouraged, watching that. It's not down-and-out despondent. I was just very disappointed. Extremely disappointed."

On offense the Jets produced just 126 total yards, their lowest total in twenty years. O'Donnell was sacked eight times. Now the 8–6 Jets were a game behind both the Patriots and Dolphins, both of whom were 9–5 and held a tiebreaker advantage over the Jets.

"I take responsibility for [the loss]," the coach continued. "I'm embarrassed by it, I really am."

The Jets would bounce back to beat Tampa Bay 31–0 the next week, then meet the Detroit Lions in the final game. There was still a chance to make it as a wild card. But win or lose, Bill Parcells had again proved himself a coach who could build a winner quickly. He had essentially the same team that had been 1–15 the year before, now at 9–6 and on the brink of the playoffs. It was apparent that he hadn't lost his touch. He had been criticized for destroying the confidence of his starting quarterback, yet still had his team winning. The Parcells stamp was already on the franchise, but the coach knew his team had a final hurdle to clear.

"This game can make you wealthy," he said. "It can make you famous. It can give you a lot of things, but it can't give you a championship. You've got to earn that."

Against the Lions, the Jets didn't earn it. The Lions were playing inspired ball because they were trying to help their great running back Barry Sanders become just the third runner in NFL history to go over the two-thousand-yard-mark for a single season. Despite this, the Jets took a 10–0 lead in the first quarter. Hall kicked a thirty-two-yarder, and O'Donnell led a seventy-yard drive with Murrell going over from the 14. Meanwhile, the Jets' defense was stopping Sanders cold. Though the Lions managed a field goal in the second quarter to cut the deficit to 10–3 at the half, Sanders had just twenty yards. It looked as if he might not make his two thousand afterall.

In the third quarter, Jets fullback Richie Anderson had a pass bounce off him and into the hands of defensive back Mark Carrier. A Lions field goal followed and it was 10–6. Then at the end of the third quarter, Sanders went to work. He broke loose for a forty-seven-yard gain that helped set up his own fifteen-yard TD run, giving the Lions a 13–10 lead. While the Jets struggled offensively, Sanders's running began to control the game. The New Yorkers coughed the ball up twice more via interceptions, one thrown by fullback Leon Johnson on an option and the other by a little-known special-teams player, rookie Ray Lucas of Hofstra. Lucas had been a quarterback in college, and Parcells surprised everyone by putting him in during the third quarter, when he actually led a drive into the red zone before being sacked, then throwing the interception.

"We had a little package of plays for him," said Parcells, in defense of using Lucas.

In the end, it was all the great Sanders. In the final minutes he broke free for another fifty-three yards, enabling his team to run out the clock. The Lions won it 13–10, and Sanders finished with 184 yards on twenty-three carries for a season total of 2,053 yards, second-best in NFL history. A season of triumph and promise for the Jets had ended on a sour note.

"I thought our team played hard," Parcells said. "We came in here, it was hostile. [The players] tried to win the game as best they could today. I'm proud of them for that. But the factors that cause you to lose stay the same. We lost the ball twice inside the 30."

The playoff dream was gone, but a 9–7 finish following a 1–15 debacle was considered one of the great turnarounds in sports history. Remember, a football team is the toughest to turn around in the major sports. Once again Parcells was lauded as a great coach. His defensive staff, working with the same players, fielded a team that allowed just 278 points, a far cry from the league high 454 a year earlier. The team cut its turnovers from forty-six to twenty-two, and all the players felt they were learning how to win.

Still, it wasn't enough for the redoubtable coach. When someone asked if he was going to watch the playoffs, he said sure, then added, "Hey, we should be playing in one of these."

He was also asked what he told his team after the final game. He answered quickly, "I told them I'm going to recommit my efforts and I need a recommitment from them to move on. We're not a talent-laden team right now. We need to get more players. That may be hard for us to do because we're missing some draft choices and we don't have any money [under the salary cap]."

Yes, there would be more players. Parcells the coach worked his magic by playing the hand that was dealt him. Now Parcells the master builder would go out and bring in his kind of pieces to the puzzle. He already had an idea of who would stay and who would have to go. The results of his maneuverings would produce some real highs, some devastating lows, and a number of shocking changes, all in the next two years.

CHAPTER EIGHTEEN

And A Guy Named Vinny Shall Lead Them

T RUE TO HIS WORD, BILL PARCELLS WENT ABOUT GATHERING PLAYers he felt would help put his team over the top. By the third week in March he had acquired veteran Keith Byars from the Patriots, a reliable third-down back who was also a great pass receiver. Next came center Kevin Mawae, guard Todd Burger, and center/guard Mike Gisler. Parcells also got a number-two draft pick from Philadelphia in exchange for defensive end Hugh Douglas. Douglas was considered a coming star, an outstanding pass rusher. For whatever reason, he just didn't come under the umbrella of a Parcells guy.

"If you don't fit his mold, then he'll find somebody who does," said Douglas, who continued to play fine football for the Eagles.

But Parcells was still far from satisfied. In the first five games of the 1997 season, running back Adrian Murrell had topped one hundred yards three times. Then in the final ten games in which he played, he rushed for a total of 495 yards and a 3.1 per-carry average. That wasn't good enough. Parcells liked running backs who could go the distance, who were stronger in the fourth quarter than the first, and who could carry the load right through the playoffs. Murrell, though obviously talented, didn't fit the Parcells mold.

Curtis Martin did. The coach had seen him up close for two seasons in New England, and once again in 1997, Martin had run for more than one thousand yards with the Pats. On March 20, the Jets surprised everyone by signing Martin to a free-agent offer sheet. The Jets were willing to pay the running back some $27 million for five years. If the Patriots didn't match the offer, Martin could sign with the Jets, who would then lose their first- and third-round picks in the upcoming April draft.

A week later, the deal was done. Parcells couldn't have been happier. He always liked having a running back who could control the ball and the clock.

"This was an opportunity that we felt was difficult to pass up," he said. "Curtis has always displayed character and passion for his job and I expect that he will bring that energy, character and passion to the team. We know the price was high, but we think we got good value in return. When I look at the draft and the eighteenth spot (where the Jets would pick in the first round), I look to see if I can get a better player than Curtis Martin, and I don't think I can."

Martin had run for 3,799 yards in his first three seasons, becoming one of just eight backs in NFL history to go over one thousand yards in each of his first three seasons. Some said he was injury-prone, but most backs get nicked up as the season progresses. Now he was coming off surgery to repair an abdominal tear, and team doctors pronounced him fit. To make room for Martin, Murrell would wind up in Arizona, where he would also play well. Again, Parcells knew what he wanted.

In July came another move, one that would turn out to be a helluva lot better than anyone even suspected at the time. Several teams had free-agent quarterbacks available. It was no secret that Parcells was not happy with Neil O'Donnell. Once again it was that sometimes indefinable, almost abstract instinct that said, *He is not a Parcells guy*. The coach simply didn't feel the veteran quarterback was the man to take the team over the top. He asked O'Donnell to restructure his contract, take a pay cut to help with the cap. O'Donnell refused, sealing his fate.

Who then was available? Parcells wasn't about to land a John Elway, Steve Young, Troy Aikman, or Brett Favre. One possibility was the Indianapolis Colts' Jim Harbaugh. A seasoned veteran, Harbaugh was a late-bloomer who had put together some outstanding numbers over the past few years. Parcells was interested.

"Bill Parcells was pretty open in his assessment that he really liked Jim, that he had some interest in Jim," said Harbaugh's agent, Leigh Steinberg. "[But then] the Ravens jumped in and moved very, very decisively."

So Harbaugh signed with the Ravens, which made Baltimore's incumbent starter suddenly available. He was thirty-four-year-old Vinny Testaverde, a pro since 1987, the year after he won the Heisman Trophy while finishing a great career at the University of Miami. In his various stops at Tampa Bay, Cleveland, and Baltimore Testaverde had put up some impressive numbers, but was always looked upon as a mistake-prone quarterback who sometimes made bad decisions and who coughed the ball up at the worst possible times. Take away that assessment, however, and you had a six-foot-five, 235-pound quarterback with an exceptionally strong arm and outstanding record of durability.

Defensive coordinator Belichick had coached Testaverde at Cleveland, while Parcells had seen the big quarterback play against his Patriots and Jets. In fact, Testaverde had driven the Ravens eighty yards against the Jets with no time-outs the season before, getting his team the tying touchdown before the Jets won it in overtime. The Jets decided to sign the veteran, ostensibly as a backup to Glenn Foley. O'Donnell was odd man out and would wind up in Cincinnati.

Parcells and his coaches felt that Testaverde always looked to throw the ball downfield. With the Jets, he would learn to throw short passes to his backs, to mix it up more. They also felt many of his interceptions came when his protection broke down and he tried to do it on his own. They would emphasize to him that it was better to eat the ball rather than making an ill-advised throw.

The consensus was that the Jets had made a mistake. Had they landed Harbaugh, he would have been penciled in as the starter ahead of Foley. Testaverde was being tabbed the backup, which many felt indicated the team didn't have a whole lot of confidence in him. Time would tell.

There was one other important acquisition for the 1998 season, one Parcells decided upon because it involved a player he thought could help light a fire under the team: inside linebacker Bryan Cox, a highly emotional player who often let his temper get the best of him. Cox had spent five years with the Dolphins and two with the Bears. During that time he amassed some $146,000 in fines, most of it for his impulsive behavior on the field. The linebacker was out of football when Parcells called.

"I don't know," Cox said, when asked if he could still play. "I'm discouraged, I'm out of shape, and I don't know whether I want to play."

"You *do* want to play," Parcells told him, in no uncertain terms. "I want you in a contributing role, not as a special-teamer. Think about it. I'll call you back tonight."

When Cox said he didn't know how soon he could be ready, Parcells replied quickly, "I don't care if you're not ready on August 1. I want you ready on September 1."

Cox signed, and he would contribute mightily all year long.

In early August, once the preseason was getting started, some reporters jumped on a remark Parcells made about how he loved the summer in Saratoga and being around the track. One of his few hobbies was horses, of which he owned several. That made some observers think he was already getting tired of his latest coaching stop.

"So I say I'm not coaching forever, is that a revelation?" he asked, rhetorically. "So I say there are things I like to do. Saratoga is starting and I watched a couple of races on TV and I got a little sentimental. Because I like it. Now all of a sudden someone is saying that I'm not coaching.

"Well, I'm coaching. I'm coaching as hard as I can. I'm committed. I don't think Jets fans should be worried, because I'm committed. I was here about six or seven Sundays in the off-season. I was here fighting over this Curtis Martin thing. . . . I don't have a crystal ball to tell me what I'm going to be doing two or three years from now. But I think I know. I think I'll be here trying to coach this team. I really mean that.'

Maybe. Maybe not. The New England situation showed how quickly the coach could change his mind. That, however, was a matter of how long. When he was on the job, Parcells was still as committed as any coach in the league, as any coach ever. Will McDonough, for one, felt that Parcells was still running the top program in the NFL.

"Players who have been with other teams and seen how they're run, then come here with Bill and see how he runs things know that he is doing the most professional coaching job in the National Football League. He's concerned about his players, concerned if they have any problems off the field, concerned about their wives and families. That's why you see the older guys with the greatest respect for him.

"He and his staff leave nothing to chance, no stone unturned from Day One of the draft all the way through the end of the season. He's on top of everything. I personally think he simply outworks everyone else. This is his life. The guy is in his office at 6:30 in the morning. He's still there at

8:30 or nine at night. I remember when he was with the Giants they had a month off. He would go away for four or five days, then suddenly come back. He was already beginning to worry. He started going to the office himself while all the other coaches were still away. That's just the way he is. He's simply driven to excel.

"I think it's the competition that really turns him on," McDonough continued. "He's a competitor. When he does take a break from football after the mini-camp in May, what does he do? He goes right to the golf course the next day. He's go out and he'll hit golf balls every single day, then go out and play each day. But just as abruptly as he starts, he stops. As soon as he has to come back to work, he drops the golf clubs and won't pick them up until one year later. A lot of [coaches] sneak out and play a round of golf during the bye week, for instance. Bill doesn't do that. It's all coaching."

Every move Parcells and the Jets made in the preseason was scrutinized and analyzed, with all kinds of conclusions being drawn without an official word from the top. When the coach announced that Testaverde instead of Foley would start the Jets' preseason home opener, the quarterback question began. Had the coach lost confidence in Foley? Was Testaverde about to be anointed the starter? Was another change in the offing, maybe another quarterback brought in? It never stopped. The coach claimed it was just a rotation, a way to get both of them into the action.

"There are certain things I'd like to accomplish with those quarterbacks," the coach said. "I want to see how each manages the team, the game, that kind of thing. It's no big deal. Teams around the league do it all the time."

Parcells was basically covering his rear. Foley had never finished a game that he started, getting hurt in each of his few starts. Testaverde was durable and a veteran. So while Foley was still considered the starter, the key hadn't been turned. Even Foley knew it.

"Nobody's job is secure," he said. "This is the way it works with Bill and his teams."

What's wrong with that? If a guy isn't cutting it, and someone else can do the job better . . . well, the name of the game is still winning. As the head coach, it's Parcells's responsibility to give his team the best chance to win every week, and that means having the players on the field that can do it.

It didn't help either quarterback or the team when the Ravens won the preseason game 33–0. Now, perhaps, there was a question. Neither quarterback had stepped up, taken control, and said, "This is my team."

"Don't say I singled out the quarterbacks," said an angry Parcells, after the game. He them ripped the entire team as "immature" in its approach. "Am I more worried [about the quarterbacks]? No, I would say I have concerns about all positions."

When the Jets were beaten, especially badly, no one was safe from Parcells's wrath. The team, however, was good enough to come together. But the quarterback situation truly was key, and a potential albatross. Foley had started just five games in two years and didn't throw a single pass in twenty-three others. Testaverde, on the other hand, had 132 career starts but had won only forty-eight of them. You could chalk some of it up to bad teams, but the doubts remained. In fact, there were doubts about both signal-callers.

It was Foley who opened the season in a game against the 49ers at Candlestick Park. The former Boston College star played very well, throwing for 415 yards, but the Jets' defense wasn't quite up to stopping Steve Young, Jerry Rice, and company. San Francisco won it 36–30. Close, but a sour beginning nonetheless. Then, a week later, the team seemed to regress, losing 24–10 to a Baltimore team not nearly in San Francisco's class. Foley was OK in the first half and terrible in the second, winding up with three passes intercepted, two of which he seemed to telegraph, making for easy pickings.

At 0–2, the Jets were already in trouble. Indianapolis was next and Parcells was facing a big, early season decision. Should he turn to Testaverde in an attempt to get more offense? If he did, Foley's confidence might be shattered, and if Vinny didn't come through . . . well. The resultant thought wasn't a good one, not good at all. That's when fate, as they say, suddenly took a hand.

Foley started Game Three against the Colts, was hit hard early on, and left the game with bruised ribs. It was yet another injury for a player the coach was beginning to view as brittle and injury-prone. On came Testaverde. Vinny didn't throw too often, completing twelve of twenty-one for 203 yards, but he made his passes count. When the game ended he had thrown for four touchdowns and the Jets had their first win by an impressive 44–6 score. They were on the board.

"I feel good about what Vinny did," Parcells said. "That's what I was

It's never over 'til it's over. Though the Jets were en route to a 48–21 victory over Carolina in 1998, the coach still looks like a worried man as he works the sidelines. (Photo Bill Lenahan)

Jets defensive coordinator Bill Belichick (shielding his eyes) and the head coach watch the field intently during a close 32–31 victory over Seattle in 1998. (Photo Bill Lenahan)

With intensity written all over his face, Parcells talks to his coaches up in the booth during game action in 1998. (Photo Bill Lenahan)

Jacksonville Jaguars coach Tom Coughlin credits Bill Parcells with being his greatest coaching influence. The two old friends don't like coaching against each other but they sometimes can't avoid it. They're all smiles before their teams meet in the play-offs following the 1998 season. This time Parcells and the Jets won, 34–24. (Photo Bill Lenahan)

Parcells and longtime aide Al Groh stand side by side during a playoff game in January 1999. Groh would emerge as Jets head coach following Parcells's sudden retirement and Bill Belichick's unexpected resignation after the 1999 season. (Photo Bill Lenahan)

Always out front and leading his team, Parcells misses nothing that happens on the field on game days. As usual, defensive coordinator Bill Belichick (l) isn't far from the head coach. (Photo Bill Lenahan)

Parcells and defensive coordinator Bill Belichick direct the Jets in the opening game of the 1999 season against New England. Before the afternoon was over, quarterback Vinny Testaverde would be lost for the season and Parcells would face the toughest coaching job of his life. (Photo Bill Lenahan)

Seattle coach Mike Holmgren, a Super Bowl winner himself when he was with Green Bay, has called Bill Parcells the best coach in the National Football League. The two never miss a chance to talk shop, as they do here before the final game of the 1999 season, which the Jets won, 19–9. (Photo Bill Lenahan)

It's a mutual admiration society when Parcells meets another Parcells guy. Before a 1999 pre-season game, the Jets coach swaps stories with former coach and current broadcaster, John Madden. (Photo Bill Lenahan)

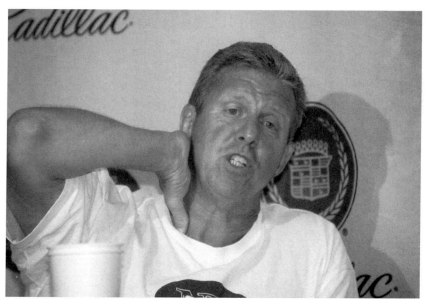

To watch Bill Parcells at new conferences can be an adventure. He can be smiling one minute and assailing a reporter for asking a dumb question the next. And his expressions never stay the same for any two questions. (Photo Bill Lenahan)

When Parcells left the New England Patriots after the 1996 season, Pats quarterback Drew Bledsoe wasn't sorry to see him go. But like many former players, Bledsoe came to realize that Parcells's harsh ways were designed to make Bledsoe a better quarterback. By the opening game of the 1999 season, Parcells and Bledsoe had mended the fences and met on the field for a friendly chat. (Photo Bill Lenahan)

Extremely loyal to old friends and former players, Parcells always has time for a visit. Hall of Fame linebacker Lawrence Taylor is a drop-in at the Jets training camp and immediately begins talking shop with his former coach. (Photo Bill Lenahan)

No, the coach isn't about to take on the heavyweight champ. He's just making a point, Parcells-style, at the Jets training camp in 1998. (Photo Bill Lenahan)

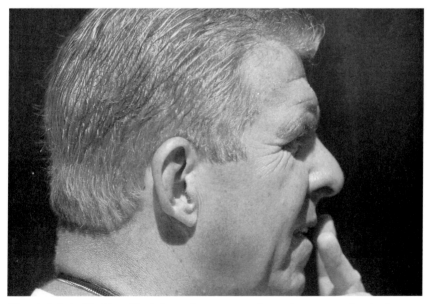

How do I deal with this problem? A pensive moment for an intense coach who lets no stone go unturned. (Photo Bill Lenahan)

The T-shirt has a message. Parcells doesn't miss a trick when it comes to motivating his team. This time it's START OVER. He wears a variety of shirts to practice with various messages that are easy to understand. (Photo Bill Lenahan)

hoping for. . . . He made good decisions. He didn't do anything to hurt us. I was very pleased with him. I'm glad I've got the guy."

The Jets had stayed with the game plan, not having Testaverde throw downfield. None of his four TD passes traveled more than twenty yards in the air. Fortunately, both the runners and receivers did a fine job. The Jets gained 302 yards on the ground, and Leon Johnson turned a screen pass into an eighty-two-yard touchdown.

Now the coach had a genuine dilemma. The rule of thumb is that a quarterback, or any player, shouldn't lose his starting job due to an injury. Miami was up next, following a bye week, and Foley vowed he would be ready. But Parcells knew better than to take a player at his word, especially when it involved an injury. Some players will say they're all right because of their competitive natures. During practice that next week, the coach walked up behind Foley and, unseen, poked him in the ribs. The quarterback nearly collapsed in pain.

"I guess you're not ready," the coach said, adding, "I have to see for myself that everything is good with Foley. I can't just hear it; I've got to see it."

The bye week also gave the scribes time to write about the way Parcells had been building the Jets since taking command in 1997. That year he had made a trade with the Rams, giving up the number-one draft choice, which turned out to be tackle Orlando Pace. Pace was on his way to becoming an All-Pro, but four of the players the Jets received in return were making major contributions. Linebacker James Farrior had become a starter before a knee injury early in the season. Wide receiver Dedric Ward was a bona fide deep threat and improving weekly. Running back/ punt returner Leon Johnson was also a player with game-breaking abilities, while defensive tackle Jason Ferguson was now one of the team's best defensive linemen.

With Foley not completely healed, Testaverde got the call against Miami and led the Jets to a big 20–9 victory. There was a temporary setback, a 30–10 loss to St. Louis, but then came another huge win, 24–14 over the Patriots. The team was now 3–3, the season still in the balance. It could go either way. Parcells had made a major decision. Vinny Testaverde, on the strength of his consistent play, was now the starting quarterback.

"We have to figure out what kind of team we are," Parcells said, after the New England game. "Are we a roller-coaster team or a yo-yo team? I know we're capable. Just because you show it once doesn't mean you're any good, though. You have to show it consistently. This week we fought it out and that's what you have to do. Hopefully, next week we get some guys back and we're fine."

Ironically, more of Parcells's former Patriots players were now beginning to praise their former coach. Remember how many Pats were glad to see him go, saying that the team had been returned to the players? Parcells was now 2–1 against his former team and could easily have been 3–0, had a John Hall field goal not been blocked in the closing seconds of regulation the season before.

"He's a great coach, no question," Patriots safety Lawyer Milloy said. "You knew he would come in here and have his team ready to play. That's why his track record is so great. We knew we were going to have our hands full and we didn't get the job done."

After a 28–3 whipping of the Atlanta Falcons, Parcells seemed cranky and irritable, playing the role of the old curmudgeon to a tee. During the game he chided Keyshawn Johnson for dropping a couple of passes, saying one more drop and someone else would be in the game. Johnson told him not to worry, went back out, and caught a twelve-yard TD pass from Testaverde.

"He's like a big, old crybaby type when something ain't going right," Johnson said. "He's a major panicker."

But nothing would placate the coach on this day. "I still got too many on this team I gotta whip too much," Parcells said. "It's always prod, prod . . . get 'em to do stuff. You run out of energy. In the end that really never works."

When asked how he prods, the coach answered, "I can't tell you what I'm gonna do because I don't know myself half the time. It's just an instinct."

Linebacker Bryan Cox, who immediately became one of Parcells's guys with his all-out effort and self-motivation, had a pretty good handle on how the coach operates.

"He's in control; that's his relationship [with the team]," Cox said. "He's in control. It's how he wants it, when he wants it, and where he wants it. If he doesn't like what he's getting, he'll get rid of you."

But Cox denied that the coach instilled fear in his players. "He's not a big 'fear' guy," the linebacker continued. "He's a realist. If he gives you a couple of warnings about your play, you're gonna be on the waiver wire.

Players respect that. I know I respect that. He's hard, but he's fair, that's how I would sum it up. [But] when he's mad, stay away from him. If he don't talk to you, don't talk to him."

It really hadn't changed much from Giants days. Maybe he was a little less tolerant, a little more antsy, a bit more impatient. But back then, one of his Giant players said something that would probably ring true with his current Jets.

"If Parcells was named king of the world on Sunday," the player said, "he'd be unhappy by Tuesday."

Despite Parcells's moaning and groaning, the team continued to play well. They topped Kansas City 20–17, soundly whipped division rival Buffalo 34–12, then lost to Indianapolis by a point before rebounding to defeat Tennessee 24–3. The team now stood at 7–4 and were still in the thick of the AFC East race. In Vinny Testaverde, the Jets had caught the proverbial lightning in a bottle. The veteran quarterback was having the best season of his career, statistically among the top quarterbacks in the league. He was firmly ensconced as the number one, with Foley relegated to backup. Once again, Parcells's decision to bring the veteran to New York had paid dividends.

After the Tennessee game, the coach was in a surprisingly jovial mood. There was nobody to pick on. "Listen," he said, "I would be hard-pressed to find anybody that didn't play pretty well. That's probably the first time I can say that. I think, overall, [it was] pretty solid. I mean, I don't think there's anybody I can look at [and question]."

It was as if he sensed something, the team coming together, the pieces in place. No longer was this Jets team teetering on the bring of self-destruction, as so many others had been over the years. Even the fans seemed to know that they now had a coach who wouldn't let the team fall apart. Losing just wasn't part of Bill Parcells's makeup. Even Leon Hess, the team's octogenarian owner, was overjoyed at the turn his team had taken.

"We have wonderful coaches, a wonderful spirit with the team," he said. "We may have a setback from time to time, but we'll come back. I hope that we do very well. I enjoy it a hell of a lot more than 1–15." Then Hess said of his coach, "He's the boss. The whole team is his, as if he owned it."

The Jets had become a fine offensive machine. Johnson and Chrebet were the top receiving tandem in the league. Dedric Ward was averaging just over twenty yards a catch. Curtis Martin was on track for another one thousand-yard season, and Vinny Testaverde was playing at an All-Pro level. The defense, though not quite as dominant, came up big when it had to, and would get stronger down the stretch. These Jets were for real. In just two years, Bill Parcells had a taken a 1–15 team to a group contending for a division title.

Victories over Carolina, Seattle, and Miami followed, giving the Jets a 10–4 record and a leg up in the AFC East. Then the Jets traveled to Ralph Wilson Stadium in Buffalo to meet the Bills. A victory would clinch the division. It was a tough game, both offenses moving their respective teams, the defenses stopping them. With just over two minutes left in the third quarter it was still anybody's game at 10–10. That's when Testaverde dropped back from his own 29 and aired it out in the direction of Dedric Ward. The speedy receiver made the grab in full stride and completed a seventy-one-yard touchdown play. Hall's kick made it 17–10.

The Bills fought to the end, driving toward the potential tying score late in the fourth period. But with just 3:52 left, Doug Flutie threw in the direction of Kevin Williams. The ball bounced off his hands and into the arms of Jets safety Victor Green. After that, the Jets ran out the clock to win it and in doing so wrapped up the AFC East, their first division title in twenty-nine years, since the 1968 team of Joe Namath.

No one was happier than Parcells. He smiled broadly, hugged his players, bumped chests with some, tapped a couple of his assistants on the back. When he finally talked to his players, the tough old coach had tears in his eyes.

"You hear 'same old Jets, same old Jets,' " he said. "Well, now you're the champs and nobody can take that away from you. You have a responsibility to keep playing that way."

A few minutes later, the coach was talking to the press. "Our guys, they just try hard for me all the time," he said. "They're not the greatest team. But mentally, they're really tough now. I'm proud and happy. It's pretty emotional for me today. I can't even recount much of this game."

When owner Hess, proud as a peacock at long last, was asked if he was surprised how quickly his team turned around, going from 1–15 to division champs in two years, he gave the credit to one man.

"I'm not surprised by anything Bill Parcells tries to do," he said.

Parcells quickly returned the compliment. "I'd be remiss if I didn't tell you how happy I am for Mr. Hess," the coach said. "It's been a long time coming for him. I just feel honored to be the one to give him this. We're going to give him the game ball. I'm honored to be able to do that."

The coach had genuine affection for this owner, whom he looked upon as a father figure as well as a man of quality and substance. He was happy for Hess and proud of his team. At the same time, he must have felt extremely gratified at his own achievement. There was still a ways to go, but he had proved to himself that he still had the touch, still had the fire, and in his fifty-seventh year could still impart that fire to much-younger players who looked up to him.

CHAPTER NINETEEN

Unfinished Business

W HEN PARCELLS HAD TIME TO REFLECT ON HIS TEAM'S SUCCESS
he seemed to wax sentimental, if only for a few moments.
"It's hard to describe [what I felt after the game]," he said.
"When you see these kids and their faces, it does get to you—even for
a person like myself, who has seen a lot of it. That's what's great
about this game. It can be very humbling and very frustrating, but also
very euphoric.

"I keep saying I'm too old to lose. Not many people understand what
that means. I have a few players who understand it, and I understand it.
If it gets to where you're just losing all the time, at my age, it's just not
worth it. It takes too much out of me. When you win, it makes it worth-
while."

It was the old hatred of losing, something that went back to River Dell
High. "You either win or you lose. There are no moral victories." That's
what young Bill Parcells said to Mickey Corcoran so many years before.
Now, as an aging coach, winning was becoming more urgent, more immediate. It was as if he knew this wasn't going to last a whole lot longer.
Win now. At this point in his career, losing was no longer tolerable or
acceptable. His legacy of winning was ingrained within him. It had become the only thing, a la Vince Lombardi.

A week after the division-clinching game with Buffalo, the Jets ended
the regular season in fine style, once against besting the Patriots, this time

246

by a convincing 31–10 margin. The team had won its final six games, eleven of its last twelve, and finished the season with a 12–4 record.

Individually, the Jets had some outstanding performances. Testaverde emerged as a Pro Bowl quarterback, leading the AFC quarterback rankings with 259 completions in 421 attempts for 3,256 yards and a team-record twenty-nine touchdowns. More importantly, he lost his reputation as a mistake-prone quarterback by throwing just seven interceptions. Curtis Martin was fourth among AFC rushers, with 1,287 yards on 369 carries and eight touchdowns.

Keyshawn Johnson and Wayne Chrebet were both outstanding. Two men with conflicting personalities who didn't really like each other, they complemented each other perfectly on the field. Johnson caught eighty-three passes for 1,131 yards and ten touchdowns. The six-foot-three, 212-pound receiver was nails-tough and often used his great physical ability to outleap or outreach defenders for the ball. Chrebet, at five-foot-ten and 185 pounds, was a possession receiver who had the knack of getting open despite not having great speed. He caught seventy-five passes for 1,083 yards and eight scores.

"I've worked with some very good receivers in my career," Testaverde said. "They're two of the best. They're versatile, tough, have great hands, and they want the ball."

On offense, the Jets had scored 416 points. In the AFC only Denver, with 501, had more. Defensively, the Jets gave up 266. Just the Dolphins, yielding one fewer at 265, did better in the entire league. So it wasn't totally inconceivable that these Jets were fully capable of winning the Super Bowl.

The Jets had a bye in the first round of the playoffs and then would play host to the winner of the game between the wild-card Patriots (9–7) and AFC Central champs Jacksonville (11–5). But before that game was even played, Bill Parcells began motivating. At the team's first practice, more than a week before the game, he did something he had never done before. He showed up wearing his 1990 Super Bowl ring. His players had never seen it before and he knew it would affect them.

"It's just a ring, it doesn't make any difference," he said, downplaying it to the press. "I didn't talk to my team about the Super Bowl or anything. Maybe they will [see the ring] and maybe they won't. [But] they'll get a chance to."

They saw it, all right. Wayne Chrebet spoke for nearly everyone when he said, "He's showing us what we can get if we work a little harder this next month. You see the ring, but it's what it represents, to go through everything you do all year, and know you are the best for a whole year. That's the ultimate."

Someone asked the coach if his Jets team could compare to that Giants team of 1990. Though he normally hated to talk about the past, Parcells unexpectedly made an exception, showing the affection and pride that he had in that Giants team of nearly a decade earlier.

"I thought that was one of the great teams in history," he said. "Don't forget who we beat. We beat the team of the decade [the 49ers] on the road and the offense of the '90s [the Bills]. We weren't aesthetically pleasing, but our defense gave up the fewest points [in the league] and we turned it over the fewest of any team in history. We had only fourteen turnovers in nineteen games, which is pretty amazing."

Though he may have felt his Giants team of 1990 was better, that didn't mean Parcells's Jets couldn't win. It was a different time, different players, different teams. When Jacksonville whipped the Patriots 25–10, Parcells began getting his team ready to face the Jags and his old protégé, Tom Coughlin. When the two teams met at the Meadowlands on January 10, the football world saw just how far this well-oiled Parcells team had come.

The Jets controlled the game for three quarters, taking a 17–7 lead at the half, extending it to 31–14 after three, then coming home with a 34–24 victory, though the Jags made it interesting by closing to 31–24 midway through the final quarter. The defense tightened again, Jacksonville finally losing the ball on downs in the closing minutes and then John Hall kicking a field goal to put it out of reach. Martin gained 124 yards on thirty-six carries, while Testaverde completed twenty-four of thirty-six for 284 yards and a touchdown. Keyshawn Johnson had a great game, with nine catches for 121 yards, scoring on a pass reception and an end-around. The offense had been great; the defense had a couple of fourth-quarter lapses. But they won, and now had to travel to Denver to play the John-Elway-and-Terrell-Davis-led Broncos for the AFC Championship and a trip to the Super Bowl.

If the Jets made it, Bill Parcells would also rewrite history. He would become the first coach to take three different teams to the Super Bowl.

Denver, however, was not only the defending Super Bowl champ, but owner of a 14–2 regular-season record with an offense that scored 501 points. Veteran quarterback John Elway could still work his magic at age thirty-eight, while running back Terrell Davis had just become the fourth back in history to run for more than two thousand yards in a season. The Broncos' defense might not have been quite as good as the Jets', but Denver usually just outscored its opponents. In addition, the Broncos were big-game tough, having upset the Green Bay Packers to win the previous Super Bowl.

Many prognosticators felt the Jets had the tools to win. The players were confident, many feeling that defensive coordinator Bill Belichick would devise a scheme to slow, if not stop, the high-powered Denver offense. By contrast, the Jets' offense had the confidence it could score on the Broncos. Quarterback Testaverde also felt that looking back at history, at the Namath-led upset of the Colts in Super Bowl III, would help inspire the ball club.

"Because of guys like Joe Namath and the team the Jets had in 1968, they make it possible for teams like us to believe that we can win this game," Testaverde said. "We know we have our hands full. But if we play good solid football and don't make mistakes, we'll have an opportunity to win this game."

The interesting thing was that Broncos fans, and maybe even some of the players, didn't fear the Jets players who would be on the field. They seemed more concerned with one man who would be standing on the sidelines. It was Bill Parcells's penchant for coaching his team in big games that seemed to be the X-factor. Many talked as if Parcells would be on the field, making tackles, running the football, throwing passes.

"Coach Parcells rarely loses at this stage of the season," was the way one columnist put it, echoing the words of many others. They would point out that he was 3–0 in conference championship games, winning two with the Giants and one with the Patriots. He did lose one Super Bowl, but won two others. It was as if he simply would not let his team lose at this time of the year.

The game, at Mile High Stadium in Denver, was played on January 17, and for the first thirty minutes of football, it looked as if the Jets had found the key. The only scoring in the first half came just as time ran out when John Hall booted a thirty-two-yard field goal. The Jets had moved forty-six yards in six plays to set up the three-pointer. In fact, they got all the yards on two Testaverde passes, a twenty-yarder to Chrebet and a twenty-six-yard strike to Dedric Ward. Otherwise, it was a defensive struggle and, better yet, John Elway did not look sharp, many of this throws badly off the mark.

Then, early in the third quarter, the Jets' Blake Spence blocked a Denver punt at the goal line. Fred Baxter recovered at the one, and on the next play Curtis Martin burst into the end zone. With 11:56 left in the third period, John Hall kicked the extra point that made it a 10–0 game. The Jets were looking good. What happened next, however, was totally uncharacteristic of a Bill Parcells–coached football team. In a nutshell, the roof fell in.

It started when the Broncos suddenly came to life on the next drive, going sixty-four yards on just three plays. Elway hit Ed McCaffrey for forty-seven yards and finished it by passing eleven yards to fullback Howard Griffith in the end zone. The kick made it 10–7. At this point the Jets were under pressure to respond. Nothing negates a score better than a quick score at the other end. But on the ensuing kickoff, the ball soared high, got caught in the wind, and bounced free without a Jet touching it. Denver's Keith Burns recovered it at the New York 31. Four plays later, Jason Elam booted a forty-four-yard field goal to tie the game at 10.

After the Jets punted on the next series, Denver quickly moved into field-goal range again and Elam converted a forty-eight-yarder to give the Broncos their first lead, 13–10. Parcells tried to rally the troops on the sideline, imploring the offense to get it in gear again. Once again, however, the Jets could do no better than three-and-out. That gave Broncos punt returner Darrien Gordon a chance to do his stuff. He brought the ball back thirty-six yards to the Jets' 38. Three plays later the Broncos were in the end zone again, Terrell Davis taking the ball in from thirty-one yards out. With just eighteen seconds remaining in the third period, Denver had a 20–10 lead and the Jets were falling apart. The Broncos had scored twenty unanswered points with just fifteen minutes of football remaining.

The Jets had already turned the ball over several times, but now they began driving again. A score now would put them back in it. The offense moved the ball to the Broncos' 46, then Testaverde threw a pass to little-used receiver Alex Van Dyke. Van Dyke caught the ball and began moving downfield, but when he was hit at the Broncos' 30, he fumbled the ball and Denver recovered. After that, the Jets offense couldn't get it going. There was no ground game and Testaverde couldn't do it alone. Terrell Davis controlled the ball with his heavy-duty running and set up the Broncos for a final field goal with 3:40 left. The game ended with the Broncos winning 23–10 and taking yet another AFC championship.

It was a bitter disappointment. Testaverde was thirty-one of fifty-two for 356 yards, but threw a pair of interceptions trying to play catch-up. Martin gained just fourteen yards on thirteen carries—nothing there. Meanwhile, Terrell Davis ran for 167 yards on thirty-two carries, more than making up for Elway's subpar thirteen-of-thirty-four passing day. The real killer, though, was the six turnovers—that sealed the Jets' fate. For Jets fans it was time to adopt a slogan left over from fans of the old Brooklyn Dodgers baseball team, in the years when the Dodgers seemed to always play bridesmaids to the New York Yankees. It was, "Wait 'til next year!"

The loss was a bitter disappointment to Jets players and coaches alike. Many of the Jets felt they could have won the game. "We could have beat these guys," tight end Kyle Brady said afterward. "We gave the ball away and when you do that, a great team like this will beat you. They played better than us. But we could beat this team."

Fiery linebacker Bryan Cox expressed his coach's sentiments when he said there were no excuses. "It was the mistakes we made, it wasn't anything great Elway did," Cox said, adding, "We didn't go where we wanted to go. I don't want to hear that we had a good season. We didn't meet our goal."

Remember, no moral victories. You either win or you lose. Despite the heartbreaking loss, it had been a great season, an exciting season, a season that far exceeded everyone's expectations. But in the end, if you lose, it doesn't mean much, at least not for awhile. It's an awfully long road to get back there again, back to where you're one game away from going for all the marbles. Parcells had experienced it once before, in 1985 with the Giants, when they lost the NFC semifinal game to the Chicago Bears despite the feeling that they could go all the way.

"I always think the same thing," Parcells said, "the same thing I felt back in 1985. It's another off-season. It's another draft. It's another training camp. It's another preseason. It's another regular season and it's another semifinal game just to get where you are standing. I can remember the feeling [from 1985] very well. I felt exactly the same way. It was the same setting, same kind of game, same kind of opportunities for our team, and a couple of freak things happened."

Star receiver Keyshawn Johnson expressed the feeling of loss that everyone had. "I don't want a small victory and say, 'Woo, we got to the AFC championship.' I don't want to smile and be happy about that. That's not the case. Everyone in this locker room is not happy about it."

A day later, however, Bill Parcells sounded like anything but a tired coach. This veteran of so many NFL wars was already looking ahead to 1999, quickly putting to rest the thought that he might be considering retirement.

"My intention is to be here," Parcells said, in no uncertain terms. "I really do always think [the future] over [after every season], but I know in my heart what I'm going to do. I'm doing to come back to coaching. I like these players. I like coaching this team. I've got people I like working with here. I've got kids that know what we want. It's not an easy job, but I like it."

Though admittedly very tired after the long season and in need of some time off, the coach said he'd soon be back at work.

"I don't think people really understand what twenty-six weeks in a row, seven days a week, is like," he explained. "A lot of nights you're not sleeping while your mind races. [But] I told the players I won't rest. I told them that last year [as well]. My whole idea is to try to improve this team each year. We'll see what we can do to do it [now]."

The coach also admitted that he felt bad leaving New England before finishing what he had set out to do there. He vowed not to do the same with the Jets.

"The singularly most sad thing that I had to do was when I left New England I knew I had kids there that would fight their [butts] off. It took four years of blood to get them that way and they were ready to do that. I'm not going to do that here without giving it my best shot."

It was a matter of unfinished business. Everyone felt it. The team had come so close in 1998 that the taste lingered long after the disappointing loss to Denver. The players felt that their coach, who had already reaffirmed his commitment, would find a way to get them over the top. Maybe it meant adding a few more key players and getting a bit more out of those returning. No one did that better than Parcells.

Before going home for a rest, Parcells was scheduled to travel to Hawaii a week after the Super Bowl to coach the American Conference All-Stars in the annual Pro Bowl game. The game was scheduled for February 7. More than a week before, however, word came out of New York that Bill Parcells would not be going. He was withdrawing, on the advice of his doctors.

"Coach Parcells was examined by his cardiologist as well as by me in my office a couple of days after the Denver game," said Jets team Medical Director Elliot Pellman. "He was clearly showing the physical effects of the long season. Given his medical history, I told him that he should not travel to Hawaii and participate in the Pro Bowl. He will remain under my care for the foreseeable future."

Parcells said he would take his doctor's advice. "I was in the midst of preparation for the Pro Bowl," he said. "But after undergoing a thorough medical examination, I feel it would be a big mistake on my part not to listen to the doctors. . . . The limited period of rest will rejuvenate me and allow me to continue to carry out my duties and commitments to the ownership and organization of the New York Jets and . . . do everything I can possibly do to improve our team."

There was no mention of a recurrence of any kind of heart problem. It was simply a matter of Parcells's medical history and the degree of exhaustion from the long season. They were simply playing it safe. Coaches don't have a long off-season, anyway. By passing up the Pro Bowl, he would have an extra couple of weeks to rest. With the time he had, the coach worked to recharge the batteries. He took a vacation, then spent a great deal of time at his Sea Gate, New Jersey, home, where he worked out on a treadmill and lifted weights, something he hadn't done in years. He seemed to be gearing up physically, getting himself in even better shape for what promised to be another long grind. How long, he couldn't have known then.

In early March, the team formally thanked Vinny Testaverde for turning in an All-Pro season by signing him to a new three-year deal worth some $19.5 million. The contract signing was put off for several week due to the death of Testaverde's father on February 14. That would be the first of several major blows that Parcells and the team would have to absorb during the year.

Several weeks later the team made another move, dealing backup quarterback Glenn Foley to the Seahawks for a draft choice in 2000. With Testaverde now firmly established as the number one, the feeling was that Foley would be better off elsewhere. He felt he had lost his job because of his rib injury and probably would find it difficult accepting the backup role. In addition, the Jets had serious questions about his durability. Now they had to look for another backup.

The team added several other veterans, players who would probably not be around long but whose experience could help put the final pieces to the puzzle. One was former Denver safety Steve Atwater, an aggressive, hard-hitting backliner, and tight end Eric Green, once an All-Pro with the

Pittsburgh Steelers but beset by injuries in recent years. The coaches were hoping he would regain some of his former skills, especially after incumbent tight end Kyle Brady departed. Because of free agency, teams had a larger turnover each year, sometimes making it difficult to keep a winning team intact. You often had to replace part A with part B and hope the results were as good.

As the coach prepared for the draft he talked about his team, and what he had learned in the past two seasons.

"Two years ago at this time, I didn't know anything about my team," he said. "We were just scrambling so badly. Last year, we had the Neil O'Donnell thing and the money, and all that stuff going on. This year, from a stability standpoint, I feel a lot better. I know a lot more about my team than I have either of those two previous years.

"It isn't any one thing that makes a good team. It's not how you draft, or how you sign free agents, but how you do all of it. It is just a matter of putting my team together. I'm just trying to make this team better. In that respect, I think it's going all right."

Then, on May 7, the entire organization was jolted by the news that team owner Leon Hess had died at the age of eighty-five. Hess had been suffering from a blood disorder that often required hospitalization and frequent transfusions. Though it hadn't been publicized at the time, there was a kind of urgency among the Jets hierarchy, and especially Parcells, the season before to try to reach the Super Bowl. They knew then that Hess was ill and that his time was limited. The beloved team owner never had the pleasure of accepting the Vince Lombardi Trophy that goes with winning a Super Bowl. Now it was too late.

"[Mr. Hess's health problems] motivated me very strongly," Parcells said, when informed of the owner's death. "I really did want to try to do something for this man. I was trying the best I could to insure that he be successful."

Parcells had genuine affection for the older man and several days before Hess's passing had expressed his regrets to team President Steve Gutman that he wasn't able to take the team all the way the season before. Yet he could take solace in the fact that Hess told many people that the 1998 season was very satisfying to him in many ways, and a source of great enjoyment. One of the highpoints came when the Jets clinched the AFC East title and gave a game ball to their owner. Hess was so touched by the gesture that he wrote his coach a personal thank-you note.

"I know that meant a lot to him," Parcells said. "I'm just happy there was one little, small thing we could do for him. [Mr. Hess] did more for me than any coach could ever ask."

Steve Gutman said there was one more thing the Jets could do for their late owner. "All of us could have no fonder wish than the 1999 season plays out in such a way that it truly becomes Leon's final year, and the one in which he does get that Super Bowl."

However, the death of Leon Hess would have ramifications for the entire Jets family, far and above the initial loss of a beloved figure and popular owner. Within weeks of his death it was learned that in his will Hess had mandated the sale of the Jets, with the investment banking firm of Goldman, Sachs & Co. managing the sale. The will was very specific, for it also barred any member of the Hess family from buying any interest in the Jets or participating in the team's future, "either directly or indirectly," in any capacity whatsoever.

In the will, Hess detailed the reason for the sale, stating, "I anticipate that the sale of my interest in the New York Jets Football Club, Inc., will substantially raise the cash needs required by my executors to pay the debts, administration expenses, and taxes borne by my estate."

This surprising turn of events raised immediate questions about both team and coach. How would Hess's death and the impending sale affect a team that seemed on the brink of some very special things? Parcells tried to end the speculation quickly. He spoke to the press at the start of a three-day veterans' mini-camp in late May. First he said that John Hess, son of the late owner, had given him assurance that there would no changes in the front office through the 1999 season.

"Nothing disturbs this season," the coach said. "That was my major concern. John has told me to run the operation as I've been running it, and if I need any help from the estate in doing that, to let him know. I was comforted a great deal upon hearing that."

He also said there was a clause in his six-year contract that protected him financially if his relationship with the team was severed prematurely for any reason. Again, he was asked if he planned to retire after the upcoming season.

"Write whatever you want," he snapped. "I haven't had anything to say about it. I coach every year, and at the end of the year I decide what's going on. There's obviously going to be some changes here and we'll just have to see what the new ownership wants to do. I get the sense, however, that they're going to be very thorough about this. I don't see anything happening for a while."

The other rumor that probably drew a few chuckles was that Parcells himself was putting a group together to buy the team. "I am not part of any group, nor will I ever be part of any group, to buy the Jets," he said, firmly. "I'm not trying to buy the Jets. Period."

That seemed unlikely. Analysts felt the going price for the franchise would be in the $500 million range, possibly more. Only heavy-hitters need apply. The coach was also right in that the sale would not take place quickly. The season would proceed unencumbered by any consequences of the impending transfer of ownership. That would wait until the season was over. By July everyone was concentrating on football, and the majority of the preseason polls were making the Jets early favorite to reach, and then win, the Super Bowl.

Of course, there were the usual "ifs." Testaverde had to prove his 1998 season wasn't a fluke. Martin had to stay injury-free and once again go well over a thousand yards. Johnson and Chrebet had to continue as the top receiving tandem in the league. The defense had to be even better than it had been in '98. And the coach would have to do his usual job of motivating, getting every player to perform to the absolute best of his ability.

Despite Parcells's constant denials, there continued to be speculation about his future. There were stories that contained quotes from anonymous sources saying that at age fifty-eight the coach wanted a more relaxed lifestyle, a chance to play golf, to become more involved with his horses, and to get away from more than thirty years of almost constant coaching. His three girls were all grown and working on their own. Jill was *Sports Illustrated*'s events marketing manager; Dallas was in the marketing department of an electronics firm; and Suzy, the eldest, was a mother and part-time dental hygienist. No one could blame the coach if he wanted to spend more time with Judy, his wife, who had spent three decades wondering what time her husband would be coming home and knowing he would not be home on weekends. An easy life it isn't for coaches' families.

To those who believed Parcells might leave, the 1999 season became the Jets' window of opportunity to finally win that elusive Super Bowl. One week into training camp, he seemed like the same Parcells. The needle was sharp, the tongue acerbic, the challenges already starting. No one was safe. Bill Parcells was back on the prowl. He kept telling them over and over that he didn't want them resting on their laurels, reminding

them that the majority of teams reaching conference championship games
don't return the next year.

"We're just not getting good production out of some of the players who
should be producing well," Parcells said, early on, "some of our superstar
central guys who think they can walk into the huddle and dial up a star
any time they want. It's just the whole coordination of it all. It's not one
guy that is responsible. . . . If you want to say I'm complaining about something, you can say that, because I am."

Because the Jets were already the big story of 1999, being the early
favorites to win the Super Bowl and having a team that was up for sale
and a coach who attracted attention like a magnet, the press flocked to
Hofstra, leading Parcells to quickly set some ground rules.

"We're gonna let you come across the parking lot to get in here," he
said, the first day of camp, "but we ask you not to talk to any of the players
as they're coming off the field. Otherwise, we're gonna have to close the
parking lot."

The Parcells relationship with the press was long a subject of controversy. He could be brutal at press conferences, especially when he thought
certain questions didn't measure up. Just as he wouldn't hesitate to tell a
player he made a dumb play, he would quickly tell a reporter, "That's a
dumb-ass question." He has been called a bully and intentionally intimidating. Some even say he's paranoid when it comes to the endless questions and the way his answers may be interpreted. There was a time back
in his Giants days when he answered a question about his then-star
Lawrence Taylor, and a second reporter, in asking a follow-up question,
seemingly misinterpreted his initial response. Parcells bristled.

"Hey," he snapped. "Don't put words in my mouth, now. 'Cause I don't
want to read that tomorrow. I'm not saying anything. I'm not confirmin'. I'm
not denyin'. I'm not saying anything other than what I do is my business
with this team. There's no premise, there's no standard. I said it before,
you guys know it. It's not my job to be consistent. It's my job to be right."

When asked if a another incident with a Giants player would have an
effect on the team, Parcells said no, it wouldn't. Then someone asked him
why he was so certain. He answered very quietly, but firmly, "Because
I'm the one in control, that's why."

That magic word again. Just as Parcells liked to control everything
concerning his team—at practices, in the locker room, during games—
he also liked to control press conferences. He would say as much as he

felt like saying. No more. Just as he had little tolerance for stupidity on the field, he had the same attitude toward stupidity in the press. He was never out to win a popularity contest with the media, so Mr. Nice Guy he often wasn't. Will McDonough, who has been at more than a few Parcells press conferences over the years, has watched the coach deal with several generations of media, both print and electronic.

"I think, overall, he has a great relationship with the press," McDonough said. "I've basically seen him do the same thing all the way through his career. He gives everybody a fair shot. When he started with the Giants he had to feel his way through at first, because he hadn't been a head coach in the NFL before. But he developed his own style with the press during those Giant years. Most of his style was developed when he was winning the two Super Bowls, rather than the first couple of years when he was struggling. Like many people, he tends to become defensive when he's struggling.

"He has a lot of great friends in the New York press, people who like him, who call him on the phone every day, and he'll respond to their calls. He still has some great friends in the Boston media, as well. What he does is treat everyone the same way starting out. But if a guy starts to put his own spin on his answers, or a guy's not a hard worker, and especially if a guy doesn't tell the truth, he will address him. I know he's said to guys like that, 'Hey, I told you before, if you want an answer, you come to me. I'll give it to you.' Or, he might say, 'You'll not telling the truth, so I'm not dealing with you anymore. I'll talk to you in a press conference, but other than that I won't talk to you.'

"This is the way he's done it. He's also very aware of guys in the electronic media coming in to get a sound bite, then putting a different spin on it. He resents that, like anyone would."

As the head coach of a New York team, one that was expected to win and go all the way, Parcells knew he would be inundated with media, probably all year long. So he had to establish the rules from the start. There are more media demands on coaches and players today than there ever have been before. It is often the league itself, whether the NFL, NBA, or major-league baseball, that mandates scheduled press conferences, often after every game. There are times when coaches who have just lost a huge game, maybe in a heartbreaking way, have to come out and address the throngs of reporters and writers almost immediately. It isn't easy to smile and be cheerful in that situation, especially when sometimes many of the questions are negative. All things considered, Parcells has handled the media well, better than some others.

Now it was back to the business at hand. The opening preseason game against Green Bay turned into a 27–16 loss. It was, however, a time for the coach to evaluate talent. Testaverde looked as sharp as ever, completing eleven of thirteen passes for 147 yards. He was apparently ready to take up where he left off in '98. So the coach yanked him early and inserted Ray Lucas, a quarterback at Hofstra who had mainly been a special-teams player since joining the Jets in 1997. Parcells liked Lucas's work ethic, his composure under fire, and his competitiveness. He was hoping Lucas might emerge as Testaverde's backup. Lucas's performance against the Packers showed he had a long way to go, as he completed just thirteen of twenty-eight passes for 140 yards and failed to get his team into the end zone. Fortunately, Parcells was not about to give up on a kid who was already a Parcells guy.

As the preseason progressed, it began to look as if the Jets' most pressing need was for a reliable backup quarterback. Second-guessers felt the team should not have traded Glenn Foley. First Parcells brought in Scott Zolak, who had been a backup in New England, but it didn't work out. Next he made a deal with Green Bay for veteran Rick Mirer. Mirer came out of Notre Dame the same year Drew Bledsoe was available and Parcells actually agonized over the selection before deciding on Bledsoe. Mirer had some big boosters then, including San Francisco's Bill Walsh, who saw him as a bigger, faster Joe Montana. Mirer eventually went to Seattle, where he enjoyed moderate success but never made that big step to the next level. He eventually went to Green Bay as a backup, but was deemed expendable. Now the Jets had him.

At age twenty-nine, Mirer still had the sometimes ominous word "potential" attached to his resume. Parcells and quarterback coach Dan Henning had transformed Testaverde a year earlier by tailoring the offense to his talents and breaking him of his career-long habit of forcing throws when plays broke down. Now they hoped they could do the same with Mirer and make him a dependable backup.

"I'll try to tell him what I've seen of him," Parcells said. "Mostly I'll try to tell him about the players we have here and what he can count on from them. If he does that, you wind up maximizing your resources because you gain confidence in your players."

As the preseason continued, the coach remained his usual testy self. If he wasn't complaining about one thing, then he was complaining about another. If he wasn't picking on one player, then it was another, or maybe two or three at a time. A 10–9 victory over Philadelphia only made him worse. He felt the team had played poorly again, and was doing everything he could to make sure his players didn't become complacent. At one point he compared the team with his 1988 Giants, a very talented crew that he felt could have done much better than the 10–6 record that saw them squeezed out of the playoffs.

"I've seen this kind of behavior on a couple of other teams I've had," the coach said. "They are misjudging what's in front of them. I've never seen this exist without a hard lesson having to be learned."

In a battle for early bragging rights to New York, the Jets whipped the NFC Giants 16–10 in the next-to-last preseason game. The good news was that Ray Lucas played just one series but completed all four of his passes and led the team on a touchdown drive that helped win the game. Martin gained 127 yards, including an eighty-yard jaunt, and showed he was ready for the season.

Then in the final preseason game against the Minnesota Vikings, the team suffered the first in a series of setbacks that would soon appear to be growing into an epidemic. In the first quarter, receiver Wayne Chrebet was running a pass route when he suddenly pulled up lame, favoring his left foot.

"I was just running," Chrebet said later, "I wasn't hit. All of a sudden, I felt a pop."

The pop was the sound a bone breaking in his foot. Now the gutsy receiver, who had been getting better every year and had never missed a game, would be out at least six weeks. The team felt they were deep at wideout, with Dedric Ward stepping in and several other competent players behind him. Tough as it was to lose a guy like Chrebet, they felt they could get through it.

"We had a little setback with Wayne," Parcells said. "But you've got to go on. Every team has them."

More good news was that the Jets rallied from a 10–9 halftime deficit to blow out the tough Vikings 38–17. Mirer threw for three touchdowns and veteran wide receiver Quinn Early stepped up to catch three passes for 124 yards. Even without Chrebet, the Jets seemed ready for the season. The coach didn't want his players to read too many of their press clippings.

Most experts were still picking the team to win the Super Bowl.

CHAPTER TWENTY

His Best Coaching Job Ever

THE JETS OPENED THE 1999 SEASON AT GIANTS STADIUM AGAINST the New England Patriots. It seemed the perfect way to start, playing against Parcells's former team, a team they seemed to have little trouble beating. It must have seemed to the Patriots as if Parcells was haunting them.

That, however, was before the Jets lost Vinny Testaverde.

The unthinkable happened with 7:12 remaining in the second quarter. The quarterback had just handed the ball off to Curtis Martin. When Martin fumbled, Testaverde's football instincts took over and he made a quick move to go after the loose pigskin. Seconds later, he crumbled to the Meadowlands turf, almost unnoticed, and immediately began pounding the carpet with his fist. It wasn't so much the pain, just the knowledge that he had ruptured his left Achilles tendon, an injury that would end his season after less than thirty minutes of football.

Testaverde had already completed ten of fifteen passes for ninety-six yards, one touchdown, and one interception when his season came to an abrupt halt. The Patriots had a 10–7 lead at the time, but the Jets were driving and had recovered the Martin fumble to keep the ball. After the man with the reputation as the strongest quarterback in the league was helped to the sidelines, Parcells had no choice but to bring Tom Tupa in at quarterback. The veteran Tupa was the team's punter and rarely played quarterback anymore. But Mirer was designated the emergency quarterback for the game and couldn't enter until the fourth quarter unless the Jets lost Tupa.

To the surprise of the packed house, Tupa came in and immediately threw a twenty-five-yard touchdown strike to Keyshawn Johnson, giving the Jets the lead at 14–10. New England then rallied to take a 27–16 lead. However, a short time later Tupa connected with Johnson on a sixty-five-yard bomb, bringing the ball to the five. Three plays later he hit tight end Fred Baxter from seven yards out. A two-point conversion failed and it was 27–22 Pats. Tupa actually played very well, completing six of ten passes for 165 yards and two scores. But the game was still up for grabs in the fourth quarter and that's when Parcells opted for Mirer.

The Jets got a break when Bryan Cox intercepted a Bledsoe pass and ran it back twenty-seven yards for another Jets TD. Again the coach went for two points and the try failed. So it was 28–27 Jets. Mirer, however, just didn't play well in the fourth, completing only four of eleven passes for twenty-eight yards. The defense hung tough until New England's Chris Slade intercepted a Mirer toss in the final minutes. New England drove into Jets' territory and Adam Vinatieri won it with a twenty-three-yard field goal with just three seconds left, 30–28.

Suddenly the Jets had to pick up the pieces. Not only was Testaverde's season-ending injury confirmed, but later in the game the team lost versatile running back/punt returner Leon Johnson to torn knee ligaments. He too was gone for the year.

"What? I'm going to put up the white flag?" Parcells snapped to a question about the team's prospects after the game. "No, I'm not going to do that. You know what? Nobody cares. . . . We just have to try and adjust and go forward."

Mirer tried to alleviate some of the fears by saying, "I'll feel better in a month than I do right now, but we don't have time for that. Hopefully, I can pick up right where Vinny left off and get this team where it deserves to be."

All the talk didn't matter. The Jets were in trouble. Three New York daily papers had stories that summed it up the general feeling.

"Say Good Night, Gang Green. Season's Over," was the headline in one story in the *New York Post*.

"Tuna Won't Admit It, But Jet Season Is Over," is how a *Daily News* story described the situation.

"Loss of Testaverde and Leon Johnson Dims Jets' Hopes," read the more conservative *New York Times*.

The meaning was the same in all three. The respective reporters didn't think the Jets could win it without a dominant quarterback. Now the only chance the team might still have was the coaching magic of Bill Parcells. Another *Post* story was headlined "With QB In ER, It's Tuna's Time To Start Operating."

That nickname again. Call him anything you want, it was Bill Parcells who now had the job of figuring a way for his team to compensate for their loss. Testaverde's was the worse, but Leon Johnson was an improving player with game-breaking tendencies. He too would be sorely missed. In addition, Wayne Chrebet would still be on the shelf for another month or more. The disaster that befell Parcells and the Jets in the opening game would present the veteran coach with perhaps the toughest challenge of his career. This was a Super-Bowl-potential team that had just lost his right arm, literally. Unfortunately, it would get a lot worse before it got better.

With the team going on the road to play division rival Buffalo, Parcells had no choice but to go with Mirer, while speculation began as to whether the Jets would try to trade for another veteran quarterback. All week, the coach tried to prepare his team, with the repetitive theme a simple one: "We can win with Rick Mirer at quarterback."

Against Buffalo, they couldn't. In fact, the team came out listless and flat. The Jets were victimized by nine penalties and five dropped passes. Not only didn't they looked like a Super Bowl contender, they looked closer to a sandlot team than a team that was a supposed lock for the playoffs. The 17–3 loss was described by one beat writer as "one of their most uninspired performances of the Bill Parcells era."

Even the coach knew that something was wrong. "This is the first time I've really been disappointed in the team in a long time," Parcells said. "I'm disappointed with the way we played. I don't think the quarterback had much to do with it. It was bad playing, that's what we have to overcome. I don't know what the solution is right at this moment. If we don't do something about it soon it's going to be a long season."

Mirer was just thirteen of twenty-eight for 121 yards. Curtis Martin ran for just forty-five, while the Bills racked up 224 rushing yards, sixty-seven of them by their elusive quarterback, Doug Flutie. Keyshawn Johnson caught a paltry three passes; Dedric Ward, subbing for Chrebet, had just one. There was virtually nothing to grasp onto and say, hey, here's a positive sign. Parcells had been around the block more than enough to know you don't dwell on an injury. Once the star goes down, the understudy comes in. It's Broadway with yard markers: The show must go on. You work with the hand that is dealt you. Ironically, the Jets had started at 0–2 a year earlier when they thought Glenn Foley would be their quarterback, and Testaverde came on to rescue the season. Now Testaverde was gone and someone else would have to step up. But who? And when?

The next five weeks may have been the most difficult of Bill Parcells's entire coaching career. There were losing seasons before, though not many. But never had he been at the helm of a talent-laden team with such high expectations that crashed so suddenly and so thoroughly. Here's a capsule glance at what happened.

Week Three—The Jets lost to the Washington Redskins 27–20, after taking a 17–13 lead into the fourth quarter and still holding it with 8:10 left. A Mirer fumble led to one 'Skins touchdown and several questionable calls by the officials helped seal it, one negating an apparent touchdown catch by Keyshawn Johnson. Mirer was seventeen of thirty-one for 227 yards and a TD. It still appeared he might be able to put it together. The 1999 Jets were the first Parcells-coached team to start 0–3 since 1993.

Week Four—Maybe there was hope yet. The Jets beat the defending Super Bowl champion Broncos 21–13, as Mirer passed for 242 yards and two scores. Problem was that this wasn't the same Bronco team as in the past season. Elway had retired and star running back Terrell Davis was out for the year. Both teams came in at 0–3, but at least the Jets left with one in the win column.

Week Five—The Jacksonville Jaguars whipped the Jets 16–6 at the Meadowlands on a Monday night as the New York offense did an about-face. Parcells had taken over the play-calling responsibility from offensive coordinator Charlie Weis. It didn't help. Parcells himself didn't make excuses. "[The offense] was as poor as we've had in a very long time— maybe ever," he said. "I can't think of anything that was this bad."

Week Six—At 1–4, Parcells made a bold move. Just two and a half hours before meeting the Indianapolis Colts, he named Ray Lucas the starting quarterback. Wayne Chrebet was also back for the first time. Lucas, who had thrown just seven career passes before this day, led the Jets to a 13–0 advantage. But he gave some of it back by throwing an interception, then sustained leg and ankle injuries on the last play of the game. Before that, the Colts had tied it, then went on to win it with a late field goal, 16–13. Curtis Martin had 128 yards, to no avail. Lucas looked good, but would now miss a game or two. Mirer's confidence was shot and Bill Parcells didn't know what to say about a 1–5 team. "It's hard for me right now to express how bad I feel about what's going on here," the coach said.

Week Seven—This was the worst one yet. The Jets were leading the Oakland Raiders by a 20–3 score with just twenty-nine seconds remaining in the third quarter when, once again, the team collapsed. With just five seconds left in the game, Oakland's Rich Gannon capped a ninety-yard drive by firing a five-yard touchdown pass to James Jett, giving the Raiders a 24–23 victory. The Jets had now lost fourth-quarter leads four times and their record dropped to an abysmal 1–6. "I don't know what to tell you," Parcells told the press. "We had a lot of guys involved [to blame] in this one. We just can't make a play under pressure. As you can imagine, I'm just fed up with this situation. I thought it couldn't get any more disappointing than last week. But this one is."

What to do? It was almost a case of divine providence that gave the Jets a bye week after the loss to Oakland. At least there would be some time to heal, some time to think, a week to try to figure a way to turn it around. There were also some who worried about the effect of this disastrous season on the coach's health. Ex-Giant George Martin felt his former coach and good friend was suffering.

"What you see on the outside doesn't matter," Martin said. "There's precious little correlation from what people perceive on the outside and what's going on inside him. This is tearing him up. He doesn't want this to be the final chapter in his coaching career."

People remembered how exhausted Parcells had been at the end of the successful 1998 season, and that his doctors advised him not to coach in the Pro Bowl. Yet he looked surprisingly fit and vigorous on the sidelines, despite the pained expressions generated by his team's often woeful performances. Will McDonough, for one, felt that it had taken all these years for the coach to learn how to handle the rigors of the business.

"I think he's learned to adapt himself better to the medication he takes and to balance it with his workouts and conditioning," McDonough explained. "For years I would tell him, 'Bill, you do too much. You just do.' I mean, he's relentless when he gets up on some of those machines, like the Stairmaster. He does too much for a guy his age and his size. It's like everyone else, when you do too much you're gonna get tired and worn down.

"I think doing too much physically, being under pressure, and eating too much as the year went along would result in his being worn out at the end of every season. I think he's done a much better job this year handling all of that."

Parcells still, however, had to figure out how to handle his floundering team. But before he could do that, he had to deal with yet another tragedy. The morning after the loss to the Raiders, a very unusual and disturbing story hit the news wires. A private Lear Jet that had taken off from Orlando, Florida, heading to Dallas, Texas, was now suddenly flying north, across the heartland of America, and no one on the ground could contact the crew or passengers. The drama continued for several hours as the plane few northward. Authorities began to assume the worst, that something that happened on the plane had either killed all aboard or rendered them unconscious. Soon the plane would run out of fuel.

The jet continued to head north, flying on automatic pilot at forty-five-thousand feet. Then the inevitable happened. The plane spiraled downward and crashed into a lonely South Dakota pasture. The names of the passengers further shocked the nation. On board was pro golfer Payne Stewart, who had won the U.S. Open earlier in the year and was one of the most popular golfers on the tour. Also aboard was Robert Fraley, Parcells's longtime friend and agent, who had represented him since his first contract with the Giants in 1983. Investigators felt that a sudden loss of cabin pressure rendered everyone unconscious and caused the temperature in the cabin to plunge well below freezing. Everyone on board had died long before the tragic crash.

"To the best of my knowledge I think I was [Bob Fraley's] first football client," the saddened coach said. "He was a friend. It just evolved to a lot more than a business relationship quickly. We've been close for a number of years. It's really hard for me to tell you how I feel about it."

It seemed almost uncanny. In 1983, when Fraley first represented him, Parcells had gone through a season of hell. The team was losing, an assistant coach died, a former player died, Parcells's parents died. Now, in 1999, Leon Hess had died, the team was losing, key players were injured, and now a very close friend was killed. As he had done in 1983, Parcells again found the strength to pull himself together and focus on trying to return his football team to respectability. He was determined not to let things continue along the same downward direction. The team was too talented for that.

"We're not that far off," he said. "Anyone who's been watching the games knows we still have a chance to do something here. It's these things that, regardless of what our situation is, if you could just do a couple things better you know you're going to win games.

"I like this team," he continued, "I don't have problems with these players. They work and do what I ask them to do. When I said [after the Raider loss] that I'm fed up, I mean I'm fed up with not being able to get them over the hump, at not being able to do enough to help them get over the win. I [still] believe we're going to win every Sunday, I really do. Do I think we can turn it around? Yes, I do."

There was no quit in this guy. Then again, there never was. The team's next game was against the Arizona Cardinals at the Meadowlands on November 7. Parcells wasn't sure whether Ray Lucas would be sufficiently recovered from his leg injury to play, but he seemed to have already made a mental commitment to go with the youngster as soon as he was ready and stick with him for the rest of the year.

"Lucas whetted my appetite a long time ago," he explained. "I like a quarterback who's a fighter. I don't think you can win in this league unless you've got a quarterback who's a fighter. We've seen some tremendous passing quarterbacks who don't have that little extra to get their teams to the promised land. I've seen the Billy Kilmers of this world who can somehow get there teams there."

Kilmer was a tough, battling quarterback who helped the Washington Redskins reach the Super Bowl back in 1973. Kilmer couldn't run, didn't have a rocket arm, and his passes wobbled through the air. But if you knocked him down, he'd get up and spit in your eye, then continue to come at you. He was a winner. That Parcells remembered and admired him tells you something about the coach. Kilmer would have been a definite Parcells guy. Now, he apparently had that same feeling about Ray Lucas. Even though Mirer had a few pretty good games, the coach seemed to feel there was something missing.

"[Mirer's] a laid-back guy," Parcells said. "I can't pass judgement. I don't know him that well."

That terse statement spoke volumes. Yet when it came time to play Arizona, Mirer was in there once more as Lucas's ankle still wasn't healed. The defense played well, and Mirer hit Keyshawn with a forty-three-yard touchdown pass that gave the Jets a 12–7 victory. Win number two—at last. But while Mirer had made a beautiful throw to win the game, Parcells again said, quickly, "You can't judge the passing game today." It all pointed to Lucas taking over the following week against the Patriots at Foxboro, in a showcased Monday night game.

Lucas it was, and for the first time all year, the Jets of 1999 looked like the Jets of a year earlier. With Curtis Martin thundering for 149 rushing yards, and Lucas completing eighteen of thirty-one passes for 153 yards and two touchdowns, the Jets beat the favored Pats 24–17. The only note of caution was that the Jets had a 24–3 lead at one point and almost fell victim to another comeback effort. Lucas, however, had passed an initial test. He was poised and tough, and ran a controlled offense that featured Martin's running and a close-to-the-vest passing game.

"I though Ray did a pretty good job of moving the team," said Parcells, not wanting to gush. "He looked pretty good out there. Like I told the team, even though we're 3–6, it's too soon to quit."

The only sour note was the loss of left tackle Jason Fabini for the season due to yet another knee injury. Key players continued to go down, yet the team was upbeat. Once again Bill Belichick's defense harassed Drew Bledsoe the entire game as Parcells's mastery over his former team continued. For the first time, a victory had the players excited, especially when their coach reminded them that they had won ten of their final eleven games a year ago.

"It's been done before," said Wayne Chrebet, who was regaining his old form with seven catches for seventy yards. "If we can put another one of those streaks together . . ."

In other words, they were thinking playoffs. Perhaps the next two weeks would tell, because the club would be meeting a pair of winning teams: the 7–3 Buffalo Bills and the surprising 7–2 Indianapolis Colts. Buffalo provided the Jets with their third straight victory. They whipped the Bills 17–7, with Lucas completing sixteen of twenty passes for 142 yards. Again he played controlled football, well within himself, and didn't make mistakes. The team was 4–6. Someone pointed out that they had lost fourth-quarter leads four times. Had they won those games, the club would have been 8–2 and again considered one of the elite teams in the league. Were they now really that far from reclaiming a lofty perch?

Indianapolis would be an acid test. The Colts were now 8–2, and with second-year quarterback Peyton Manning emerging as a bona fide star and the AFC's top-rated passer, the Jets knew they would have their hands full. This was a tough game, both teams slugging it out and refusing to yield their turf easily. What it came down to was this: The Colts had a 13–6 lead late in the fourth quarter when Lucas had the Jets driving. He completed seven straight passes to bring the ball to the Colts' seventeen–yard line with 3:20 left. But a penalty nullified a Martin run to the 10. Finally, the Jets had their last chance, with the ball back on the 26.

Lucas dropped back again, saw Chrebet breaking into the end zone, and fired. The ball brushed through the usually sure-handed receiver's palms, bounced off his face mask, and fell to the ground. There was just 1:39 left, allowing the Colts to run out the clock and secure the 13–6 win. Like so many of the others, this one hurt.

"It's a catch I've made thousands of times in practice and in games over the course of my career," said Chrebet. "I've got to catch that ball. . . . I pride myself on making plays on third or fourth down when the team needs me to make them."

"This is probably the worst loss of the season, even worse than the Raiders game," Parcells said, " because I know it should have been better."

"The defense was awesome," said quarterback Lucas. "Offensively, we didn't get it done. We gave the game away."

No excuses. Ray Lucas didn't make any. He had already learned the same lessons that Harry Carson, Phil McConkey, Ottis Anderson, and the other Giants players had learned a decade or so earlier. That's why Lucas had become a Parcells guy so quickly. The downside of it all was that the team had fallen to 4–7. Now, even if they ran the table to finish at 9–7, the playoffs would still be in doubt.

A week later, the team bottomed out for the second time. Playing a New York Giants team that didn't have the same level of talent, the Jets wouldn't have to worry about the bragging rights to the city for very long. Instead, they had to deal with a blitzkrieg, an invasion of Panzer tanks wearing Giants uniforms. It was one of those magical days when nothing seemed to go wrong for the Giants offense. Coach Jim Fassel's team scored four touchdowns and two field goals on their first seven possessions. At that point they had a 34–7 lead and the game was all but over. The final was 41–28, with the Giants outgaining the Jets in total yardage 490 to 291.

Like his players, Parcells made no excuses. He also didn't hide his feelings. "It's the first time in three years that I have been ashamed," he said, afterward. "I take responsibility for the lack of preparation and the lack of effort on the part of our team. They didn't play well, and I really don't know the reason why. We were certainly outplayed, outprepared, outcoached and out-everythinged, and I am ashamed."

Whether the team suffered a letdown after the lost to the Colts is hard to say. But that game pretty much dashed their playoff hopes. Perhaps it was a delayed reaction, or maybe the Giants just had a perfect day. Didn't matter. It was a crushing loss, a painful remainder that the team simply hadn't played up to its talent level all season long, the rash of injuries notwithstanding. At 4–8, they were once again on the brink of losing the season. Teams in this kind of a funk sometimes simply quit. It wasn't difficult to envision the Jets coming in at 5–11 or maybe even 4–12. The headlines the next day were a painful reminder:

"BIG BLUE RULES BIG APPLE"

"JETS FEELING LOST AFTER PUNY EFFORT"

"SHAME ON GANG GREEN"

"AN ASHAMED PARCELLS SEARCHES FOR ANSWERS"

There's little doubt that Parcells had to be down. The team had apparently weathered the loss of Testaverde and the others, and had righted itself from its 1–6 start to win three straight and keep some semblance of playoff hopes at 4–6. Now, the tough loss to the Colts followed by the debacle against the Giants really sounded the death knell. The coach must have been wondering how to re-energize his team, how to bring them back to play the final four games without having them mail it in.

Chances are he was also looking at the bigger picture. Leon Hess was gone, the team on the auction block. He had no idea as yet who the new owner would be, but he surely remembered what had happened when James Orthwein sold the Patriots to Bob Kraft. It could happen again, a new owner thinking he knew more about football and running a team than his coach. Parcells was simply too old to tolerate that kind of situation again. He had also lost his friend and agent Robert Fraley, another tragedy that undoubtedly dampened his spirits and made it difficult to come to work each day.

On the other side of the coin, he was a football coach, a man who had devoted his entire life to the sport. He knew he had to look at these upcoming four games as games his team *had* to win. There was no other way. If he had to start yelling and screaming, he would. If he had to challenge the players, challenge their manhood, appeal to their pride, he would. If it meant making some personnel changes to infuse new life into the team, he would do that, too. According to Will McDonough, who had covered many of the great coaches in the NFL since the 1960s, there was a common link. It coursed through the veins of the yellers and screamers, as well as the quieter, more low-key coaches. It was present in coaches who are wired on emotion, and those who rely on more cerebral methods to get the job done. All were winners, and McDonough feels he knows why.

"The great coaches all have the same thing in common," he explained. "[Don] Shula, [Bill] Walsh, [Tom] Landry, [Chuck] Noll, Paul Brown—completely different personalities in every way, seven or eight guys. The one thing they always had is toughness. Every one of them in their own way is tough. When it came time to make the tough decisions, whether it was in personnel, cutting guys, drafting guys, challenging guys, screaming at guys. No matter how they did it, every one of those guys would cut your heart out. None of them would say, 'Well, I'm keeping this old timer around for another couple of years because he's a wonderful guy.' They'd say, 'Hey, time to go. We have to move on.' I've been around all those guys and that's the common thread that links every one of them."

McDonough also felt that the Jets were working through a snake-bit season, that it was injuries that had taken them down, that no coach could have had the team in contention under these circumstances.

"Had Testaverde not been hurt they would have been so far ahead in most games that they wouldn't have had to worry about the fourth quarter. That's the only reason they aren't up with the Colts at the top of the AFC. They lost Vinny without him getting hit. They lost Leon Johnson in the first game. Eric Green has been in and out. Now Ryan Young and Jason Fabini, their two best tackles are gone. Jason Ferguson, their best defensive lineman, he's gone. Bryan Cox has been hurt. Otis Smith is out for the year. [Linebacker] Chas Cascaden went out without being hit. Chrebet went out in training camp the same way.

"Look, even if they just had Vinny, you know, Vinny's worth seven, ten, fourteen points a game. Look at the average score from last year to this. They just haven't been scoring enough point to be a good team."

Find a way. That was always something Parcells was able to do, whether preparing his team for the game or making halftime adjustments. All the years of coaching had made him one of the best, or so people had said. No one, however can live on his reputation. That was then and this was now. With four games left, Parcells was once again faced with finding a way. Next up were the always-tough Miami Dolphins.

Playing before a packed house at the Meadowlands, the Jets set the tone for the rest of the season. It was a game in which the Jets finally did to someone else what had been done to them all year. They rallied in the fourth quarter, scoring twenty-two unanswered points, turning a 13–6 deficit into a 28–20 victory, the kind of victory that was just what the doctor ordered. Lucas had his best game of the year, completing twenty-two of thirty-eight passes for 230 yards and a pair of touchdowns. He had now thrown 130 consecutive passes without an interception. He was doing something all good quarterbacks do, taking care of the football.

Lucas also showed the kind of toughness Parcells liked. In the fourth period he took a huge hit on a helmet-to-helmet collision with defensive tackle Daryl Gardener. Lucas was dazed, had a hard time focusing, and came to the sidelines. One play later he was back in the game and promptly fired a twenty-four-yard touchdown strike to Johnson.

"He has the attitude of a hard-hitting safety," said tackle Jumbo Elliott. "Maybe that's from his special teams days. It's kind of neat."

Keyshawn Johnson also had his best game of the year, grabbing a career-high eleven passes for 144 yards. Aaron Glenn had a key interception in the fourth quarter, helping set up the drive that tied the score. Martin ran for seventy-five yards to keep the defense honest. It was a total team effort, epitomized by rookie Randy Thomas, who said, "The spirit was up. We got our emotions involved. We had a spark, some kind of spark."

As for the coach, he told the media that he had used a different approach during the week. "I tried to practice my team on the mental part of the game this week,' he said, "and take it easy on the physical part. I wanted to eliminate that 'We're tired, we're beat up,' and all that stuff. I tried to eliminate that excuse, and they responded pretty well."

Find a way. Apparently, Parcells had done that once again, varying his approach and his practice schedule, letting his team rest a bit physically while getting sky-high mentally. And it worked! At 5–8 and with three games left, there was still a mathematical possibility of making the playoffs, albeit a small one. Next came a meeting with the Dallas Cowboys, another team struggling to make the playoffs. The Cowboys were at 7–6, but still a formidable team.

Once again Parcells had the Jets ready. Dallas was hungry, looking for a playoff spot and possible division title, and they took a 21–13 lead into the fourth quarter. For a team that blew four fourth-quarter leads earlier in the season, the odds didn't seem good. But these were not the Jets of September and October, these were the Jets that had stormed back against Miami a week earlier. Now they went to work again.

Once again it was Ray Lucas, improving weekly, who stepped up. He went to work like a seasoned veteran, hitting Chrebet for thirty-eight yards, then Johnson for fourteen, before culminating the drive with a two-yard TD toss to Blake Spence. An attempt at a quarterback draw for a two-point conversion failed, but the Jets had the Cowboys' lead down to 21–19. Then the defense did its job, stopping Troy Aikman and the Dallas offense, giving Lucas a chance to win it.

The Jets took over at their own 40 with less than six minutes left. Once again they began moving on the Dallas defense. With Martin producing a thirty-eight-yard run to highlight an eleven-play drive that took minutes off the clock, the Jets moved to the Cowboys' 19. From there, John Hall booted a thirty-seven-yard field goal with just 1:35 left that proved to be the game-winner. The Jets had taken a 22–21 decision. In completing twenty of thirty-four passes for 229 yards, Lucas was again the toast of the town.

"That field was his today," said Wayne Chrebet, who had eight catches for 108 yards. "[This game] shows you what kind of player he is."

Parcells, in his understated way, also felt that Lucas had now justified his confidence as well as his instinctive feeling that the former Rutgers star could make a good NFL quarterback. "It's been good the last couple of outings," the coach said, "but this puts him over the top as a starter."

In typical fashion, the coach couldn't help taking a few jabs at the media and at the armchair quarterbacks who thought Lucas was nothing more than a special-teams player. "He's improving, he's come a long way," Parcells said. "You guys had him out of here after the Green Bay game," he said. "Now you're giving him his job for [for 2000]. Close your eyes and tell me what's next."

By this time Lucas had a 4–3 record as a starter, and the seven teams he had gone up against had a combined record of 61–35. He was earning his "pelts" against quality teams and his emergence had clearly brought the Jets out of their early season funk. Despite all the injuries, the team was suddenly looking upper-echelon once again. Their playoff hopes were slim, but they were giving it their all and certainly were playing as well as many of the teams that would be in the postseason.

Miami was next. At 9–5, the Dolphins still weren't in the playoffs and were not playing well. They needed this game, but the time for teams pushing the Jets around and pressuring them into mistakes has passed. The Jets were now the ones applying the pressure. It turned into a game that almost mirrored those of the last two weeks. This one was hard-fought and close for three quarters. When the Dolphins' J. J. Johnson scored on a one-yard plunge with 13:32 left in the game, Miami took a 28–24 lead. Against these late-season Jets, however, fourth-quarter leads were no longer safe.

Bring on Ray Lucas for an encore. He wasn't having a strong game until that final session. Then, he came alive, hitting all five passes in the closing minutes, including touchdown tosses of fifty yards to Chrebet and fifty-six yards to Dedric Ward. When the smoke cleared the Jets had their third straight victory, 38–31, and were now a game away from finishing at .500, something that no one thought possible after the 1–6 start.

Ray Lucas was again the story. Earlier in the season he rarely threw the ball downfield. Now, with his own confidence soaring and the coach's confidence in him growing, he was beginning to air it out with success.

"If he gets that going," Parcells said, talking about Lucas throwing long, "he's going to be dangerous. He went through a dry spell early in the game, but he rallied back."

The game also featured a ninety-eight-yard return of an interception by improving cornerback Marcus Coleman. Now a number of the younger players—Lucas, Coleman, guards Randy Thomas and Kerry Jenkins, and tackle Ryan Young—were all contributing. Some got the call because of injuries to veterans. Others earned it with their talent and desire. All of them responded to the prodding of their veteran coach.

"I think we have some developing players that I'm starting to see a little something from, and it's encouraging," Parcells said, in typically understated tones. "I'm pleased about that."

He had to be more than pleased. His team was one game away from finishing at 8–8 and winning its last four games. A few minutes later, he couldn't hold his enthusiasm back any longer.

"This is the best win of the year for us," he said. "That was a gut check.

There weren't many people who thought we could come down here with nothing on the line and beat these guys, who were playing for everything. This is not an easy team to beat and this is a tough place to play. I'm real proud of these kids."

Both coach and team seemed fully rejuvenated. Parcells looked rested and healthy on the sidelines each week, coaching his heart out, as usual, and showing no signs of the exhaustion that had crept in at the end of the last season. It was almost as if the youthful exuberance of his team was re-invigorating the coach. In addition, there had been a feeling all year, what with the death of Leon Hess and the impending sale of the team, that Parcells might consider stepping down after the season. All the players, especially the younger ones, wanted the coach back. That was their self-motivation and, in a sense, it was ironic. Parcells was always known as a great motivator; yet perhaps in the closing week of the 1999 season, the greatest motivation may have come from the fact that his players wanted him back—another tribute to a coach who always seemed to win over the majority of his players, despite the tough, biting way he worked them and a tongue that could cut the heart out of the strongest of men.

Ray Lucas spoke for many on the team when he talked about Parcells returning for the 2000 season. "I would be shocked, definitely, if he didn't come back for one more year," the quarterback said. "He wants to go out on top, as a winner. Coach is a winner, and if we go out 8–8, that wouldn't be a winning season. I'm sure he wants to come back and have a better go of it without worrying about who's having surgery this week and who'll get hurt next week. He wants to win."

Now there was one game left and this one, too, was against a team trying to make the playoffs. The Jets were out of it now, but the Seattle Seahawks could still clinch the AFC title with a win at the Meadowlands. If they lost, the Seahawks would need Oakland to beat Kansas City later in the day to take the division. Mike Holmgren's Seahawks were 9–6 but had lost four of their last five after an 8–2 start. Holmgren was perhaps *the* hottest coaching commodity in the league. He had led the Green Bay Packers back to respectability, bringing them to two straight Super Bowl appearances and one championship, the one in which the Packers topped the Parcells-led New England Patriots. Like Parcells, Holmgren wanted complete control over his football operation and wouldn't get that in Green Bay, where General Manager Ron Wolf directed personnel matters. So Holmgren left for Seattle, another franchise hungering for a winner, and was given the silver-platter treatment, including the control he wanted as well as the highest-dollar coaching contract in history. When his team arrived in New York, however, Holmgren just wanted to talk about his longtime rival.

"Bill Parcells, in my opinion, is probably the best coach in football," Holmgren told the New York press. "There are a lot of good coaches, but he probably gets as much out of his players as any coach I've ever seen. Bill is one of those guys I admire and I've tried to take some of his ideas and incorporate them into my philosophy. The best thing you can say about him is, he wins. He just wins."

Parcells, in turn had the same kind of respect for Holmgren, then added an interesting take on Holmgren's exodus from Green Bay and arrival in Seattle.

"[Mike] had a great support system in place in Green Bay," Parcells said. "Now Mike is trying to prove to himself that he can do it on his own [as the coach and GM]. That's another challenge. Guys that are like us need that. You need something to keep you going."

Would the challenge of bringing a third team to the Super Bowl be enough to bring Parcells back? *Guys like us need something to keep us going.* The challenge this year was an unexpected one, to return a 1–6 team to respectability by the end of the season, to instill confidence in young players and put all the pieces back in place for 2000. The coach had apparently met that challenge. Despite the Seahawks' winning record, the two teams were going in different directions. It would surprise no one if the Jets won.

Parcells had certainly received his share of "best coach" accolades over the past two years. But perhaps the most flattering came from his first boss, longtime Giants owner Wellington Mara. Mara had watched Parcells not only rebuild his struggling franchise, but win a pair of Super Bowls as well. According to Will McDonough, Mara was another who thought the 1999 season was special. He called Parcells during the Jets' resurgence and flat-out told him,

"Bill, this is the greatest coaching job you have ever done."

CHAPTER TWENTY-TWO

A Tough Decision
Made Tougher

THE SEASON FINALE WAS PLAYED ON JANUARY 2, 2000, THE TEAM'S first game of the new millennium. This wasn't one of the Jets' better games, but good teams don't always have to be at their best to win. All it took was a single touchdown and four John Hall field goals, coupled with a very strong defensive effort, to produce the 19–9 victory that finally brought the team back to .500 for the season.

Lucas was efficient, no more, but Curtis Martin turned on the burners and gained 158 yards on thirty-four carries to finish the year with a new Jets rushing record of 1,464 yards. The defense held Seattle quarterback Jon Kitna to a second-half log of seven completions in twenty-three tries. In addition, they kept Ricky Watters and the Seattle runners at bay, allowing just a total of thirty-three yards on twelve carries.

"[The Jets] feel good about themselves," Parcells said, afterward. "I really think they played like champs the second half of the season. Not that it makes any difference because 8–8 is 8–8. [But] this kind of evidence will carry over, that there's a way to come back from a big hole."

The irony was that Seattle made the playoffs when Oakland did beat Kansas City. At the same time, Seattle's loss enabled the Dolphins to slip in as a wild card, and the Jets had beaten the Dolphins twice over the regular season.

"The way the NFL is, we've got a good enough bunch that we can beat anybody we play, if we play well," said veteran tackle Jumbo Elliott. "It's great now, but it's going to be hard later. Right now we're happy, because we battled back [from a 1–6 record]. But as we watch the playoff games, we're going to be kicking ourselves."

Or, as Ray Lucas said, "The clock struck twelve for me, and it's time to go home."

Lucas was going home to the tune of being the second highest–rated passer in the AFC, behind only Peyton Manning. That's how far he had come. But statistics and number were not what was on the players' and fans' minds as soon as the final gun sounded. In fact, the chant that came cascading down from all corners of the Meadowlands in the game's final minutes expressed everyone's feelings:

"One more year! One more year!
One more year!"

That was a message clearly intended for Bill Parcells. It wouldn't be surprising if some of the players chimed in, if only mouthing the words. Perhaps no one will ever know the feelings that were swirling in the coach's mind at that moment. He was extremely proud of a team that had come back from the brink of extinction to win their last four games, all against playoff-bound teams, as well as seven of their last nine, to finish at 8–8. Had they manage to stave off just one of those early season fourth-quarter collapses, they would have been in the playoffs. Then there was no telling how far they might have gone. That, however, was pure conjecture and it paled in comparison to the conjecture about Parcells's future.

His final address to his team was an emotional one. He had choked up some, then went around the room hugging his players, telling them how proud he was, and already motivating them to continue next year. But what about next year? After the game he spoke to the media.

"I'm not trying to be nostalgic now, but you know when I think about football, it's going to be right here," he said, speaking of Giants Stadium, the home of both his New York teams. "This is my home, and nobody can be luckier to have done this where I've done it. There's no coach in the league ever that's been as lucky as me, that's had that good fortune. I realize that."

Was it a kind of farewell address? The question was asked quickly. When would the coach make a decision about his future? He gave his usual answer, leaving much open to interpretation.

"I'm going to think this over real quick," he said. "We've got imminent changes here in the organization. I have a responsibility to the organization, and I will adhere to that responsibility. I'll do the best I can to get things squared away very quickly. Don't try to interpret what might happen. I have a few things to think over. I have to talk to some people."

There was no doubt as to what was the number-one topic of conversation in the New York sports media, and around much of the NFL. The players seemed to think he would be back, that the team had built such a solid foundation for the next season that Parcells wouldn't be able to resist taking one more crack at it. One person on the team who was close to Parcells said he thought the coach would return for his fourth season, yet an assistant said, "I don't think he knows yet."

There were, however, many different factors at work. One was the impending sale of the team. The two prime bidders were Charles Dolan, the chairman of Cablevision, a company that had already bought Madison Square Garden, including the basketball Knicks and hockey Rangers. The second serious bidder was Robert Wood Johnson, heir to the Johnson & Johnson pharmaceutical fortune. Both men could obviously afford the price, with the bidding now thought to be up around the $600 million mark. It was thought that both would be essentially "hands-off" owners, the only kind Parcells could tolerate.

Another key ingredient in his decision was, of course, the death of Leon Hess. Had Hess lived, the team would not yet be up for sale. In addition, Parcells had such a genuine and caring affection for the late owner that chances were he would have stayed on to try once more to give Hess that elusive Super Bowl title. In addition, had the team not come out of its tailspin and finished with an embarrassing record, a 3–13 or 4–12, chances were the coach would probably return for the simple reason that he wouldn't want his final season to be remembered in such a negative light.

Then there was the Bill Belichick factor. When Parcells was in the midst of his bitter breakup with Bob Kraft and the Patriots, the Jets first announced that his longtime defensive coordinator would become head coach and Parcells a consultant. Once Parcells was cleared to coach, it was written into Belichick's contract that whenever Parcells decided to step down Belichick would automatically be elevated to the head coaching slot. Just a year earlier, Leon Hess gave Belichick a one-million-dollar bonus not to interview with other teams for a head coaching job. The meaning of the bonus was clear: Wait for Parcells to step down and take his job. Yet in the closing weeks of the season, rumors began circulating that the Patriots would fire Pete Carroll and that Belichick was Bob Kraft's first choice to replace him.

Prior to the season finale, NFL Commissioner Paul Tagliabue had told the Jets that they could not stop Belichick from talking to other teams, despite a rather confusing contract. Teams cannot tamper with a head coach under contract if they are offering the same job. But they can speak to an assistant under contract if they are offering him a promotion, i.e., the head coaching job. Technically, Belichick was still an assistant. If Parcells stepped down, however, he would instantly become the head coach. Though it was first thought that Parcells would wait for a new owner before making a decision, he might step up the timetable to keep his old antagonist, Kraft, from pirating Belichick away.

"The only reason [Parcells] is going to make a rapid decision is that he thinks the Patriots are offering a job to Belichick," an anonymous source said. He also felt, the source said, that some of his assistants would follow Belichick to New England. It was interesting how many "anonymous sources" began feeding information to the media. There was also some talk of friction between the two longtime friends because of the possibility that New England wanted Belichick. Yet with less than a minute remaining in the Seattle game, Parcells had walked over to Belichick on the sidelines and put his arm around him, observers calling it a rare show of affection between the two men.

So speculation ran rampant on the Monday morning following the Seattle game. Would he or wouldn't he? Everyone had an opinion and, knowing Parcells as they did, the opinion was always tempered with a "but . . ." One of the coach's favorite phrases was "I reserve the right to change my mind." Obviously, he had changed his mind several times in his career, saying one thing and, a short time later, saying the opposite.

Will McDonough, a longtime Parcells friend, didn't have any firsthand information, either. But writing in the *Boston Globe* Monday morning, he reported that people close to the coach expected him to retire, maybe as early as Monday afternoon.

"He didn't say anything official after the game," McDonough quoted someone who had worked with Parcells for years as saying, "but he looked and acted like a guy who was at peace with himself and a guy who had made the decision about his future."

McDonough concluded his column by saying, "After the [Seattle] game, Parcells . . . went out of his way to thank the members of his coaching staff, many of whom have coached with him for more than fifteen years. If Parcells leaves, Belichick is expected to keep the staff and the system in place. . . . Parcells always said he wouldn't be coaching when he was sixty. He is fifty-eight."

It sounded as if McDonough, who perhaps knew Parcells better than any of the beat writers, also expected a retirement announcement. As it turned out, the coach was true to his word. He made his decision almost immediately. In reality, he had made it even before that. The word spread quickly on Monday, January 3. Everyone who loved playing for him, watching him work the sidelines, or rooting for his team saw their worst fears realized.

Bill Parcells was retiring.

He had told Belichick of his decision Saturday morning, before the Seattle game. Immediately after the victory over the Seahawks, the coach informed Jets President Steve Gutman of his decision. Though Parcells didn't officially tell his players until Monday morning, Keyshawn Johnson said many of the players suspected what was coming just by the way the coach spoke to them after the game.

"You look a guy in the eyes, and see what I've seen—he doesn't give kudos to everybody, he doesn't say anything to players," Johnson explained. "[But] to tell a person they've done superb and they're champions and they're going to always be a success, you know he's sending a subliminal message by saying that, that he's getting ready to step aside. I think a lot of players caught that."

That night, Parcells told friends and family of his decision, then had dinner with his mentor Mickey Corcoran at a local restaurant near Giants Stadium. "My thoughts were really very personal and I didn't even tell my own immediate family, my daughters and my wife, until the night before I was going to actually do this," he would say.

What he said, basically, was that it was time to step down, that he felt he was leaving the franchise in good shape with Bill Belichick taking over. As he told his players, he didn't feel he had the energy to give the job one hundred percent any more. It was the right time to go.

"Could I coach sixteen more games? Yeah, I could probably do it," he said. "Maybe thirty-two or forty-eight. But you have to have the committed

effort to do it and want to do it at the level I would want to do it. I demanded
a lot from my players in terms of commitment, and they have the right to
expect the same from me."

He also read his players part of a poem called "The Man in the Glass,"
written in 1934 by a man named Dale Winbrow. It was a poem that said
a man should listen to the voice in his own head and be true to the person
he sees in the mirror every morning.

When he finished speaking to the team, he read the final lines of the
poem

> *You may fool the whole world down the pathway of life,*
> *And get pats on the back as you pass,*
> *But your final reward will be heartaches and tears,*
> *If you've cheated the man in the glass.*

In other words, he'd be cheating himself, the fans, and the players if
he didn't step down at this time. Looking deep within himself, he knew it
was over. The Jets players, who heard it first, were shocked and then
saddened by the news.

"He was heartfelt in there today when he talked to us," Ray Lucas said.
"I know it hurts him inside. We're going to miss him a lot. He gave me an
opportunity. . . . He saw me grow and believed in me when I was a nobody.
And he stood by me when everybody else didn't give me a chance."

"It was very quiet," said linebacker Dwayne Gordon. "You could hear
a pin drop. Players were just sitting there looking at each other as if to
say, 'What do we do now?' "

Safety Victor Green put it this way. "It was Parcells's game. It was his
moment, and it was a good moment. He's a proud man. There's nothing
wrong with it. When it's your time it's your time. He left a good legacy."

Defensive back Ray Mickens, picking up on Parcells's observation that
he could no longer give one hundred percent, had an observation of his
own. "Bill Parcells at seventy-five percent is better than most coaches in
the league. For him to go out in this way it sort of hurts, because you enjoy
playing for a coach like him."

At his news conference, the departing coach talked some more about
his decision, saying it had nothing to do with his health, which was fine.

"If we hadn't finished the way we had, I think I probably would have
considered even more strongly staying on," he continued. "But the way

we finished, on a positive note and knowing that the team felt positive and felt good about itself and that we won thirty games in three years, I think they will approach next year with a confidence that they know they can certainly complete."

He also alluded to Leon Hess and confirmed what many thought, that if Hess were still alive his decision may have been different. "There was no way I could have ever left him—and I mean that," he said. "It's very hard to describe to you what this guy was like. It really is. He was just in my corner. . . . He was a wonderful man."

There were more questions, more answers, capsules of his career, and comments on the resignation from everyone, even those who didn't follow football closely. He was even asked if he had resigned just to keep the New England Patriots from getting Bill Belichick.

"What the Patriots wanted to do had nothing to do with my decision to leave coaching . . . nothing whatsoever," he said. "I had known pretty much for the last month that I was going to give up coaching at the end of this season, and Saturday I spoke with Belichick about it.

"I have been talking with Belichick all the way along throughout the season. Saturday morning I met with him and asked him if he wanted to be the next head coach of the New York Jets. He told me, 'I've been planning on it,' and he said this is the job he wanted. If he was upset about not having the chance to go to New England, he's never said anything to me about it. I don't think that's the case at all."

There had been a previous report on television channel ESPN that Belichick was upset because he did not have a chance to speak with the Patriots and perhaps consider any offer they might make. Parcells said it wasn't true. He also said that no matter what rumors might start, he would never coach another football game. It was over. However, he was supposedly going to remain with the team as its chief operating officer for an undetermined time. He said, however, that he would not interfere with the football operation.

"I don't know what my title is going to be, football operations director, something like that," he said later that day, in an interview on radio station WFAN. "I think an experienced coach like Bill Belichick, who has been in the league twenty-five years, should have the right to make football decisions. I'm going to relinquish that to him and act as a confidant and consultant to him, and keep the rest of the operation going well so we don't miss anything."

On the radio show, Parcells repeated the reason for his resignation, that he had told Leon Hess last winter that the 1999 season would probably be his last year. He then talked again about how the job had become a year-round grind.

"If you don't feel you can do it with the commitment that is necessary now, which is really 365 days a year, you can't do it. I mean, the season is over today and the first thing I'm doing is talking to the doctors about players who have to be operated on, things like that. There's really no end to it. I wouldn't feel right telling [people] I was going to do it if I didn't feel I could. Remember, this has been my life since 1964, so you just don't take thirty-five years and say you're not going to do this anymore without some trepidation."

He also talked about how lucky he was to have coached fifteen years in the NFL; about people such as Wellington Mara, who gave him his first chance with the Giants; and about some of the players in whom he believed and who made him proud over the years, the last being Ray Lucas, who had justified the coach's faith in him by producing when finally given a chance—the last of the many "Parcells guys."

So it all seemed neat and final. No loose ends. The only thing that could mar this smooth transition was the new owner, still unknown. But a smart new owner would leave the status quo, let Parcells dissolve into Belichick, and hope the winning would continue. As difficult as it was to believe that Parcells was leaving, at least all the pieces were still in place. That's what everyone thought . . . for one day.

Then the dream turned into a nightmare, completely unexpected and mind-blowing in its implication. The day after Parcells resigned, Bill Belichick stepped to the podium for a packed news conference, ostensibly to talk about his first day as head coach of the Jets and his plans for the team. Surprise. It didn't happen that way.

Instead, Bill Belichick stepped to the podium and abruptly resigned!

Looking somewhat disheveled and nervous, Belichick dropped the bomb as soon as the press conference began by saying he was going to read a short prepared statement, a copy of which he had given Steve Gutman just moments before the conference started. Belichick read:

"Due to various uncertainties surrounding my position as it relates to the team of new ownership, I've decided to resign as the head coach of the

New York Jets. I've given this decision very careful consideration. I would like to wish the entire New York Jets organization, the players, coaching staff, and new ownership the very best of luck."

Four sentences equaled a fait accompli. Belichick just quit the job he supposedly had wanted so badly, the job he had been prepared for, contracted for, and paid for, including the one-million-dollar bonus he received a year earlier from Leon Hess. Just like that he was kissing it goodbye.

From there Belichick launched into a kind of rambling, twenty-five-minute statement before he even took a single question. He continued to insist that the problem was "the uncertainly surrounding the ownership of the team and a number of other things." The sale was schedule to be completed by December 15, but still hadn't been settled. "I know the commitment that needs to be made, and I don't feel in the current situation I can lead the Jets with one-hundred-percent conviction."

Speculation ran rampant. The most obvious reason, some felt, for Belichick's sudden resignation was that he really wanted the Patriots job. His Jets contract, signed back in 1997, wouldn't pay him nearly as much as a brand-new head coaching contract with another team. It was apparent, despite denials, that he was Kraft's number-one choice now that Pete Carroll had been fired. Since Belichick couldn't negotiate for another head coaching job without the Jets' permission, it looked like a situation that might go to the courts.

Belichick's sudden resignation opened a whole new can of footballs. Whether Belichick wound up in New England, somewhere else, or nowhere else, one thing was certain. He was through in New York. The Jets needed a coach. There was immediate speculation that this turn of events might cause the departed Parcells to return. Remember, Parcells was a guy who never said never, and always said he reserved the right to change his mind. Even Belichick admitted that Parcells's occasional indecisiveness gave him cause to wonder.

"We've had so many scenarios," Belichick said. "It seems like every time we talk, a new scenario takes place that's different than what we talked about previously. There hasn't been a consistent pattern." Belichick said he didn't inform Parcells of his decision until minutes before he announced it to the rest of the world.

"We all know how Bill is," Belichick continued. "Sometimes he reacts emotionally to a loss or a bad season, or a series of bad performances. Every time Bill says that, I take it with a grain of salt. It's been like that for the last twelve, thirteen years."

It was almost as if Belichick was worried about Parcells suddenly appearing and reclaiming his throne, signed contracts notwithstanding. Parcells, for his part, had no comment immediately after the abdication. There were, however, people already calling for his return to once again save the franchise. Some said he would have no choice. He had to come back. Even his players felt that way.

"I'd be all for [him coming back]," said Vinny Testaverde. "For him, it would be like riding into town on a white horse, saving the day. He's our knight in shining armor. I guess he's still in charge, right? So it's up to him to make sure everything is taken care of. He's still the leader. When stuff like this happens, he's the one we look to."

Testaverde was speaking for many of the Jets players, especially the ones who knew the kind of turmoil the team had experienced before Parcells came. They were concerned that with Parcells gone, Belichick gone, and a new owner on the way, the team might quickly slip into pre-Parcells days.

"Coach Parcells had the train on the right track," Testaverde continued. "And it would have been a smooth transition to Coach Belichick. Now all the stability is gone. It's wiped out. I don't want a situation where someone is going to come in and rebuild the team. At my age I don't have time for that. I think we're good enough to win now."

It was a situation that almost begged for a Parcells return. Strangely enough, a number of additional theories began circulating, perhaps the strangest one being that the entire scenario was orchestrated by none other than Bill Parcells himself. It was a way for him to set up a number of situations.

1. By resigning quickly, Belichick couldn't go to New England without compensation. He would then negotiate with Bob Kraft for draft choices, just as the Jets had to give Kraft choices when they wanted Parcells.

2. By allowing Belichick to go to New England, Parcells's longtime friend could be out from under his rather substantial shadow and get a huge head coaching contract with the Patriots.

3. Parcells could offer himself to the new owner as the only person who could "save" the Jets, and then command the largest contract ever given to an NFL coach. Some estimated that the new owner, desperate to begin his tenure with a winner and paying more than $600 million for the fran-

chise, would be willing to pay Parcells upwards of $10 million to coach for that begged-for one more year.

Far-fetched? Maybe. But in today's sometimes out-of-control sports world, nothing was impossible or implausible. When Parcells finally re-emerged, however, the first thing he said was that he would not return to coaching. "I'm pretty adamant about not doing that," he said. "What I said the other day is what it's going to be."

He also promised that he would not let the Jets founder. "I'm on the job," he said. "This is still my watch." He promised that as the team's chief football operations officer he would begin working immediately to find and hire a new coach. Then, less than a week later, the ownership question was finally settled.

The new owner was Robert Wood Johnson, IV, the great-grandson of one of the three founders of Johnson & Johnson. He agreed to buy the team for the incredible sum of $635 million, the highest price ever paid for a United States sports franchise without a stadium included. The fifty-three-year-old Johnson, who went by the nickname of "Woody," was a quiet, unobtrusive man who had the job of overseeing his family's exten-sive philanthropic interests. He was obviously excited about the Jets and promised he would become involved quickly.

"I do intend to have preliminary conversations with both Steve Gutman and Bill Parcells at the earliest possible moment," Johnson said. "We hope that we can be successful in fulfilling Mr. Hess's dream of developing the New York Jets into a championship team."

Johnson had to wait about a week until the NFL formally approved his ownership, which they did. Then things began moving quickly. Johnson, by all indications, would be the kind of hands-off owner that Parcells, and many other coaches, always liked. Produce for him and he would leave you alone. The first name on Johnson's lips when he went to work was Bill Parcells. The two men soon had the first of several meetings.

"He's not the easiest person to read," Johnson said of Parcells, echoing a thought those in the football community had known for years. "In fact, he is very difficult to read. But he is a quick study, very direct, very honest. I would love to have him coach. We will know—I guarantee we will know—by the end of the week."

It soon became apparent that Parcells still did not want to return to the sidelines. His choice for coach seemed to be longtime friend and ally Al Groh, who was his linebackers coach and was slated to become defensive coordinator under Bill Belichick. Groh was one of those long-term Parcells disciples, having worked with him at Army, Air Force, and the Giants, Patriots, and Jets. He was considered a good teacher and communicator. Johnson also mentioned he was looking outside the organization, something that didn't make Parcells or the players too happy. Nothing, however, was decided immediately and speculation continued. There were still many who thought that in the end, Johnson would open the vault and Parcells would return. One of those who thought Parcells would come back was his old quarterback, Phil Simms, who always stayed in touch and often interviewed his former coach in his job as a CBS television commentator. Simms, in fact, co-hosted Parcells's CBS show.

"I'll tell you what," Simms said. "I'm sitting here reading the papers and I think there is a definite chance this guy is going to come back and coach. I don't know why, but it's starting to add up that Bill Parcells is going to come back and coach the Jets again. I haven't heard [him] say he's not going to coach. Not hearing that [from Parcells] makes me think there is something there."

Asked for a reason, Simms quickly cited the new owner. "[Robert Johnson] sounds like a Wellington Mara, Leon Hess type," the former quarterback explained. "He sounds like a man who wouldn't interfere with the football operation, a man who lets the coach coach."

Opinions remained divided while the process continued. There were still many who felt Parcells would come riding in on a white horse at the last second, that if appeals to his pocketbook failed, appeals to his ego wouldn't. He couldn't, some reasoned, resist coming to the rescue of the franchise and taking them to the promised land. If he had even the slightest misgiving about resigning, here was the perfect chance to return without appearing to be a mind-changing, opportunistic maneuverer. It would certainly be easy for him to say, well, I didn't really want to coach, but there really is no other way this year, what with Belichick's defection, a new owner, the players' concern about losing what had taken to long to build, and so on.

In the end, however, Parcells was true to his word. On January 24 it was announced that the fourteenth head coach in the history of the New York Jets would be Al Groh, the man Parcells had recommended immediately after the Belichick resignation. Parcells would remain as the club's director of football operations and would reassess his future with Woody Johnson at a later date.

Parcells's coaching days, apparently, were really over. "I'm going to act in a support role," he said, "and basically going to try to be a consultant to Al and a supporter and an adviser, and will do that until such time as Woody and I get a chance to review my status much later on."

Parcells also said that Al Groh would have the last word on trades, the draft, and free-agent acquisitions. "I think you all know that I have a very strong belief that a coach must be allowed to shape and form his team the way he wants to," he said. "I've been an advocate of that. I think it's important. I think he has enough experience coaching and has seen enough programs in operation to do that."

Three days later, the final chapter in the odyssey that had become the Jets postseason was played out. Parcells picked up the telephone and placed a call to a man he hadn't spoken with in three years—Bob Kraft.

"I told him it was Darth Vader," Parcells quipped, when revealing the call to the press, "and he knew who it was."

The purpose was to resolve the dispute over Bill Belichick. When the two men hung up, all the problems were solved. The Jets would allow the Patriots to hire Belichick and in return would receive the Pats' first-round draft pick, the sixteenth choice in the upcoming college draft, as well as the Patriots' fourth- and seventh-round picks the following year. The Jets gave the Patriots their fifth-round selection in 2001 and seventh-round pick in 2002.

That evening the Patriots announced that Belichick would be their next head coach, which was apparently the place he wanted to be all along.

"We mended a lot of fences," said Parcells. "We came to an agreement that regardless of what happened with Bill Belichick, this border war with the Jets and Patriots needed to come to a halt. I was anxious that we make an attempt to repair the relationship. [Bob Kraft] is a good businessman, and I knew that if there was an opportunity, regardless of who is presenting it, that would improve his franchise, he would consider it.

"I think it's win–win for everybody," Parcells said. "If I were him, and things were reversed, I would have paid it, too. Now, we're in a position to help our team."

He was already sounding like a businessman, an executive working the phones upstairs, away from the field, away from the cracking of pads, the split-second decisions, the immediacy of the competition.

"My diplomacy is directly proportional to the scoreboard," Bill Parcells said. "I don't think anybody won. I think we made a business deal."

Funny, they always said he was a great coach, but a lousy businessman. It was finally time to change hats. At last.

Epilogue: The Parcells Legacy

OR ALL INTENTS AND PURPOSES, BILL PARCELLS'S COACHING CA-
reer ended on a cold January day at the Meadowlands when his
New York Jets topped the Seattle Seahawks to end their 1999
season. It was a career that spanned more than thirty years, fifteen of them
as a head coach in the NFL. The raw numbers tell only part of the story,
but they are significant. Coaching three different teams, Parcells won 149
games, lost 106, tied one. He took his teams to three Super Bowls and
won two of them. By themselves, the numbers bespeak of a successful
career. Bill Parcells, however, will not be remembered only by a ledger
of wins and losses.

He will be remembered as a coach with a powerful personality who
commanded respect from his players, but only after they worked to earn
his respect. That didn't come easily. He was difficult and demanding,
expecting the same kind of commitment and dedication in return that he
was always willing to give. He had, perhaps, the sharpest tongue of any
coach, using it with a cutting sarcasm that could be as withering as it was
effective. Parcells spoke and his players got the message. You measured
up to his standards, or you were gone.

More than that, he will be remembered as a winner, a coach capable
of taking over a struggling franchise with a paucity of quality talent and
a losing mentality, and changing it quickly by imposing his tremendous

will in addition to making shrewd personnel decisions. The players he felt would win for him might not always be the most talented, but they were the kind of guys ready to go to war. *Parcells guys*, they were called. Once there were enough Parcells guys in tow, the team won. He proved it with three different franchises.

Though every great coach is an individual, making comparisons difficult, Will McDonough, who has covered the NFL for decades, says that Parcells reminds him of another legendary coach from an earlier time.

"I think Parcells is a lot like Vince Lombardi," the *Boston Globe* columnist said. "They both had a lot of that New York–New Jersey guy in them. They both went through West Point [as assistant coaches]. They both saw the military combined with football. Both could be despotic yet loving with their players at the same time. They were both driven to win. Neither was afraid to gamble and take chances during a game.

"Bill had the best record in football for years going for it on fourth down. Look at Lombardi. Being foolhardy and risky cost him a chance at his first championship when the Packers played the Philadelphia Eagles [in 1960]. Twice he had chances to kick easy field goals and he didn't do it, trying instead for a first down they didn't make. After the game he admitted those six points cost him the championship. The challenge for both of them is not to be afraid in critical situations, to do whatever you have to do to win a game."

McDonough wasn't the only one to compare Parcells to Lombardi. Both were tough and uncompromising, yet inspired the utmost respect and—though it's not often a word associated with football—love among many of their former players, hard men who often attributed their success after football to lessons learned from their coach during their playing days. Can there be a better testament to a coach than to have a lasting influence on so many former players? Football is a violent sport, not for the faint of heart. For a coach to do what is necessary to mold his team, be a winner, and at the same time inspire and influence his players is not an easy balance to achieve.

His methods were not for everyone and some players simply couldn't deal with him. That's why there were *Parcells guys*, players who could persevere with him, earn their pelts, and finally capture the coach's total respect. Outwardly, he'll be remembered as a coach who turned franchises around. Bring in Parcells and you would soon have a winner, as assuredly as knowing the sun will rise. To many of his players, his legacy was more than that. He was a man who touched their lives and made them better men for knowing him.

Yet old images never really die. Phil McConkey, who became a quintessential Parcells guy when he played for the Giants, was asked what he thinks of first when someone mentions Bill Parcells. Without missing a beat, McConkey said,

"I always think of him standing at practice with his warmup jacket on, that ugly plastic thing he wore to sweat and lose weight, his grey sweats on, one leg of the sweats brought up to his knee, his arms folded, and with a great big perpetual scowl on his face."

That from a player who, like many others, genuinely loved his coach.

Index